Women's leisure in England
1920–60

This Book
belongs to the Library of
King Edward VI's
Grammar School,
Guildford, Surrey

D1514345

MANCHESTER
UNIVERSITY PRESS

Z6Z15
Women's leisure in England 1920 - 60

STUDIES IN POPULAR CULTURE

General editor: Professor Jeffrey Richards

R.G.S. GUILDFORD.
J.C. MALLISON
LIBRARY.
WITHDRAWN

Women's leisure in England 1920–60

CLAIRE LANGHAMER

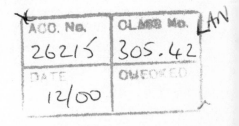

ACC. No.	CLASS No. LAN
26215	305.42
DATE 12/00	CHECKED

Manchester University Press

Manchester and New York

distributed exclusively in the USA by St. Martin's Press

Copyright © Claire Langhamer 2000

The right of Claire Langhamer to be identified as the author of this work
has been asserted by her in accordance with the Copyright, Designs
and Patents Act 1988.

Published by Manchester University Press
Oxford Road, Manchester M13 9NR, UK
and Room 400, 175 Fifth Avenue, New York,
NY 10010, USA
http://www.manchesteruniversitypress.co.uk

Distributed exclusively in the USA by
St. Martin's Press, Inc., 175 Fifth Avenue, New York,
NY 10010, USA

Distributed exclusively in Canada by
UBC Press, University of British Columbia, 2029 West Mall,
Vancouver, BC, Canada V6T 1Z2

British Library Cataloguing-in-Publication Data
A catalogue record for this book is available from the British Library

Library of Congress Cataloging-in-Publication Data applied for

ISBN   0 7190 5736 1   *hardback*
        0 7190 5737 X   *paperback*

First published 2000

07 06 05 04 03 02 01 00   10 9 8 7 6 5 4 3 2 1

Typeset in Monotype Garamond by Illuminati, Grosmont
Printed in Great Britain by Biddles Ltd, *www.biddles.co.uk*

STUDIES IN POPULAR CULTURE

General editor's introduction

There has in recent years been an explosion of interest in culture and cultural studies. The impetus has come from two directions and out of two different traditions. On the one hand, cultural history has grown out of social history to become a distinct and identifiable school of historical investigation. On the other hand, cultural studies has grown out of English literature and has concerned itself to a large extent with contemporary issues. Nevertheless there is a shared project, its aim, to elucidate the meanings and values implicit and explicit in the art, literature, learning, institutions and everyday behaviour within a given society. Both the cultural historian and the cultural studies scholar seek to explore the ways in which a culture is imagined, represented and received, how it interacts with social processes, how it contributes to individual and collective identities and world views, to stability and change, to social, political and economic activities and programmes. This series aims to provide an arena for the cross-fertilization of the discipline, so that the work of the cultural historian can take advantage of the most useful and illuminating of the theoretical developments and the cultural studies scholars can extend the purely historical underpinnings of their investigations. The ultimate objective of the series is to provide a range of books which will explain in a readable and accessible way where we are now socially and culturally and how we got to where we are. This should enable people to be better informed, promote an interdisciplinary approach to cultural issues and encourage deeper thought about the issues, attitudes and institutions of popular culture.

Jeffrey Richards

For Mum and Dad

Contents

Illustrations

General editor's foreword

In her ground-breaking and thought-provoking study, *Women's leisure in England 1920–60*, Claire Langhamer sets out to reconceptualise the question of women's leisure in the period between the end of World War One and the advent of the 'swinging sixties'. In doing so, she draws on feminist theory to establish the importance both of social and cultural context, and of the meanings which women themselves assigned to the concepts of work and leisure. In addressing these issues, she makes extensive use of oral evidence. But this evidence does not stand alone. It is consistently backed up by systematic reference to contemporary newspapers and periodicals, and to a wide range of social surveys such as Mass-Observation, as well as by a thorough mastery of the current historiography on the subjects of women's lives and their leisure activities. Armed with this evidence, she challenges and interrogates the received meanings of leisure as applied to the lived experience of women during the four decades of her study. While being continually alive to the elements of both continuity and change, the existence of diversity and variety and the ever-present constraints related to time, money, parental demands and society's expectations, she concludes that for most women the life cycle was the fundamental determinant of the nature and structure of their leisure. She persuasively demonstrates the crucial difference between youth, the years between leaving school and getting married, when leisure was seen as a right and 'going out' (to the dance hall or the pictures) a necessity; and married life, when leisure became decisively focused on home and family, and notions of duty and service superseded those of freedom and independence. Sensitive, thoughtful, judicious and thoroughly documented, this study is enlivened and illuminated again and again by the memories and observations of the women who lived through the forty years which Claire Langhamer has so effectively anatomised.

Jeffrey Richards

Acknowledgements

During the course of this research, I have received help and support from a number of quarters. Initially, I would like to thank the series editor Jeffrey Richards and Vanessa Graham and Louise Edwards at MUP for giving me the opportunity to write this book and Elizabeth Roberts, who made some valuable suggestions for improvements. Dave Russell and Cathy Lubelska supervised my doctorate and were unstintingly generous in the time and effort they dedicated to advising and encouraging me. This book has benefited enormously from their help, support and friendship during my four years at Preston. I must also thank the University of Central Lancashire for the studentship which funded my doctoral research, and the staff and graduate students of the department of Historical and Critical Studies, who offered friendship as well as intellectual stimulation. I would also like to offer heartfelt thanks to Andy Davies of Liverpool University for encouraging me through the dark days of post-doctoral unemployment, and for his invaluable advice and friendship since the inception of this project. Also to be thanked are my Ph.D. examiners, Carol Jones and Pat Thane, who offered valuable comments on the thesis, and Sean O'Connell, who commented on my book proposal. Over the past year, I have accumulated yet more debts of gratitude. I would like to thank my colleagues in the history subject group and the School of Cultural and Community Studies at Sussex University, my students in the years 1998 to 1999 for keeping me on my toes, and Dorothy Sheridan and her team at the Mass-Observation archive, who make research there such a pleasurable experience. (Mass-Observation materials are reproduced with permission of Curtis Brown Ltd, London. Copyright the Trustees of the Mass-Observation Archive at the University of Sussex.) I am also grateful to Paula Moorhouse, at the local studies unit, Manchester Central Library, for her help regarding illustrations, and to Longman for allowing me to reproduce small parts of a chapter entitled 'Towards a feminist framework for a history of women's leisure', in Gallagher, Ryan, Lubelska and Webster (eds), *Changing the Past. Women, History and Representation* (Longman, London, 2000).

Friends and family also, of course, merit a huge thank you for helping me through the ups and downs of the thesis and book; they include Catherine Kennedy, Alison Kirby, Karen O'Farrell, Annabel Kiernan, Pietro Columbi, the late and very much missed Elaine Walker, Joss Alexander, Ron and Maira Torjussen and my own immediate family. In particular I must thank Martin Torjussen for offering love and support throughout, and for casting a critical eye over the final draft. Finally, and most importantly, I would like to thank those women who allowed me to interview them. Without their willingness to give so freely of their time, this research would not have been possible. The kindness and hospitality which I encountered made the project more enjoyable than I could ever have anticipated.

Introduction

Over the past three decades, historians have conducted research into a wide range of leisure forms and pursuits, yet the experiences of women in the twentieth century remain only partially explored. Leisure history has, on the whole, tended to concern itself with the activities of working-class men, within a periodisation that has often ended with the onset of the First World War. Against the backdrop of the transformative impact of industrialisation, historians have pursued research into areas such as sport, music-making, the pub and the seaside holiday. Of prime concern to many has been the relationship between social class and the destruction or development, use and 'control' of particular leisure forms.[1] Our knowledge of the specific leisure experiences of women has consequently been limited to an assessment of their engagement in, or exclusion from, pre-defined leisure forms. Moreover, fields of research have sometimes been chosen more for the opportunities they provide for an intervention in established debates concerning political, social and economic developments than for their centrality to the experiences of working men and, crucially, women.

Women's leisure in England argues that the limitations in our knowledge of women's experiences can be explained neither in terms of an earlier academic 'gender blindness' nor as arising out of 'the nature of the documentary sources'.[2] Rather, it suggests that a preoccupation with certain forms of leisure has led historians actively to ignore or misrepresent women's experiences. At a basic level, surveys of the field have pointed to the tendency of researchers to focus upon 'institutional', commercial, or organised, out-of-doors, leisure 'activity'. As Clarke and Critcher write: 'Much of the day to day fabric of life has eluded historical analysis.'[3] Yet, as historians are beginning to recognise, inattention to the informal realm of family, street and neighbourhood can produce only a partial picture of leisure experience.

Recent research has attempted to access informal and street-based leisure patterns, and it is this which forms the immediate historiographical background to this book.[4]

The pursuit of the informal illuminates the stage upon which many women act. However, illumination is not the same as explanation. In this book I will argue that the existing conceptual frameworks of leisure history are not appropriate to the study of women; the definitions of leisure employed by historians have been drawn from a specific type of male experience. In essence, historians have implicitly located leisure in direct opposition to paid labour, and have conceptualised it as freely chosen reward for that labour, unambiguously structured in terms of time and space.[5] As Bailey writes: 'modern leisure is a certain kind of time spent in a certain kind of way. The time is that which lies outside the demands of work, direct social obligations and the routine activities of personal and domestic maintenance; the use of this time, though socially determined, is characterised by a high degree of personal freedom and choice.'[6] Indeed, the chronology of leisure development, utilised by historians in the field, highlights the crucial role of industrialisation in promoting a spatial and psychological separation of work and leisure from the mid nineteenth century onwards.[7] Such a separation is contrasted with the more integrated experiences of the pre-industrial age.[8]

As feminist sociologists have argued within the field of leisure studies, a conceptualisation of leisure as fundamentally distinct from work is unhelpful to the study of women's experiences.[9] In essence, 'leisure' as constructed by many historians is a gendered concept; understandings of the category assume the male wage-earning experience to be normative. In contrast, my aim here is to reconceptualise the category 'leisure' in the light of the experiences of women in the period 1920 to 1960. The study recognises the complex and ambiguous relationship between leisure and work, and explores the problems inherent in the characterisation of leisure as 'reward'. In particular, it explores the fluidity within which specific experiences gain definitional validity as 'leisure' or 'work', and pursues this across the historical period and, crucially, over the course of the life cycle.

This book is a study of women's leisure in England, yet it also offers a detailed picture of leisure at the local level, through a case study of Manchester which draws upon oral history interviews with twenty-three Manchester women, local newspaper evidence,[10] and social surveys of the period.[11] Manchester is selected, in part, because it enables case-study findings to be situated alongside existing work in the field, notably that of Davies on leisure and Fowler on youth.[12] Manchester was also a large city, with a population of 730,307 in 1921, which acted as a leisure capital for its region. [13] The city offered a diverse and competing array of commercial and informal leisure opportunities including cinemas such as the Paramount, dance halls like the Ritz, opportunities for participant and spectator sport, parks and open spaces, and the numerous attractions of the Belle Vue Zoological Gardens on Hyde Road. However, this Manchester case study is firmly located within a national context of changing attitudes and shifting experiences. Indeed, the study makes detailed use of a number of documentary sources which deal with different parts of the country. Substantial use is made of previously underexploited Mass-Observation material, notably a series of major leisure surveys conducted in the late 1940s, and replies to the monthly 'Directive' sent by the organisation to its group of volunteers, a number of which deal with leisure activities. Other national and local social surveys from the period are utilised to examine both leisure behaviour and provision across the country,[14] while the print media, a leisure commodity for many, is also used to address representations of women's leisure.[15]

This book provides a great deal of empirical detail concerning women's leisure experiences in the local and national context. Of course, all historical accounts must, by the nature of their production, remain partial. What follows here is grounded in the particular experiences and self-representations of the Manchester women interviewed, and the nature of the documentary sources consulted. My own role in co-constructing the interview material and in 'reading' the textual sources also fundamentally determines the nature of what follows.[16] Moreover, significant areas remain to be addressed, and I will outline some of these in my Conclusion. While it does not claim to be fully comprehensive in its coverage, however, this book does offer an alternative *approach* to the history of women's leisure. In effect, it suggests a feminist framework to a field which has, hitherto, largely lacked the conceptual tools necessary to access the complexity of women's lived leisure experiences.

Approaches to the history of women's leisure

The history of women's leisure forms a small, but growing, field of study. A scattered literature exists, with various articles and books looking at narrow parts of the terrain. Much of the existing work exhibits a tendency

to approach women's leisure within one or more of the following parameters. First, taking the lead from the wider field of leisure history, studies
have, until recently, foregrounded the Victorian and Edwardian experience.
Secondly, research in this area has been of a 'topic-based' nature; approaches
have utilised the 'out-of-house', activity-based understandings of 'leisure'
which I take in this book to be fundamentally problematic. Thirdly, historians have worked within a class-specific framework: within the historiography of the nineteenth century there has been an emphasis upon the
activities of middle-class women; within that of the twentieth century the
focus has been upon those of the working class.[17]

The most substantial literature in the field of women's leisure relates to
the study of organised sport and physical exercise: specifically, the experiences of upper- and middle-class women of the nineteenth and early
twentieth centuries. Work by a number of historians has indicated that
women's involvement in sporting activity was more extensive than has
previously been supposed.[18] Areas which witnessed particular growth in
the late Victorian and Edwardian period included tennis, golf, hockey,
badminton, cycling and ice-skating.[19] Much of the literature here places the
growing participation of women in active, competitive sports within the
wider context of changing ideas of 'natural' womanhood. For example,
Vertinsky explores the role of scientific knowledge, medical practice and
social perception in defining the particular types of physical exercise seen
as being appropriate to women at different stages in the life cycle; McCrone
and Mangan assess the challenge which women's sporting activities posed
to existing ideas of femininity.[20] Elsewhere, Rubinstein characterises the
bicycle as a symbol of women's emancipation: 'Cycling brought the sexes
together on equal terms more completely than any other sport or pastime.
It also gave women a striking sense of independence and self-reliance.'[21]
Recent work has, however, advanced a more cautious view of the relationship between increased sporting participation and the wider movement for
women's emancipation.[22] Certainly, historians of women's sport are careful
not to overplay the extent, or speed, of change, nor to underplay continued antagonism towards the sporting female. Moreover, they note that
even among middle-class women, engagement in sport rarely extended
beyond the years of youth.[23] As we shall see, this discontinuity in women's
sporting activity continued into the period 1920 to 1960.

The overriding concern of the works surveyed above is not an analysis
of leisure as experienced by women in the nineteenth century, but the

study of a specific form. Sport and physical activity are selected not for their centrality to most women's lives, but because of a perceived – if complex – relationship to wider changes in ideas about 'women' and the movement for women's emancipation. As such, these studies tell us much about this relationship, but somewhat less about the leisure experiences of the majority of women in the nineteenth century. Indeed, as Hargreaves points out, only a tiny minority of working-class women participated in organised sport before the First World War.[24]

Other historians have illuminated the place of women within particular leisure institutions, notably the music hall. Hoher has pointed to the presence of women in music-hall audiences, noting the extent to which patterns of attendance were influenced by changing life-cycle and work-cycle position.[25] Elsewhere, the role of women in music-hall performance as well as audience has been addressed.[26] Within the wider field of popular musical culture, Russell has indicated the limited opportunities for women presented by Victorian choral societies.[27] Once again, however, these are studies of particular activities, providing valuable information concerning the specific, rather than the general, leisure experience.

Women's leisure in the twentieth century has received less attention from historians. Beyond the minimal discussion in Stephen Jones's *Workers at Play*,[28] the work of Fowler and Osgerby on youth culture,[29] and Andrew Davies' ground-breaking study *Leisure, Gender and Poverty* (to be discussed shortly),[30] existing work again tends to be rooted in the 'topic' approach. Invaluable research has been conducted into aspects of women's leisure such as youth organisations, physical exercise, magazine-reading and car ownership. For example, Warren and Proctor have traced the history of the Girl Guide Association in Britain, Oliver has uncovered the surprising popularity of rounders among Bolton cotton-workers, Tinkler has addressed the role of magazines in girls' lives over the period 1920 to 1950, and O'Connell has explored the relationship between gender and the design and consumption of the motorcar in the first part of the twentieth century.[31] Yet, these remain studies whose starting points are particular activities rather than the more general subject 'leisure'. Indeed, overall, the issue of what women actually did in their leisure or spare time has rarely been directly addressed by historians. Particular activities have been studied, but these are activities selected by historians as important, and do not necessarily reflect the leisure priorities of women themselves. This study, in contrast, suggests a more holistic approach to the history of women's leisure. 'Leisure' is approached as an area of conceptual ambiguity rather than as constituting particular, pre-defined forms. The overriding aim is an exploration of the very nature of the concept as it operated within women's everyday lives and across a particular historical period.

The immediate historiographical background to this book is provided by one text which, in contrast to other work in the field, takes as its starting point the subject 'leisure'. *Leisure, Gender and Poverty* by Andrew Davies is the first published work to approach twentieth-century leisure from an explicitly gendered perspective; in fact the book explores the leisure experiences of men, women and youths.[32] Davies' central focus is upon the constraints which poverty placed upon leisure forms, and he stresses the need to place gender differences within the context of economic circumstances, exploring the constraints upon leisure which this entailed. His work draws upon a series of oral history interviews to examine leisure activities such as drinking, cinema-going, visits to the fortune-teller and, most notably, informal street-based pursuits which include sitting-out on the doorstep, gossiping, street entertainment, street customs such as the annual Whit Walks, trips to Saturday night markets and visits to public parks.

The emphasis of Davies' work is ultimately upon 'out-of-doors' leisure defined in terms of time and activity; as such it remains partly within the established school of leisure history. *Leisure, Gender and Poverty* does not fundamentally challenge definitions of leisure. None the less, Davies' emphasis upon informal leisure forms clearly widens our understanding of the nature of 'leisure', and suggests that a belief in the inexorable progress of commercialisation across all social classes must be viewed with caution.[33] This book builds upon Davies' pioneering work by similarly attempting to extend our body of knowledge concerning women's leisure experiences. However, in contrast to Davies' study, *Women's leisure in England* explicitly problematises 'leisure' as a category of historical analysis. Rather than 'adding in' gender to an analysis of working-class communities, this book seeks to reconceptualise our understanding of the very nature of women's leisure as a subject of historical enquiry.

This book also adds a new dimension to the field of leisure history in terms of its class focus and chosen periodisation. While Davies examines the experiences of both men and women of the working class, this study concentrates upon the specific experiences of women of contrasting social backgrounds. The cross-class focus allows for the examination of both divergence and similarity in women's experiences, as well as illuminating the complexity of class definitions for women. While *Leisure, Gender and Poverty* examines the period 1900 to 1939, this book examines a different period, that of 1920 to 1960. This period is bounded by significant social change, starting just after the First World War and ending on the eve of the so-called 'second wave' of British feminism. The period is, in fact, a contradictory one in the history of women. Significant changes across both the so-called 'public' and 'private' spheres were accompanied by considerable continuity of experience, rooted in notions of gender difference which persisted throughout the period. As Jane Lewis writes: 'Socio-economic changes which might have been expected to result in the blurring of sexual divisions were often balanced by attitudes and beliefs which served to reinforce those divisions.'[34] There are, of course, problems with this periodisation, which largely concern the potentially dislocating impact of the Second World War upon women's leisure experiences. While the importance of this dislocation is not denied, it is suggested that in approaching this period as a whole, there is more scope to access continuity in women's experience, as well as change, than is possible in a more limited interwar study. [35]

Chapter content

The first part of this book explores the nature of leisure within women's lives: it outlines the conceptual frameworks within which women's experiences are best understood, and unpicks the category 'leisure' in the light of lived experiences. Chapter 1 establishes the foundations of the approach to women's leisure developed within the book: an approach informed by feminist scholarship within the field of leisure studies. It opens with a discussion of the theoretical underpinnings of the study, outlining the valuable insights offered by feminist researchers and suggesting ways of integrating this work into a historical study. Attention is then turned to the concept at the centre of this book: 'leisure'. After tracing the history of the term itself, I demonstrate how oral history methodology can provide an invaluable means of reconceptualising understandings of leisure in the light of interviewees' understandings and representations of their everyday experiences. Particular attention is paid to the alternative terms used by women to describe their experiences. Here the aim is both to unravel and to reformulate the category 'leisure' as it relates to women's experiences.

Where Chapter 1 establishes a framework for the historical study of leisure, Chapter 2 explores the ambiguities inherent in defining both 'work' and 'leisure' within women's lives by focusing upon key sites of definitional uncertainty. The relationship between work and leisure is explored first through an examination of the nature of housework: unpaid labour, often defined in terms of duty rather than work. The chapter explores the relationship between work in the home and the time and space available for leisure, and critically evaluates the impact and prevalence of historically specific definitions of housework as more akin to leisure than to work. Chapter 2 then pursues definitional ambiguity through analyses of the family holiday, shopping and sales, home crafts and personal grooming or 'beauty', thereby demonstrating that 'work' and 'leisure' are historically shifting categories, which gain meaning only if they are fully contextualised within women's everyday lives.

The second part of the book focuses, in detail, upon the life cycle as a changing and crucial context for women's leisure. Chapters 3, 4 and 5 examine the ways in which women experienced leisure in their passage through the life cycle within a particular historical period. In so doing they provide useful empirical evidence concerning the particular forms of leisure enjoyed by women in England at different stages of their lives. Cinema-going and dancing are the dominant *activities* in youth, but these must be understood within the context of close female friendships and relationships with men. In adulthood, social life and home-based 'leisure' take centre stage. Crucially, however, these chapters also explore changing conceptualisations of 'leisure' as women moved from youth, through the years of courtship, to adulthood. They explore the impact which cultural constructions of leisure as 'reward' for paid labour had upon women's own notions of appropriate leisure behaviour, as well as attending to the ambiguity which framed the women–leisure relationship. Specifically, Chapter 3 explores a characterisation of youth as a period of legitimate leisure, albeit within the context of gendered material and social constraint. Chapter 4 acts as a short bridging chapter between youth and adulthood. In its examination of the influence of courting upon the leisure experiences of young women, it introduces many of the themes concerning the relationship between men, women and leisure which are integral to the final chapter on leisure in adulthood. Finally, Chapter 5 outlines a movement in adulthood away from the personal towards a family-orientated leisure, rooted in notions of duty and service to others.

Notes

1　See P. Bailey, 'Leisure, culture and the historian: reviewing the first generation of leisure historiography in Britain', *Leisure Studies* 8:2 (1989), for a detailed survey of the field and an extended bibliography.

2　*Ibid.*, p. 118.

3　J. Clarke and C. Critcher, *The Devil Makes Work: Leisure in Capitalist Britain* (Macmillan, London, 1985), p. 50.

4　A. Davies, *Leisure, Gender and Poverty: Working-Class Culture in Salford and Manchester, 1900–1939* (Open University Press, Buckingham, 1992).

5　See for example, P. Wild, 'Recreation in Rochdale 1900–1940', in J. Clarke, C. Critcher and R. Johnson (eds), *Working-Class Culture: Studies in History and Theory* (Hutchinson, London, 1979).

6　P. Bailey, *Leisure and Class in Victorian England: Rational Recreation and the Contest for Control, 1830–1885* (Routledge, London, 1978), p. 6.

7　*Ibid.*, p. 4.

8　R. W. Malcolmson, *Popular Recreations in English Society, 1700–1850* (Cambridge University Press, Cambridge, 1973).

9　E. Wimbush and M. Talbot (eds), *Relative Freedoms: Women and Leisure* (Open University Press, Milton Keynes, 1988).

10　The study employs a detailed study of the *Manchester Evening News*, chosen because it was Manchester's most widely read local evening newspaper of the period: D. Griffiths (ed.), *The Encyclopedia of the British Press 1422–1992* (Macmillan, London, 1992), p. 399. The *Manchester Evening News* cost one penny in 1920, rising to a price of threepence over the period.

11　Several social surveys focus upon leisure experiences in specific districts of Manchester. For example, J. L. Harley, 'Report of an enquiry into the occupations, further education and leisure interests of a number of girl wage-earners from elementary and central schools in the Manchester district, with special reference to the influence of school training on their use of leisure', M.Ed. dissertation, University of Manchester, 1937; H. James and F. Moore, 'Adolescent leisure in a working-class district', *Occupational Psychology*, 14:3 (1940).

12　Davies, *Leisure, Gender and Poverty*; D. Fowler, *The First Teenagers: The Lifestyles of Young Wage-Earners in Interwar Britain* (Woburn, London, 1995).

13　*Census of England and Wales, 1931*, County of Lancaster, p. 1.

14　For example, P. Jephcott, *Girls Growing Up* (Faber & Faber, London, 1942); M. Kerr, *The People of Ship Street* (Routledge & Kegan Paul, London, 1958); H. Llewellyn Smith (ed.), *The New Survey of London Life and Labour. Volume IX. Life and Leisure* (P. S. King and Son, London, 1935); B. Seebohm Rowntree and G. R. Lavers, *English Life and Leisure: A Social Study* (Longmans, London, 1951).

15　Here I use *The Times* and a selection of women's magazines, including those targeted at a middle-class market, such as *Good Housekeeping*, and those which addressed a wider audience, such as *Woman's Own*.

16 For a discussion of the construction of feminist knowledge, which employs a case study of the Mass-Observation day diaries, see L. Stanley, 'Women have servants and men never eat: issues in reading gender, using the case study of Mass-Observation's 1937 day-diaries', *Women's History Review*, 4:1 (1995).

17 Although a recent contribution by Catriona Parratt has explored the constraints of time and money which 'rendered leisure time a scarce resource' for working-class women in the late Victorian and Edwardian period. C. Parratt, '"Little means or time": working-class women and leisure in late Victorian and Edwardian England', *International Journal of the History of Sport* 15:2 (1998). Liz Stanley also makes some suggestive methodological comments concerning the use of diaries for the study of Victorian working-class women's leisure: L. Stanley, 'Historical sources for studying work and leisure in women's lives', in Wimbush and Talbot (eds), *Relative Freedoms*, pp. 21–2.

18 C. Parratt, 'Athletic womanhood: explaining sources for female sport in Victorian and Edwardian England', *Journal of Sport History*, 16:2 (1989), pp. 141–2.

19 N. Tranter, *Sport, Economy and Society in Britain, 1750–1914* (Cambridge University Press, Cambridge, 1998), p. 83.

20 P. Vertinsky, *The Eternally Wounded Woman: Women, Doctors and Exercise in the Late Nineteenth Century* (Manchester University Press, Manchester, 1990); K. McCrone, *Sport and the Physical Emancipation of English Women, 1870–1914* (Croom Helm, London, 1988); J. A. Mangan, 'The social construction of Victorian femininity: emancipation, education and exercise', *The International Journal of the History of Sport*, 6:1 (1989).

21 D. Rubinstein, 'Cycling in the 1890s', *Victorian Studies*, 21:1 (1977), p. 68.

22 J. Hargreaves, *Sporting Females: Critical Issues in the History and Sociology of Women's Sports* (Routledge, London, 1994), p. 42.

23 A. Warren, 'Sport, youth and gender in Britain, 1880–1940', in J. C. Binfield and J. Stevenson (eds), *Sport, Culture and Politics* (Sheffield Academic Press, Sheffield, 1993), p. 57.

24 J. Hargreaves, *Sporting Females*, pp. 68, 107.

25 D. Hoher, 'The composition of music hall audiences, 1850–1900', in P. Bailey (ed.), *Music Hall: The Business of Pleasure* (Open University Press, Milton Keynes, 1986).

26 For examples of this work, see E. Aston, 'Male impersonation in the music hall', *New Theatre Quarterly* (August 1988); J. S. Bratton, 'Jenny Hill: sex and sexism in Victorian music hall', in J. S. Bratton (ed.), *Music Hall: Performance and Style* (Open University Press, Milton Keynes, 1986); S. Maitland, *Vesta Tilley* (Virago, London, 1986).

27 D. Russell, *Popular Music in England, 1840–1914: A Social History* (1987; Manchester University Press, Manchester, 2nd edition 1997), p 255.

28 S. Jones, *Workers at Play: A Social and Economic History of Leisure 1918–1939* (Routledge & Kegan Paul, London, 1986). Jones's discussion of women's leisure is largely confined to pages 58–61.

29 Fowler, *The First Teenagers*; B. Osgerby, *Youth in Britain since 1945*, (Blackwell, Oxford, 1998).

30 Davies, *Leisure, Gender and Poverty*.

31 A. Warren, 'Mothers for the Empire? The Girl Guide Association in Britain, 1909–39', in J. A. Mangan (ed.), *Making Imperial Mentalities: Socialisation and British Imperialism* (Manchester University Press, Manchester, 1990); T. Proctor, '(Uni)Forming youth: Girl Guides and Boy Scouts in Britain, 1908–39', *History Workshop Journal*, 45 (1998); L. Oliver, '"No hard-brimmed hats or hat-pins please." Bolton women cotton-workers and the game of rounders, 1911–39', *Oral History*, 25:1 (1997); P. Tinkler, *Constructing Girlhood: Popular Magazines for Girls Growing up in England, 1920–1950* (Taylor & Francis, London, 1995); S. O'Connell, *The Car in British Society: Class, Gender and Motoring, 1896–1939* (Manchester University Press, Manchester, 1998).

32 Davies, *Leisure, Gender and Poverty*.

33 Here, Davies provides an importance counterbalance to Stephen Jones's *Workers at Play*, which foregrounds the expansion of commercial leisure in the interwar period.

34 J. Lewis, *Women in England 1870–1950: Sexual Divisions and Social Change* (Harvester Wheatsheaf, London, 1984), p xi.

35 There, is of course, debate among historians concerning the long-term effect of the war upon women's lives. For an up-to-date account, see P. Summerfield, *Reconstructing Women's Wartime Lives: Discourse and Subjectivity in Oral Histories of the Second World War* (Manchester University Press, Manchester, 1998).

Part I

The nature of leisure in women's lives

'A planned night out'?
Conceptualising 'leisure'
in historical research

The field of leisure history, on the whole, lacks the conceptual tools needed to access and explore women's experiences; the historian must look for inspiration elsewhere if she is to approach a better understanding of those experiences. Chapter 1, therefore, sets out the theoretical underpinning of *Women's leisure in England*. It begins by outlining the feminist leisure studies research upon which the book draws, identifying those approaches which have been of most use in helping me to reconceptualise the category 'leisure' as a subject of historical analysis. Specifically, I demonstrate the value of an approach to women's leisure within which context and meaning take centre stage, and argue that such an approach is better suited to a study of women's experiences than the frameworks hitherto employed by historians in the field. In the second part of this chapter, attention shifts to the term 'leisure' itself. Here, the historically unstable meanings allocated to 'leisure' are addressed, with a particular focus upon the meanings which women themselves attach to the term within oral history interviews. In effect, the chapter explores the ways in which an oral history methodology which values the subjective realm of meaning can help the historian to rethink the very nature of 'leisure' as a topic of research.[1] To this end, Chapter 1 closes with an exploration of alternative languages of leisure, surveying the words and phrases which women themselves choose to articulate their experiences within a defined historical period. Here the prime concern is to open up the category 'leisure' and, in so doing, establish the different components of a conception of leisure which has real meaning for women, and more fully encapsulates their experiences.

Feminist theories of leisure

A feminist critique of 'common-sense' notions of leisure – defined as time off from paid employment, enjoyed outside the home – is, then, available to the historian if she turns from the field of leisure history to that of leisure studies. Over the past two decades, feminists working within this field have argued that a conceptualisation of leisure as fundamentally distinct from work is unhelpful to the study of women's leisure and, indeed, actually *invalidates* the experiences of women.[2] Unwaged domestic labour is excluded from the category 'work' in this conception; consequently, the leisure experiences of those who work in the home are ignored. Indeed, Lenskyj notes an underlying assumption in leisure studies, based upon notions of intuitive mothering and maternal fulfilment, that most of a woman's day is 'free', and that her labour is closer to leisure than it is to male-defined work.[3] As McIntosh notes, it is this assumption that is at the root of the opinion that women who do not go out to work do not actually 'work' at all, and therefore neither need nor deserve leisure in the same way as men.[4] Wearing and Wearing discern a tendency for women to internalise this idea, being reluctant to put aside time for themselves or experiencing feelings of guilt if they do.[5]

Feminists also argue that a conceptualisation of leisure as separate and opposite to paid work *distorts* the experiences of women. Many women – notably those with family responsibilities – do not necessarily experience a sharp distinction between work and leisure, and for many the two interact, often occurring simultaneously. For example, a 'work' activity such as ironing may be accompanied by the 'leisure' of listening to the radio. Other activities may be work or leisure at different times (an example would be cookery), and in other circumstances, work and leisure can be different dimensions within a single activity, the self-catering holiday being one such case.

Researchers working within this field argue that the blurring of work and leisure for women stems, fundamentally, from the nature of domestic labour. Both housework and childcare are forms of work with little self-sufficient shape; they are to some extent self-defined, but subject to stringent external and internalised standards.[6] For women working in the home, there is no one point when the working day ends and leisure time begins. The work is dictated by task, not time, with given tasks revolving around the actions of other family members. Consequently, 'time off' is fitted around the timetables of others. Time itself is fragmented, and leisure is slotted into any available space. Moreover, because the workplace also acts as the living place, chores are ever present, a constant reminder of work to be done. It is within this context that the leisure experiences of women must be understood.

Thus, feminist scholarship offers a fundamental challenge to definitions of leisure which assume an oppositional relationship to paid labour. Researchers point to other shortcomings in the definitions of leisure used within the field of leisure studies. In particular, Liz Stanley has criticised the use of predetermined, activity-based conceptions of leisure, arguing that such definitions actively ignore the experiences of many women, who are, therefore, excluded from leisure studies research. As she explains: 'By including swimming, golf, pub-going and dancing, but not knitting, drinking tea with neighbours, or simply sitting and reflecting, a whole host of assumptions and interpretations are built into research which inevitably structure and so construct its outcomes.'[7] Instead of an approach to the subject which assumes definitional certainty, Stanley suggests one which emphasises complexity. Rather than approaching both 'work' and 'leisure' as given activities, she proposes that they should be addressed as conceptual constructions.

While feminist researchers differ in their particular emphases, it is possible to identify a characteristic approach to women's leisure arising out of their critique of leisure studies. Within this approach, key importance is assigned to the *meaning* that women themselves give to their actions as leisure, work, or a combination of the two. It is acknowledged, however, that the meanings attached to particular activities differ between individuals and over the course of the life cycle. Consequently, researchers emphasise the importance of establishing the *context* within which actions take place. For Stanley, 'leisure' should be examined within the context of everyday, lived experience. As she writes: '"Leisure" certainly does not make sense on its own; it has to be understood as part of a conjunction of interests, needs, skills, commitments and obligations in women's lives most importantly including those of "work".'[8] She therefore argues for a rejection of abstraction in favour of an examination of women's leisure experiences 'in the round'.[9] For other researchers, the process of contextualisation demands an emphasis on the structural constraints upon women's leisure: socialist-feminist analyses foreground the ways in which patriarchy and capitalism interact to structure and constrain women's leisure.[10] Elsewhere, postcolonial theorists employ the concept of 'otherness' to explore the nature of leisure within the lives of women of colour.[11]

Thus feminist researchers point to the constraints which frame women's experiences of leisure. More recently, however, work influenced by poststructuralist approaches, 'has explored the possibilities that leisure offers for liberation', emphasising 'resistance' and 'difference' over structure and a perceived universalism.[12] This work emphasises the ways in which leisure constitutes an opportunity to resist and re-create gendered roles and identities.[13] Certainly, one of the most helpful lessons which the historian of leisure can draw from leisure studies concerns the consistency with which women carve out 'personal space' for leisure.[14] McRobbie and Garber, for example, have demonstrated the importance of the bedroom in providing a cultural space for young working-class women.[15] Dixey and Talbot have shown the invaluable role of bingo in creating a legitimate public arena for working-class women's leisure, providing: 'a home from home, an invaluable source of companionship, a refuge which offers excitement'.[16] Other studies have shown how women whose leisure is spent predominantly within the home carve out areas of their life for relaxation and sociability – albeit against a background of fragmented time, and the ambiguities of 'work' and 'leisure' in women's lives.[17]

Liz Stanley has emphasised the particular importance of a historical understanding of women's leisure; arguing that contemporary leisure experiences can be better understood in the light of historically changing ideas around 'work' and 'leisure'.[18] However, historians themselves have largely failed to engage with the work of feminist leisure researchers, and have been slow to utilise the insights into the nature of women's leisure outlined above. This omission has led to serious weaknesses in representations of women's leisure by historians: our historical understanding has been limited by researchers' preoccupations with a 'male' model of leisure. In contrast, the chapters which follow place feminist concerns at their heart. 'Leisure' and the inextricably linked category 'work' are approached as fluid concepts, open to changing meanings and inseparable from the contextual and historical background against which they are experienced.

Defining 'leisure' within women's lives

In his 1980 work on leisure in the industrial age, Hugh Cunningham describes how the word 'leisure' developed in meaning from its eighteenth-century association with the activities of a specific class, to its end-of-the-nineteenth-century characterisation as the non-work activities of the mass of the people.[19] By the 1920s, the word 'leisure' had certainly entered the public domain as a descriptive term for particular spare-time experiences. For example, Manchester's Ardwick Green Empire used the term in its newspaper advertising: 'Make your leisure time pleasure time as a matter of principle. All work and no recreation is a sure road to breakdown. A merry heart goes all the way – usually all the way to the Ardwick Empire.'[20] Elsewhere, writers of the period utilised the word to refer to a variety of activities ranging from the formal 'leisure occupation' to the less structured and often commercial amusements of youth.[21]

As the interwar period progressed, concern as to the 'proper' use of leisure – against a background of rising wages and shorter hours for some, and 'enforced leisure' in the form of unemployment for others – was widespread.[22] As *The Times* noted in 1929: 'Leisure, indeed, has become that serious thing, a "problem".'[23] National and international conferences were dedicated to the subject, and numerous printed works explored 'the leisure problem'.[24] Concern centred around the dangers posed by 'excessive' leisure of various types; the need to plan for ever-expanding leisure time; the perils inherent in recourse to commercial entertainment alone; the issue of legitimate Sunday leisure; and, above all, the need to educate children for a lifetime of leisure which would be of benefit both to self and to the wider community.

This concern with the proper use of leisure continued into the war years and beyond. As we shall see in Chapter 3, the use made of leisure time by young men and women preoccupied some policy-makers during the Second World War. In 1948, *The Times* outlined the comments of the Minister of Education on the subject:

> Mr. Tomlinson said that among the most disturbing facts about modern life was the number of people who went about half dead, in the sense that they had no interest in the things going on around them. In place of real interests and worth-while amusements, people drugged themselves with constant visits to the cinema, football pools, fun fairs and all the rest of the meaningless paraphernalia of commercial entertainment.[25]

As Fielding, Thompson and Tiratsoo have shown, the postwar Labour government was actively critical of the public preference for 'escapist' forms of leisure such as the cinema, the pub and gambling, and periodically attempted to improve leisure through public policy initiatives.[26] Certainly, by the end of our period, 'leisure' was of sufficient political importance to merit policy documents from both political parties on the eve of the 1959 election.[27]

'Leisure' was, then, part of the vocabulary of recreation across the period 1920 to 1960. However, the relevance of this single term to women's lives is less certain. The second part of this chapter explores individual women's understandings and perceptions of the term in order to assess its applicability to their particular experiences.

In their study of Sheffield women's leisure, Green, Hebron and Woodward observed that the term 'leisure' was not one readily used by the women they interviewed to describe aspects of their lives.[28] My own oral history interviews were informed by a suspicion that asking women for their 'leisure' experiences might not fully encompass the range of those experiences.[29] In particular, I was determined that the language used should encourage recollections of a wide range of experiences, rather than exclude some on the grounds that they did not fit commonly held assumptions about the nature of 'leisure'. To this end, a variety of different words were used in contacts with interviewees, including 'spare time', 'pleasure' and 'enjoyment'. However, women were also questioned about their own understanding of the term 'leisure' and the extent to which they would have used the word to describe particular activities and situations in the period 1920 to 1960.[30] The responses gained seemed to justify a concern that the term 'leisure' does not provide the best verbal route into accessing the experience academics label 'leisure'. They also attest to the value of oral history as a means of reconceptualising understandings of leisure, in the light of individual respondents' interpretations of their everyday lives.

When questioned about the term 'leisure', Alice, a working-class woman born in 1926, answered:

> I don't think the word was used much, there was a lot of activities going on and there was a lot of leisure, but it … it wasn't termed that in the earlier days, in the earlier days you'd say, erm, are you, are, how are you going to enjoy yourself, that, that would be more the term that you would use, you know, what are you doing tonight, are you going out, are you going away this weekend, are you going to a picture or what have you. But erm, er, leisure, the word leisure became more prevalent around the fifties because the community centres built up and in the community centres, er, er, it would say leisure pursuits … Er yes, it started to be referred to around the fifties, but, er, I think before that it was er, it was just enjoying yourself, you know just pleasure, pleasure.

Joyce, a lower-middle-class woman born four years later, responded to the same question in a similar way:

> *Would you have talked about having 'leisure time?'* No *You wouldn't have used that term?* No. No. No. No. Have you found that generally? *mmm* Yes. No you don't talk about leisure time. No it doesn't ring any bells really. I, I only really associate it really with the development of leisure centres. *Right, so sporty things?* Yes, that's what you know, these leisure centres that have … that have all cropped up in the last, what, fifteen, twenty years. Erm, that's … that's why I think it's, er, become leisure.

For these women of different class backgrounds, 'leisure' constituted a historically specific concept, associated with the provision of particular facilities such as the community and leisure centre. Neither believed that she would have used the term during the period under consideration as a name for her *own* experiences.

Other interviewees responded to the question in ways that revealed very clear assumptions concerning the nature of 'leisure'. Jane, for example, said:

> No I don't think we would have called it leisure. Leisure wasn't a word that was in our vocabulary at that time. I don't think, no, I … I don't think we would have talked about it. No. I don't think it would have been, erm, an issue … But I mean it was never classed as leisure, well this is your leisure time, you can't use this for studying because it's your leisure time, there was never any diversions or divisions of time like that. Erm, you know … it was either, things that you did or you didn't do. I don't think there was an issue to it.

Here there is a view of 'leisure' as a distinct entity, something clearly demarcated, which did not form part of her own experience. Similarly, Freda remembered: 'It was just ordinary life. You took it for granted that you went to the pictures. It was the thing in those days', and Jean reiterated: 'I don't think we really, we didn't really think of it as leisure in that sort of way. You know, it was just going out, you know.'[31] For these women, use of the term 'leisure' would have added undue formality to experiences grounded in everyday life. Other terms provided more accurate accounts of their activities. As Doris explained: 'No, I think, you said … Yes, what does he do in his spare time, spare time. Yeah, I suppose I don't know, erm, [pause] I don't think you used the term leisure like you do now. You know like, erm, no I don't think you did. Just called it spare time, erm, yeah.'

For many of the women interviewed, the term 'leisure' was not one that they would have automatically used to describe their experiences. Indeed, oral testimony suggests that 'leisure' conjured up very specific images related to physical exercise and other activities experienced within fixed time boundaries, from which women felt excluded. Those who did use the word often employed it to describe only particular stages of their passage through the life cycle. Dorothy, for example, clearly associated 'leisure' with her youth: 'Really my leisure ended when I started my family ... I mean my husband and I did other things, erm, after we were married.' Here, 'leisure' was associated with the freedom and independence of youth. Other women used the term in a way which demonstrated the complicated relationship between work and leisure in their lives, exemplified in the words of Edith: 'Well, my ... my leisure was like coming home and seeing to kids and cooking for 'em, because I, you know, I ... I bake and you know. Er, I enjoy it.' This ambiguity in defining leisure and work within women's lives will be explored in further detail in Chapter 2.

Alternative languages of 'leisure'

For many of the women interviewed, alternative words provided more accurate accounts of their activities. These labels cannot be used unproblematically; like the word 'leisure', they carried different meanings for different women. Consideration of these descriptive terms, however, enables the researcher to open up the category 'leisure', and to explore the complex and sometimes contradictory elements that constituted women's experiences within this period.

The term 'spare time' was one frequently used by the women interviewed, as well as one used in preference to 'leisure' in initial contacts with interviewees. Dorothy chose this term rather than 'leisure', and Freda repeatedly referred to her use of 'spare time'. For other women, however, the term proved problematic. A letter from one respondent, Annie, revealed some of the problems attendant upon its use: 'You ask how we spent our spare time. I'm afraid we didn't have any, we were too busy with a great many activities run by our local Methodist Church.' For this woman the term would not have included the church-based activities which, she later acknowledged, constituted her leisure. As she explained when she was interviewed: 'Yes, I don't know, we never had any what you call "spare time", because we were always busy.' In a similar vein, Kathleen defined spare time as 'virtually spare ... you'd nothing planned for it', adding: 'I think you weren't expected to be lazy. You know, and to sit about doing nothing.' Clearly, for these women, 'spare time' was time left over after more organised leisure activities; it would not include church activities or even trips to the cinema, for as another interviewee noted with reference to the cinema: 'Well, it used to be a planned night out, love.'[32] The demands of family life often ensured that in adulthood, a single visit to the cinema was, indeed, accompanied by considerable strategic planning.

Alternative terms used by oral respondents included 'pleasures' and 'enjoyment'. Joan spoke of the period after the war: 'Well by that time you had to find out what your pleasures would be'; and Elsie noted: 'I don't remember any regular pleasures except escaping now and again to dance.' These words, however, did not provide an unproblematic description of particular leisure experiences either; in many instances they reflected the ambiguities inherent in the concept of leisure for women. For example, Alice spoke of the pleasure her mother apparently derived from sewing: 'People don't understand, er, that you could get pleasure out of just doing, making a garment'; and Ada professed her own enjoyment of household labour: 'Often pleasure isn't anything like as pleasurable as work.'

Other women talked about the enjoyment of productive 'hobbies' as leisure activity. As Dorothy recalled: 'We had a lot of hobbies in those days that were hobbies that kept you in the home.' She went on to name patchwork and sewing as her particular interests. Elsewhere, it was noted that 'making things' was the most popular hobby for women, although Freda did not include handicrafts in her own understanding of the term: 'Er, as far as women and girls were concerned we spent our life sewing and knitting and making things. Erm, I don't think we had anything in the way of hobbies, no.' Others spoke of gardening as a hobby, and Margaret regarded driving as her foremost hobby. The majority of women interviewed, however, did not use the formal name 'hobby' as a label for their experiences. As Kathleen said: 'Er … I didn't really have any hobbies. I don't think. I was always too busy. I'd lots of boyfriends.'

As later chapters will demonstrate, much of the leisure enjoyed by both young and adult women was founded upon friendship and opportunities for socialising. Certainly 'social life' was a term sometimes used by women as an alternative to 'leisure'. Joan directly equated social life with leisure, remembering that after her marriage: 'Social life as such wouldn't have, erm, bothered me after the war … I wouldn't have thought I needed leisure.' For others the term was used to describe an essential element of leisure, one which was often the real reason for engaging in particular activities at different stages of the life cycle and in different contexts. Mary, for example, spoke of her married life in the 1940s and 1950s: 'We had quite a nice social life. We used to go out a lot to dinner dances and my husband was a Mason and we went to Ladies' evenings.' Of her work as a lower-middle-class housewife with one child, she observed: 'I quite enjoyed it. Yes, because I'd always got friends to go out with, it was afternoon teas, morning coffee and, er, all that sort of thing.' In contrast, Jean, a working-class woman, experienced her social life through her paid employment, where she built up a network of friends who would regularly visit each other's houses for 'high tea': 'I was a bit bored with the work at an engineering firm, and people said funnily enough recently, why did you stay there, Mum? You know ... and I said, cos I liked the people, you know, and it was this same social thing again.' For both these women, socialising was an important part of their working days.

The experiences of many of the women included in Margery Spring Rice's survey of the social conditions of 1,250 married working women add another dimension to the construction of leisure for women: the notion of leisure as rest.[33] As Spring Rice observed: 'Leisure is a comparative term. Anything which is slightly less arduous or gives a change of scene or occupation from the active hard work of the eight hours for which she has already been up is leisure.'[34] Many of the women included in that survey equated 'leisure' with 'rest'. Asked directly about their leisure time, they responded with evidence of their hours of relaxation. However, what was termed 'rest' often actually constituted work, albeit of a less strenuous nature than that performed at other times in the working day. As a woman in Caerphilly reported: 'after my children go to bed, I gets two hours' rest, if call it rest, I am mending my children's clothes and tidying in those few hours I get.'[35] Spring Rice confirmed this: 'It is much more usual to read that in effect such leisure as there is is spent in some sedentary occupation as a rest from the long hours of standing, and that it is spent entirely in mending.'[36] The memories which many of the interviewees held of their mothers' leisure time revealed a similar equation between leisure and rest. Both Margaret and Dorothy observed that the only times their mothers sat down was at the pictures.

Examination of the alternative words used by women to describe their 'leisure' enables the historian to construct a broader understanding of the concept as it operated in women's everyday lives in the period 1920 to

1960. Spare time, pleasure, enjoyment, hobbies, social life and rest constituted different aspects of the 'leisure' experienced by the women interviewed here. The evidence demonstrates contradictions between women
over the use and meanings of particular words. With the exception of the
less commonly used term 'hobby', however, these words ultimately point
to a common experience among the women interviewed. Personal leisure
time, albeit characterised in different ways, generally constituted a snatched
experience; something 'fitted in' to everyday life. In contrast, more organised
forms of leisure had to be planned for, and – as Chapter 5 will demonstrate – were often beyond the reach of adult women, whose time was
both limited and fragmented.

In spring 1947 at the height of the postwar leisure boom, Mass-
Observation conducted a major nationwide survey of leisure activity, posing
the question 'What is your favourite way of spending your spare time?'[37]
A quarter of the women interviewed replied quite simply that they had no
spare time, or that they were so exhausted by their domestic work that any
spare time was spent in rest. Comments such as 'don't get any', 'what
spare time?' or 'I have no time' were commonplace among women from
both working-class and lower-middle-class backgrounds. As one forty-five-
year-old with three children from Dagenham stated: 'I have no spare time.
When I am through with my work I am ready to sleep.' A twenty-eight-
year-old mother of two from York said: 'I like to sit. I just like to sit and
I like to have a cigarette.' Moreover, the notion of leisure as less exhausting
work, so apparent in Spring Rice's prewar survey, was evident here too.
Many of the women dedicated any spare time they did have to domestic
labours. As a woman from Becontree explained: 'I don't have much spare
time, do I? I'm mostly mending indoors.'

For a significant proportion of women, then, leisure of any type, and
however defined, was largely unattainable. Mass-Observation concluded
simply: 'Women are more likely than men to say that they have no leisure
time.'[38] Oral evidence, too, is suggestive of this trend. For example, Edith,
a working-class woman born in 1911, resisted all prompts to discuss her
use of spare time when she was interviewed, preferring instead to structure
her life story around her experience of working in a foundry, a position
which she maintained throughout her working life. She was keen to express
her enjoyment of her paid employment: 'It was really, I ... I loved it, I
mean all them years I worked there it was like going from home to home.'
As the interview progressed, it became clear that the reason Edith did not

discuss her 'spare time' was because she had very little. Working full-time and bringing up four children, with minimal help from her largely unemployed husband, quite simply left her with little time for herself. Indeed, asked directly whether she had had any leisure time, she replied: 'No. Only to have babies, when I've had the children, you know, that's the only time I've been off.' Clearly, then, no matter how 'leisure' is defined to include the experiences of women, there were those from whose lives it remained absent.

This chapter has established the theoretical and conceptual parameters of the book. The theoretical approach is one which utilises, and develops, the ideas of leisure studies researchers. In a study informed by feminist exhortations to approach 'leisure' as a problematic concept, the category itself has been critically unpicked and reformulated by drawing upon the interviewees' own self-representations. In Chapter 2, the exploration of the nature of leisure in women's lives continues as we examine particular sites of definitional ambiguity across the period 1920 to 1960.

Notes

1　As Portelli observes: 'Oral sources tell us not just what people did, but what they wanted to do, what they believed they were doing, and what they now think they did.' A. Portelli, *The Death of Luigi Trastulli and Other Stories: Form and Meaning in Oral History* (State University of New York Press, Albany, 1991), p. 50.

2　C. Griffin, 'Young women and leisure', in A. Tomlinson (ed.), *Leisure and Social Control* (Brighton Polytechnic, Brighton, 1980), p. 117.

3　H. Lenskyj, 'Measured time: women, sport and leisure', *Leisure Studies*, 6:1 (1989), p. 236.

4　S. McIntosh, 'Leisure studies and women', in Tomlinson (ed.), *Leisure and Social Control*, p. 105.

5　B. Wearing and S. Wearing, 'All in a day's leisure: gender and the concept of leisure', *Leisure Studies*, 7:2 (1988), p. 114.

6　For examples of these standards, one need only examine a range of women's magazines or parenting manuals.

7　L. Stanley, 'The problem of women and leisure – an ideological construct and a radical feminist alternative', in Centre for Leisure Studies (ed.), *Leisure in the 1980s* (University of Salford, Salford, 1980), p. 88.

8　L. Stanley, 'Historical sources for studying work and leisure in women's lives', in E. Wimbush and M. Talbot (eds), *Relative Freedoms: Women and Leisure* (Open University Press, Milton Keynes, 1988), p. 18.

9 *Ibid.*

10 See for example, E. Green, S. Hebron and D. Woodward, *Women's Leisure: What Leisure?* (Macmillan, London, 1990); and, more recently, S. Scraton, 'The changing world of women and leisure: feminism, "postfeminism" and leisure', *Leisure Studies*, 13:4 (1994).

11 B. Wearing, *Leisure and Feminist Theory* (Sage, London, 1998), pp. 162–76.

12 *Ibid.*, p. ix.

13 See, for example, E. Green, '"Women doing friendship": an analysis of women's leisure as a site of identity construction, empowerment and resistance', in *Leisure Studies*, 17:3 (1998).

14 Informed by poststructuralist insights, Wearing conceptualises leisure to signify 'personal spaces, physical and metaphorical': Wearing, *Leisure and Feminist Theory*, p. 149.

15 A. McRobbie and J. Garber, 'Girls and subcultures: an exploration', in S. Hall and T. Jefferson (eds), *Resistance Through Rituals: Youth Subcultures in Post-war Britain* (Hutchinson, London, 1975), p. 213.

16 R. Dixey and M. Talbot, *Women, Leisure and Bingo* (Trinity and All Saints College, Leeds, 1982), p. 170.

17 See, for example, Radway's research on romance reading: J. Radway, *Reading the Romance: Women, Patriarchy and Popular Literature* (1984; Verso, London, 1987), pp. 86–118.

18 Stanley, 'Historical sources for studying work and leisure in women's lives', p. 19.

19 H. Cunningham, *Leisure in the Industrial Revolution, 1780–c.1880* (Croom Helm, London, 1980), pp. 12–13.

20 *Manchester Evening News* (hereafter *MEN*), 20 February 1920, p. 1.

21 O. Morgan, 'A study of the training for leisure occupations offered in a senior girls' school in an industrial area, together with an enquiry into the use made of this training by the girls, after their entry into employment'. M.Ed. dissertation, University of Manchester, 1942.

22 For example, in the period 1900 to 1940 working hours per week for manual workers decreased by 54 hours to 46.5: A. H. Halsey (ed.), *Trends in British Society Since 1900* (Macmillan, London, 1972), p. 120.

23 *The Times*, 17 September 1929, p. 15, col. d.

24 For example, *The Times*, 24 February 1920, p. 11, col. b; 6 April 1933, p. 9, col. d; 7 February 1939, p. 8, col. f.

25 *The Times*, 21 December 1948 p. 2, col. c.

26 S. Fielding, P. Thompson and N. Tiratsoo, *'England Arise!' The Labour Party and Popular Politics in 1940s Britain* (Manchester University Press, Manchester, 1995), pp. 135–68.

27 Conservative Political Centre, *The Challenge of Leisure* (C.P.C. series no. 203, 1959); Labour Party, *Leisure for Living* (London, Labour Party, 1959).

28 Green, Hebron and Woodward, *Women's Leisure: What Leisure?*, p. 5.

29 As Devault observed of the difficulties she had in categorising her own

research on household routines for planning, cooking and serving meals; a topic more specific than 'housework' and more wide-ranging than 'cooking': 'The categories available from the discipline to construct "topics" for research do not necessarily correspond to categories that are meaningful in women's lives.' M. Devault, 'Talking and listening from women's standpoint: feminist strategies for interviewing and analysis', *Social Problems*, 37:1 (1990), p. 98.

30 Respondents were asked the following question: 'Can I ask you about what people thought about the things they did? Did they talk about having "leisure", did they actually use that term at all?'

31 Freda's lower-middle-class background is an important factor here. As Spring Rice's study of working-class wives demonstrated, not all women did take visits to the cinema for granted. As she observed: 'The cinema is very rarely mentioned, and many women say they have never been to the pictures.' M. Spring Rice, *Working-Class Wives: Their Health and Conditions* (Penguin, Harmondsworth, 1939), p. 103. Class-based differences in access to leisure will be addressed in Chapters 3 and 5.

32 Margaret.

33 Spring Rice, *Working-Class Wives*, p. 99.

34 *Ibid.*

35 *Ibid.*, p. 110.

36 *Ibid.*, p. 114.

37 Mass-Observation Archive (hereafter M-O A): Topic Collection Leisure, 80/2/B-E, 80/3/A-C, Questionnaire responses, Spring 1947.

38 M-O A: File Report (hereafter FR) 3067, 'A report on work and leisure', November 1948, p. 5.

'Waiting for the pie to brown': leisure, work and definitional ambiguity

Chapter 1 demonstrated how a historical study of women's leisure can benefit from the application of insights drawn from feminists working in the field of leisure studies. Informed by this body of work, this book approaches 'leisure' not as a given category of historical analysis but as a problematic concept, and one which must itself be critically examined. As Green, Hebron and Woodward have observed: 'Leisure has a chameleon-like quality, changing its skin in relation to its surroundings, context and the seriousness of its competitors.'[1] Chapter 2, then, continues a necessary examination of the concept 'leisure' over the period 1920 to 1960, focusing particularly upon the relationship between 'work' and 'leisure' within women's lives. In particular it explores the ambiguities inherent in attempts to define these concepts. First, I examine constructions of housewifery as both less and more than 'work', assessing the impact of such definitional ambiguity upon experiences of, and attitudes towards, leisure. Then my attention shifts to the family holiday as a critical example of the interactive nature of work and leisure within women's lives. Finally, I turn to three additional areas – shopping, home crafts and 'beauty' – where the question of 'what is leisure and what is work?' is historically shifting and conceptually unclear.

The nature of work in the home

As feminist sociologists have recognised, the ambiguous relationship between 'work' and 'leisure' within women's lives often stems from the nature of work in the home: housework and childcare, unpaid labour often defined in terms of duty rather than work.[2] As Mass-Observation observed in a 1951 report based upon the daily diaries of married working-class housewives in five suburban London areas: 'the housewife's activities are necessarily multifarious – one leading on where another is left off, according to the need or urgency of the moment. She does not clock on or off, there are no job cards. Her every action is guided by an inner logic, which only she, perhaps, can fully comprehend.'[3] A concern with the nature of housework and its relationship to 'leisure' for women is evident in local newspaper evidence and women's magazines from across the period. More specifically, replies to a 1948 Mass-Observation directive on 'Housework' demonstrate the problematic relationship between (house)work and leisure in women's lives.

In her reply to the 1948 Directive, one thirty-four-year-old housewife stated: 'A man goes out to work and returns at fixed hours, but a woman begins first and ends last – the work is never-ending and even much of the so-called leisure has to be devoted to household tasks like mending.'[4] Another, a thirty-six-year-old married shorthand typist, said: 'Too often a man regards his day's work as done when he "downs tools" at 5.30 p.m. whereas a woman's work, if she is at all conscientious, is literally never done.'[5] The all-encompassing nature of women's work in the home is clear. Indeed, as early as 1925 one *Manchester Evening News* article addressed the problematic nature of housework, offering advice on how to cope with its enormity. While the suggested solution was simplistic (the housewife was advised to concentrate on organising herself better, making a list of her daily jobs), the problematic nature of housework as work without end was clearly addressed.[6] Thirty years later, the problems posed by a work lacking in definite time boundaries were the concern of Phyllis Mills, who asked her readers: 'Do you sacrifice all leisure to CLEAN, CLEAN, CLEAN?', and urged that a 'sense of proportion' in housework should be adopted.[7] In the same year, Marjorie Lloyd asked: 'Why not a day off for housewives?', noting the problems of broken time which prevented women from having a full day off every week. Instead, Lloyd argued:

> A full day in the garden or greenhouse … an afternoon spent in the local art school taking pottery, basketry or some such … uninterrupted hours cutting out and making a frock, doing Constance Spry-ish flower arrangements, cooking fancy buns just for fun, having a friend to lunch and trying out a new dish which a husband would greet by "what in heaven…?" all leave a sense of personal achievement which is a wonderful boost to one's ego.[8]

Recognition that the nature of housework precipitated a fragmentation of women's time is also evident in Spring Rice's national survey of working-class wives in the interwar period. Referring to a 'typical' housewife's routine, she observed: 'When once she is up there is no rest at all till dinner ... Dinner may last from 12 till 3. Her husband or a child at work may have quite different hours from the school children, and it is quite usual to hear this comment. Very often she does not sit down to meals.'[9] Here the extent to which the work of housewifery revolved around the timetables of other family members is clear. Indeed, as Spring Rice herself put it: 'Whatever the emotional compensations, whatever her devotion, her family creates her labour, and tightens the bonds that tie her to the lonely and narrow sphere of "home". The happiness that she often finds in her relationship of wife and mother is as miraculous as it is compensatory.'[10]

Certainly the need to fit leisure into otherwise busy schedules was evident in the 1935 *Manchester Evening News* article 'What do you do on the tramcar?'[11] Many of the women asked used the tram journeys as valuable time for themselves. One used the time to write poetry, another to 'study dress', and a third simply to relax. The mother of a large family explained: 'It's one of the few chances I get between 7 in the morning and 11 at night, and believe me, I make the most of it.' In the early 1950s, Mass-Observation found that 'one housewife in two had to content herself with two hours or even less to spend on her own devices, at least on week days'.[12] The following 'typical example' demonstrates the nature of one housewife's working day (Saturday), and is worth quoting at length:

7.30 a.m.	Got up, washed and did hair.
8.00 a.m.	Got breakfast which lasted until ...
8.30 a.m.	Put water on for baby's bath.
8.45 a.m.	Water ready, started to bath baby.
9.00 a.m.	Finished bathing baby and dressing; fed baby (20 minutes)
9.30 a.m.	Dressed myself. Put breakfast things in bowl. Tidied but didn't stop to wash up.
10.00 a.m.	Went out shopping. Bought meat, vegetables, fruit, sweets. Bought myself a pair of stockings and rubber pants for baby. Brought laundry back.
11.00 a.m.	Came back. Took baby's outdoor clothes off. Changed nappy. Made myself a cup of tea.
11.30 a.m.	Washed up breakfast things and made beds until ...
12.00 noon	Cooked dinner. Sat down at ...
12.45 p.m.	Dinner
1.00 p.m.	Got baby's feed ready. Gave baby his feed. Put baby in cot. Sat down and had a cup of tea.

2.00 p.m.	Did some of baby's washing. Took it easy – didn't rush over it, it being Saturday.
3.00 p.m.	Got baby ready to take on walk around. Husband went out on his own.
4.00 p.m.	Came in. Husband already made tea. Sat down and chatted with my husband until …
4.30 p.m.	Baby woke. Nursed him until …
5.00 p.m.	Got bottle ready for baby – prepared everything for the feed. Fed baby for 20 minutes and put him to bed. Busy with baby from 4.30 to 6.00
6.00 p.m.	Went over to library to change books. Hung around library until…
6.45 p.m.	Came back. Washed up tea things.
7.15 p.m.	Did some baby's ironing. Had wireless on while ironing. Finished by mending, darning socks and sewing on buttons.
8.30 p.m.	Started to get supper ready.
9.00 p.m.	Listened to news. Looked at evening papers. Dallied over supper.
9.30 p.m.	Started collecting baby's things together. Got his feed ready.
9.45 p.m.	Fed baby. Changed him and put him back in his cot.
10.20 p.m.	Cleaned up
10.30 p.m.	Went to bed.[13]

While the very nature of housework impacted upon women's experience of time, the location of the home as both workplace and the site for 'family' leisure also complicated the work–leisure relationship for women.[14] In 1925, one newspaper article noted that the constant presence of work to be done within the home, combined with feelings of guilt or 'conscience', prevented the wife from taking time for herself: 'To a man it seems incredible that a woman should almost boast of her inability to sit down all day because of her household duties. "Sit thee dahn lass; sit thee dahn", he will say, but conscience, that relentless slave-driver of housewives replies, "Not till the work is done."'[15] Towards the end of our period, a 'Woman Doctor' advised female readers on relaxation techniques, observing: 'So many women, housewives especially, do not know how to relax because they are always worrying about all the jobs to be done.'[16] Noting the tendency of women to take a 'half-hearted' break from their daily labours, perhaps reading a magazine while watching the clock for the cooking, she promoted the importance of more complete rest.

As these articles acknowledged, women working in the home simply did not experience a distinction between workplace and site of leisure. While husband and children generally did view the home as a leisure venue,

Advertisements such as this one for 'Leisure Kitchens' reinforced the idea that housework was not real work.

the wife and mother was differently positioned; indeed, her work was often a prerequisite for the leisure of other family members, as Chapter 5 will demonstrate. Spring Rice articulated these difficulties when she observed: 'The pleasure which husband and children find in such comforts as the home provides, is denied to her, who may be too exhausted to enjoy them, and whose only real relief would be an hour or two right away from the scene of her labour.'[17]

Documentary sources recognised the impact of domestic work upon notions of time and space. They also provide evidence of – and sometimes directly criticised – contemporary assumptions concerning the nature of women's work. For example, in several *Manchester Evening News* articles there was both an awareness and a rejection of the tendency to regard housework as more akin to leisure than work. Indeed, one woman writer felt it necessary to argue in 1930 that: 'housekeeping remains a job and not a pleasant recreation'.[18] In 1955 an inclination to regard the housewife as primarily a woman of leisure was questioned by Joyce Stranger in an article entitled 'The Little Woman's No Lady of Leisure'. Referring to 'the delusion that the housewife has all the time in the world', she proceeded to catalogue her own day's work, describing housewives as 'very busy women, working to a far stricter routine than many shop and office workers'.[19] The strictness of this routine seemed to stem from the fact that it was organised around the activities of other family members. Similarly, Spring Rice recognised the extent to which housework could be viewed as less than work:

> With the best will in the world, it is difficult for a man to visualise his wife's day – the loneliness, the embarrassments of her work, the struggle to spend every penny of his money to the best advantage. In most cases he can count upon her devoted service to himself and to their children – and he feels instinctively that her affection gives a pleasant flavour to her work which is absent from his own – and that she is fortunate in not being under the orders of an employer, and subject to regulations of time and speed of work.[20]

Particular magazine advertisements over this period seem to have played upon this notion of housework as not quite work because it was rooted in the family. For example, a 1955 advertisement for a range of kitchen equipment called 'Leisure Kitchens' pictured a woman seated at her kitchen table stirring the contents of a bowl with the caption 'Look ahead to leisure like this'.[21] Another from that year attempted to sell kitchen utensils with the slogan 'And now make cooking fun'.[22] An earlier advertisement for Mainstat-controlled gas cookers entitled 'The Joyous Kitchen' actually

Some advertisements did acknowledge that labour-saving equipment in the home could increase a woman's personal leisure time, although it is unclear whether this particular woman viewed gardening as a form of leisure or a necessary chore.

2

pictured five women dancing round a cooker.[23] Other advertisements, however, did imply that the addition of labour-saving equipment in the kitchen could increase a woman's overall leisure time, thereby admitting that there was time-consuming work to be done in the home. One such example is a 1937 gas cooker advertisement which showed a woman, on her way out to the garden, exclaiming: 'Cooking won't keep me out of the garden. I'm a regular "Regulo" fan!'[24] Without an understanding of her material circumstances and personal preferences, however, it is impossible to know whether that particular woman regarded gardening as an enjoyable leisure pursuit or as a necessary chore.

Perhaps partly because of such advertising campaigns, there remained, throughout, a suspicion that the housewife's day was not a working day – a suspicion which fuelled definitional ambiguity concerning the 'work' of a wife and mother. A 1925 article in the *Manchester Evening News* entitled 'Too Little To Do' asked: 'Do we middle-class young wives do a full day's job?', and reported the popularity of cinemas and theatres in the afternoon, observing that cafés, dress parades, golf links and tennis courts 'are thronged with the young married women of to-day striving to keep themselves amused and occupied'.[25] Interestingly, this constitutes one of the rare examples of the newspaper addressing an audience in terms of its class, and reflects the interwar development of housewifery as a 'job' performed by women of the middle class. In 1960, Victor Anderson exclaimed: 'You poor little housewife', berating the housewife for wasting her day: 'In many homes increased leisure has meant work for the masculine home help. But not a few husbands of this type would be astonished at the time many wives spend during the day gossiping and tea-drinking with their neighbours.'[26] As Chapter 5 will demonstrate, reports such as these misinterpreted the role of neighbourliness within the working day; they also assumed the applicability of time-driven work frameworks to labour which was task-based. Crucially, however, critiques like this undermined the status of domestic labour as hard work deserving of a leisure reward and, in turn, generated guilt among those women who sought to take time for themselves.

The 'family' holiday

Conceptions of leisure as directly opposite to work and the workplace are problematised by an examination of the nature of domestic labour and its location within the home. Elsewhere, 'work' and 'leisure' could be difficult to separate out in women's lives and, in some circumstances, constituted different dimensions within a single activity. The family holiday was one such event.

Within our period, the growth of holidays with pay, coupled with rising living standards for many, enabled increasing numbers to spend time away from their homes as a family. The *New Survey of London Life and Labour* (1935) thought it probable that about half London's workpeople took an annual holiday, although it noted that a large proportion of working-class families 'have to be content with day outings on Bank Holidays or Sundays', and that there were those for whom even this limited pleasure was economically impossible.[27] Five years earlier the *Manchester Evening News* had proclaimed:

> Cheap transport and the facilities offered by great tourist agencies have made it possible for humble people not only to see Britain, but holidays in strange countries are also within their reach. Lancashire mill workers, with their characteristic genius, forget their troubles amid new joys and pleasures at the coastal resorts of France and Belgium, and likewise Continental holiday-makers visit these shores in search of holiday adventures.[28]

This upbeat image of mass holiday-going was clearly overoptimistic, as the majority of workers entered the war with no paid holiday entitlement. Certainly both Davies and Jones claim that significant numbers of working-class families could not afford a yearly holiday, and that holidays without pay could be a cause of real hardship.[29] Even in the late 1940s, following the Holidays with Pay Act of 1938, trips away from home of at least a week's duration were enjoyed by only half of the population.[30] None the less, as our period progressed, the family holiday rapidly became an established fixture in the calendar for many. By 1950, 91 per cent of United Kingdom employees were entitled to paid holiday, the majority being permitted to take two weeks.[31] Yet, as I will now demonstrate, different members of the family experienced this event as different degrees of 'holiday'; in particular, women with children often found that this apparent leisure activity was infused with continued elements of work.

The way in which some *Manchester Evening News* writers wrote about the family holiday demonstrated a clear recognition of its complicated nature as 'leisure' for women. In 1925, Valerie Rutland observed that for mothers, the annual holiday could include elements of both work and leisure. Arguing that the 'family' holiday signified an enjoyable rest for the husband and

constant joy to the children, she observed that for the mother, it necessitated packing and unpacking, worrying and looking out for the children,
as well as a much-needed rest.[32] A decade later, the problematic nature of
the family holiday as leisure for women was again addressed in the article
'Include Your Wife In This Year's Holiday'.[33] Here, husbands were urged
to consider their wife's enjoyment, and to ask themselves, 'Is her holiday
just a continuation in other surroundings of the work and worry which is
normally her lot?' Identifying the tendency of husbands to plan holidays
to suit themselves, not their wife, the writer advocated 'holidays which will
mean a real holiday for the womenfolk as well'. It was further suggested
that this would entail a change from housework, washing up and the preparation of meals, *and* relief from the duties of childcare. This article clearly
acknowledged that activities generally regarded as constituting 'leisure' often
involved real work for women. Later in the period, 'Holiday Bureau' received a letter from a 'Bothered Mother' keen to take a holiday that would
please all her family. Her assessment of one form of self-catering holiday
which grew in popularity in the 1950s neatly sums up the problematic
nature of the family holiday for women: 'We've tried caravans, but with the
shopping, cooking, bed-making etc., that's no holiday for ME.'[34]

Oral testimony also provides evidence of the work involved in the
family holiday for women. For example, both Dorothy and Joan remembered the 'apartments' system of holiday accommodation from the seaside
holidays of their interwar childhoods. As Joan explained:

> You didn't, er, full board there. If you know what that means, to us, you
> bought your own food, er, your ... er ... landlady cooked your dinner, er,
> you'd buy the meat and take it to her and she'd cook that er, you had to have
> a cold tea, which you provided yourself. She gave you a little cupboard, put
> your butter and your bread in and usually it was mice-ridden or something
> like that, you know so very few people, unless you were wealthy, er, boarded,
> you, you used to call it apartments, you see ... So of course you spent half
> your day foraging for food, for the next day, you know.

Asked who took responsibility for purchasing the food on holiday, both
women remembered it as daily work for their mothers: '*Your mother bought
the food for her to cook?* Yes. She went out shopping each day and bought the
food and ... oh she'd probably buy meat and, you know, fish and vege-
tables.'[35] Under this arrangement the landlady supplied basics such as bread,
milk and hot water for tea, at a small extra charge. Joan remembered that
the unscrupulous would charge for absolutely everything, including sauces

and the use of the cruet: she recalled one Blackpool landlady who charged ninepence for the use of salt and pepper alone.[36]

In the postwar period, too, women performed work while simultaneously being 'on holiday'. The increasing availability of a range of self-catering holidays allowed for flexibility and economy in holiday-going; however, the work of childcare was often more burdensome within an unfamiliar setting. Certainly the holidays which Dorothy took in her postwar married life did not constitute an uncomplicated form of leisure. The camping trips which her family so enjoyed gave no respite from the work of feeding and clothing them: she merely had to perform the same work in more difficult circumstances. As she stated: 'It's hard work. Not a holiday as such.' Asked why she continued to take holidays which she did not enjoy, she replied that she did it for her family: 'You don't mind what you do for your kids really, but I was quite delighted when I didn't have to go camping.' Here, leisure activity was clearly viewed as an arena for service and duty to the family – an association which will be pursued further in Chapter 5. Margaret, in contrast, noted that her holidays were a real rest for her: a time when her husband took over responsibility for the family finances and she had money in her pocket to spend entirely on herself. As she recalled:

> That was a real holiday. And we never went camping or in caravans or anything. We went in hotels. He said they might go camping or hire a flat next door, he said, what holiday does Mrs Ramsey have? If you go in a flat you've still got to cook, wash, iron and everything. Go in a hotel you're looked after.

For similar reasons, the holiday camp – of which the Butlins chain remains the best-known – was particularly popular among working-class women who could afford it. The absence of housework and food preparation duties and, importantly, the provision of childcare gave such women a real opportunity for a holiday rest.

Areas of acute definitional ambiguity

Close attention to the discourses surrounding housework and the family holiday reveal the ambiguities inherent in defining 'work' and 'leisure' in women's lives. In the final part of this chapter, I want to focus upon three additional areas where the question of what leisure is and what work is was shifting and unclear: shopping and sales, home crafts, and personal grooming or 'beauty'. In all instances the need to consider the historical context as well as the context of individual women's lives becomes apparent.

The sources consulted here reveal real ambiguity concerning the role of shopping and sales in women's lives. Generally they were regarded as a leisure activity, despite their status as real work for women with families. In the first half of this period, *Manchester Evening News* reporters referred to shopping and sales as differing degrees of leisure for women. In 1920, sales were described as 'women's joy days',[37] and in 1925 one writer employed a clear leisure metaphor in her assertion that 'there are ladies who look forward to these sales with all the ardour with which firstnighters at the theatre look forward to the first performance of a play by a well-known dramatist'.[38] Shopping was also referred to as 'a fascinating winter sport'.[39] While it might be thought that the *Manchester Evening News* was addressing a middle-class audience here, Andrew Davies' evidence also suggests that within the single activity shopping, work and leisure often interacted. In his study of working-class leisure, Davies demonstrates that Saturday-night markets, such as Shudehill in Manchester, provided a cheap form of entertainment for courting youths, married couples and even whole family groups.[40] Yet for the poorer working-class woman, such visits were only rarely a purely leisured experience. The opportunity presented late on a Saturday evening to buy food at rock-bottom prices ensured that market-visiting constituted an essential strategy for family survival.

Oral evidence supports this view of shopping as a complex mixture of work and pleasure for women. One respondent, Jean, recalled her mother's shopping trips into Manchester in the 1930s as 'a social outing', noting that 'she would really get dressed up.' Other interviewees remembered women of the same decade incorporating an element of socialising into the shopping which was an integral part of the daily routine. Ivy, for example, recalled one particular corner shop in 1930s Ancoats, which provided a focus for women in the community:

> *And did she, did you do much visiting, er, with the neighbours or anything like that?* She used to go and sit in the corner shop. And that was like a little community, you know, the … the mothers'd go in, for the shopping and they had erm, you know, orange boxes and things like that, and they'd all sit on there, and they'd be in the corner shop for about two hours, you know (laughs).

Similarly Joyce, whose parents owned a corner shop in Hulme noted that,

> we had a … high chair with a back in the corner by the counter called the rest-you, it was called the rest-you, there must've been some brand of thing called rest-you, and people would sit there and while they were ordering their stuff then, you know, the local gossip would come out.

In both these cases there is evidence of women making the work of shopping more enjoyable by engaging in conversation or 'gossip'.

The status of shopping as leisure, work or both was also, of course, subject to change across the life cycle and historical period. In 1935, the *New Survey of London Life and Labour* observed those to be found in the London streets of an evening: 'Older women, sometimes with a small child and a large basket, are chiefly engaged in buying, while the younger ones, usually in couples, appear to be mostly interested in the shop window, or in the young men, when they are not queuing up for the cinemas.'[41] Mass-Observation found that 26 per cent of 200 London girls interviewed in July 1949 had been shopping on the previous Saturday. However, as the report noted: 'this may have been more of a duty than an entertainment'.[42] An examination of wartime representations of shopping reaffirms the fluidity with which definitions of the activity must be approached. Under titles such as 'Now is the time to be hunting for bargains as never before!', the emphasis in the *Manchester Evening News* was on the 'good buy', not the enjoyment of the sale as a leisure activity in itself.[43] Sensible shopping became valuable and time-consuming war work, thus providing a key example of the influence of historical context upon leisure meanings.

Home-based activities such as knitting, sewing, cooking and baking were similarly open to confusion concerning their nature as activities. Was knitting, for example, leisure for women, or was it a productive use of time? Was it, in fact, a leisure legitimated by its productive nature? In a wartime study of young women's leisure, Olive Morgan recorded the merits of needlework as a leisure occupation for adolescent girls, emphasising, in particular, its usefulness and its sociability.[44] A *Manchester Evening News* article in 1925 pointed to the popularity of knitting, noting: 'it is just the thing while we wait for the pie to brown or for a husband to come in to tea; it is as much an expression of our busy crowded days as our shingled hair and one piece garments'.[45] For this writer, knitting reflected the fragmented nature of women's time, and constituted an activity which could be fitted around the activities of other family members.

The popularity of needlecrafts is confirmed in Mass-Observation's national postwar leisure survey. Approximately 50 per cent of the women interviewed cited 'sewing, knitting and mending' as their chief leisure activity.[46] Certainly, many of the Manchester interviewees spoke about these activities as enjoyable in themselves, and they will be dealt with as leisure in Chapters 3 and 5. However, there was also a recognition that both enabled time to be used productively. Jean, for example, remembered taking her knitting with her when she visited relatives: '*Was that because you enjoyed it or because you wanted to make something?* Bit ... bit of both really, erm, you know it was nice to have these embroidered clothes and, and covers for ... for your home, erm, and you felt that, erm, that you were making use of your time.' Indeed, for many of the women surveyed by Spring Rice in the mid 1930s and Mass-Observation a decade later, needlecraft was an essential part of their daily work. As one woman put it: 'I can always find plenty a darning and patching if not that I am refooting socks and knitting them and jumpers for the kiddies.'[47] Yet despite its status as work which had to be done, the sedentary nature of this activity led some working-class wives to regard sitting down and mending as their leisure time.

As with shopping, historical context played a part in defining the nature of knitting and sewing as activities. By 1940, needlework was characterised as war work, as women knitted items for the troops,[48] and a glance at women's magazines of this period reveals frequent exhortations to make this or that item for family members. In a situation of make-do-and-mend, the leisure became necessary work. Again, it is context which is vital here. It is essential to look at why the woman knitted or sewed, and the meanings which she herself attached to the activity.

Other interviewees expressed their enjoyment of cooking; Alice describing it as 'a real joy'. Often their comments reveal not only that the same activity could be both work and leisure in different contexts, but that the two meanings could coexist simultaneously. For example, Kathleen described the work of cooking for British Legion events as both duty and enjoyment: 'It was a good thing to do and we enjoyed doing it as well.' Moreover, particular activities could shift in meaning over the life cycle. In youth, the absence of compulsion led a number of the women interviewed to regard particular aspects of housework, such as cookery, as pleasurable activities. As Doris recalled of her lower-middle-class youth in the 1930s: 'Before I was married, you know, Friday night I used to make cherry cake or, erm, sponge sandwich, something like that, and I used to like doing it, I wasn't keen on other cooking, really, but I liked to bake.' Later in the life cycle such activities became an essential part of the working day. Mary, in contrast, noted her dislike of cooking before her marriage in 1939 (in fact she did not know how to cook), but claimed to have grown to enjoy it over the years: 'Yes, if you've got to do it, you do it and I quite liked it in the end, I did quite a lot of baking and entertaining.' The sentiment 'if you've got to do it you may as well enjoy it' adds another dimension to the intermingling of work and leisure in women's lives, and may well explain why many of the women interviewed professed their enjoyment of particular household chores despite their nature as work which had to be done.

Definitional ambiguity is evident in other aspects of women's daily lives; the final area to be examined here is that of personal grooming and the maintenance of 'beauty'. Often viewed as leisure for women, this could involve expensive and time-consuming work. As *Woman's Own* remarked in 1934: 'Men don't realise that it costs time and money to look nice, that pretty skin can't be got without pots of things from the chemist, that frocks soon look dowdy when you haven't many of them and have to wear them all the time.'[49] In a study of adolescent girls conducted in 1945, Pearl Jephcott identified the particular importance of appearance within the lives of those working-class girls to whom marriage, rather than paid work, offered the best prospect of a secure future: 'The "poor" girl's personal appearance is her main stock-in-trade. Her face literally *is* her fortune: and a girl can more quickly be a success through this than by her job.'[50] Once she was married, the pressure to maintain an interest in the realm of beauty continued. Women's magazines, and the advertisements therein, often emphasised the wife's duty to maintain her appearance for her husband's sake, if not her own. The advice of Mary Carlyle, 'Woman's Own beauty specialist', was advertised in the following way: 'Remember, looks do count after marriage. With her aid you can make the very best of yourself now and always.'[51] In a more sinister vein, another *Woman's Own* writer asked: 'Has the job of wife and mother so filled your time and interests that you have neglected yourself? Well remember how proud HE used to be of your appearance and then take yourself in hand before it is too late!'[52]

During wartime, beauty was presented as necessary to the upkeep of morale: 'Women are willing to help in every way and to give up any luxuries, but there is something about the lack of beauty aids that takes the starch out of their backbone.'[53] Moreover, as Goodman has demonstrated, female appearance was constructed as an essential element in the upkeep of male morale too.[54] The *Manchester Evening News* attempted to aid wartime women with the provision of some thrifty advice and, under the title 'Raid the larder for beauty', showed readers how to incorporate food products into their beauty routine.[55] In wartime, as elsewhere, there was a perceived link between women's appearance and ability, evident in advice offered to those in pursuit of outdoor activities: 'Don't let skin blemishes rob you of confidence'.[56] Advertisers throughout the period used this association between appearance and success to sell their products. Glymiel hand jelly was sold on the premiss that its purchase enabled one woman to rise to the post of private secretary,[57] and Eno's Fruit Salt was suggested to a secretary whose manager commented: 'Oh she's very capable, but I can't stand her complexion.'[58] By the 1950s, the popularity of the beauty contest intensified the idea of beauty as work with the appearance of newspaper headlines such as 'Beauty's Big Business'.[59] Interviews with contestants portrayed the competitions as a rational way of earning a living.

Part I of this book has demonstrated that common understandings of the term 'leisure' do not, on the whole, reflect the lived experiences of many women. In particular, the evidence presented so far has emphasised the weakness of a conception of leisure which places it in direct opposition to work and the workplace. Instead, I have argued that 'leisure' is better understood as a concept that is reliant upon the meanings which are given to particular experiences and the context, of both life cycle and historical moment, within which they are placed. Of course, the blurring of work into leisure was not exclusively the province of women. The postwar movement towards 'family leisure', and the growing popularity of home-based activities, had profound implications for masculine leisure too. New types of housing encouraged occupants to engage in home improvement and gardening in their 'leisure time'. In 1950, some 10 million males as well as 8.5 million females defined themselves as garden enthusiasts, and the time spent on 'home-hobbies' was extensive.[60] 'Leisure' of this type could also be hard, time-consuming and productive work, depending upon the context within which it was conducted. However, in contrast to the experience of many adult women with families, men largely continued to perceive the home as primarily a site of leisure; the tasks they performed were of a time-specific nature. Moreover, conceptions of leisure as 'reward' for paid labour endowed masculine leisure with a legitimacy often missing from the experiences of adult women. In Chapter 3 the focus will be upon the leisure experiences of youth. Here, the concept of legitimacy in leisure will be developed, as attention is drawn to a belief that young women, like men, earned their leisure through their engagement in full-time, paid employment.

Notes

1 E. Green, S. Hebron and D. Woodward, *Women's Leisure: What Leisure?* (Macmillan, London, 1990), p. 1.

2 H. Lenskyj, 'Measured time: women, sport and leisure', in *Leisure Studies*, 6:1 (1989), pp. 235–6.

3 Mass-Observation Archive (hereafter M-O A): 'The housewife's day', *New Series Bulletin*, no. 42 (May/June 1951), p. 2.

4 M-O A: Directive Respondent (hereafter DR) 53, reply to March/April 1948 Directive.

5 M-O A: DR1831, reply to March/April 1948 Directive.

6 *Manchester Evening News* (hereafter *MEN*), 20 November 1925, p. 10.

7 *MEN*, 18 May 1955, p. 2.

8 *MEN*, 20 October 1955, p. 5.

9 M. Spring Rice, *Working-Class Wives: Their Health and Conditions* (Penguin, Harmondsworth, 1939), pp. 96–7.

10 *Ibid.*, p. 106.

11 *MEN*, 7 November 1935, p. 4.

12 M-O A: 'The housewife's day', p. 12.

13 *Ibid.*, pp. 3–4.

14 As Chapter 5 will demonstrate, so-called 'family leisure' became the dominant experience as the period progressed.

15 *MEN*, 20 November 1925, p. 10.

16 *MEN*, 2 March 1955, p. 2.

17 Spring Rice, *Working-Class Wives,* p. 128.

18 *MEN*, 4 December 1930, p. 3.

19 *MEN*, 31 March 1955, p. 3.

20 Spring Rice, *Working-Class Wives*, p. 104.

21 *Good Housekeeping*, September 1955, p. 13.

22 *Ibid.*, p. 87.

23 *Good Housekeeping*, July 1937, inside front cover.

24 *Ibid.*, p. 143.

25 *MEN*, 30 June 1925, p. 7.

26 *MEN*, 16 September 1960, p. 7.

27 H. Llewellyn Smith (ed.), *The New Survey of London Life and Labour* (P. S. King & Son, London, 1935) pp. 5, 86–7.

28 *MEN*, 29 May 1930, p. 4.

29 A. Davies, *Leisure, Gender and Poverty: Working-Class Culture in Salford and Manchester, 1900–1939* (Open University Press, Buckingham, 1992), p. 41; S. Jones, *Workers at Play: A Social and Economic History of Leisure, 1918–1939* (Routledge & Kegan Paul, London, 1986), p. 39.

30 S. Fielding, P. Thompson and N. Tiratsoo, *'England Arise!' The Labour Party and Popular Politics in 1940s Britain* (Manchester University Press, Manchester, 1995), p. 150.

31 J. I. Gershuny and K. Fisher, 'Leisure in the UK across the twentieth century', *Working Papers of the ESRC Research Centre on Micro-Social Change* Paper 99–3 (Colchester, University of Essex, 1999), p. 16.

32 *MEN*, 27 August 1925, p. 7.

33 *MEN*, 9 May 1935, p. 3.

34 *MEN*, 15 February 1955, p. 2.

35 Dorothy.

36 The 'apartments' system declined steadily over the interwar period, replaced by the boarding-house system whereby meals were provided: J. Walton, *The Blackpool Landlady. A Social History* (Manchester University Press, Manchester, 1978), p. 4.

37 *MEN*, 29 December 1920, p. 2.

38 *MEN*, 5 January 1925, p. 4.

39 *MEN*, 30 May 1935, p. 4.

40 Davies, *Leisure, Gender and Poverty*, pp. 130–8.

41 Llewellyn Smith (ed.), *The New Survey of London Life and Labour*, pp. 51–2.

42 M-O A: File Report (hereafter FR) 3150, 'Teen-age girls', August 1949, p. 3.

43 *MEN*, 27 June 1940, p. 2.

44 O. Morgan, 'A study of the training for leisure occupations offered in a senior girls' school in an industrial area, together with an enquiry into the use made of this training by the girls, after their entry into employment', M.Ed. dissertation, University of Manchester, 1942, p. 71.

45 *MEN*, 23 October 1925, p. 10.

46 M-O A: FR3067, 'A report on work and leisure', November 1948, p. 10.

47 Spring Rice, *Working-Class Wives,* p. 50.

48 *MEN*, 12 March 1940, p. 7.

49 *Woman's Own*, 6 October 1934, p. 785.

50 P. Jephcott, *Rising Twenty*, (Faber & Faber, London, 1948), p. 63.

51 *Woman's Own*, 22 October 1932, p. 54.

52 *Woman's Own*, 6 October 1934, p. 785.

53 *MEN*, 30 October 1940, p. 4.

54 P. Goodman, '"Patriotic femininity": women's morals and men's morale during the Second World War', *Gender and History*, 10:2 (1998), pp. 280–1.

55 *MEN*, 9 January 1940, p. 2.

56 *MEN*, 3 April 1940, p. 2.

57 *Good Housekeeping*, January 1937, p. 86.

58 *Good Housekeeping*, March 1935, p. 107.

59 *MEN*, 3 May 1955, p. 3.

60 S. Constantine, 'Amateur gardening and popular recreation in the 19th and 20th centuries', *Journal of Social History*, 14:3 (1981), p. 387; R. McKibbin, 'Work and hobbies in Britain, 1880–1950', in J. M. Winter (ed.), *The Working Class in Modern British History* (Cambridge University Press, Cambridge, 1983), p. 132.

Part II

Leisure and the life cycle

3

'Stepping out with the young set': youthful freedom and independence

The nature of leisure within women's lives in twentieth-century England can be understood only if attention is paid to a series of contextual frameworks including historical moment, material circumstance and life-cycle stage. The evidence presented here emphasises the significance of life-cycle stage in actively structuring the leisure patterns of women from 1920 to 1960. As Mary explained:

> You can't live the same way all the time. I mean there's different chapters in your life. Always look on it as different chapters. Like when you're a child and then you're in your teens and that's a different chapter and then you get in your twenties and you've different ideas, then, and you're married, that's another chapter. And then you have your family, another sort of different life, another chapter.

Life-cycle stage influenced individual's expectations concerning their leisure opportunities and experiences. It also determined society's opinion of appropriate behaviour and, indeed, provided an organising concept for this. Even the experiences of those women who did not follow the usual route through youth to married adulthood were often constructed according to life-cycle dictates.

Chapter 3 addresses the particular life-cycle stage of youth, defined here as the period between leaving school and marrying – or, in the case of those who remained single, reaching the average age at marriage for their historical cohort. Youth was frequently seen as the pre-eminent period of leisure for women in their passage through the life cycle: Hoggart described it as a 'brief flowering period' for working-class girls.[1] The majority of respondents characterised the years between leaving school and marrying as a time of freedom and independence; a period with no major responsibilities and no developed sense of duty to others. In effect, youth constituted a period of legitimate leisure. As Dorothy put it: 'I'm awfully sorry that really my leisure ended when I started my family which was 1948. But I thought you might just be interested in, you know, before that.' Margaret, recalling her early leisure experiences in the interwar period, said: 'I had nobody to bother about.'

Certainly the experience of earning a wage and being engaged in clearly defined hours of work does seem to have engendered an assumption among young women that they were entitled to time for themselves. As Pearl Jephcott observed of the 152 elementary-school-educated 'working girls' who responded to her wartime questionnaire: 'the girls say that when you begin to work you want to go out at night'.[2] An underlying theme of this chapter, therefore, is the contention that the paid work of a woman's youth endowed her with a notion of 'earned' leisure. The first section pursues this concept of legitimacy in leisure by exploring the association between youth and leisure over the years, assessing shifts in this relationship over time and exploring the validity of a concept of 'youth culture' across the period. Having examined attitudes towards leisure entitlement in youth, I turn my attention to changing leisure experiences between 1920 and 1960. Here, particular consideration is given to the cinema and the dance hall as the two dominant leisure venues. Oral evidence, however, will show that young women's leisure was more complex and wide-ranging than a focus upon specific leisure *activities* might indicate.

Moreover, youth cannot be seen as a period of unproblematic leisure experience. Despite perceptions of independence in youthful leisure, the constraints of time and money could undermine any notion of unmitigated freedom. The organisation of procedures such as 'tipping up' (the handing over of wages to the family economy) and the allocation of 'spends' (the money retained or received back as pocket money), which were often influenced by gendered assumptions, acted as a control upon leisure opportunity. Similarly, the performance of household chores and other family duties, such as caring for ailing parents, could have an impact upon a young girl's access to leisure. Historically specific and class-based notions of appropriate behaviour, and constraints on behaviour informally enforced by the local community, also acted as a break upon unimpaired freedom. More directly, harsh parental discipline could prove a major barrier to the enjoyment of freedom and independence in leisure. After an exploration of those areas where young women did carve out personal spaces for pleasure, therefore, the final section of this chapter considers the constraints often placed upon the young in their pursuit of leisure.

Leisure as the preserve of youth

Chapter 2 demonstrated that a definitional opposition between work and leisure actually distorts our understanding of the lived experiences of women, particularly those who were married and performed the work of housewifery and childcare. This chapter suggests that a notion of leisure as 'reward' for paid labour actively framed both social constructions of the relationship between women and leisure, and women's own ideas concerning their personal leisure time. Within the life-cycle stage of youth, it seems probable that this notion of leisure as 'reward' precipitated an uncomplicated status in terms of leisure entitlement – a status which was founded upon some measure of economic independence.

Certainly, historians have highlighted the opportunities for leisure available to the young woman worker within the interwar period. Referring to his Manchester and Salford case study, Davies asserts: 'Prior to marriage, young women enjoyed much greater freedom and financial independence, and for a spell in their late teens, they were relatively privileged as consumers of leisure.'[3] Similarly, Hargreaves notes: 'the uneven pattern of poverty and prosperity left by the Depression made it easier for middle-class women, and working-class women who were relatively affluent, *or young and single*, to participate in sports, than for the masses of poorer working-class women'.[4] In his study of young men and women in interwar Britain, David Fowler has claimed that a distinctive youth culture, founded upon the consumption of new leisure products and autonomy in the workplace, predated the emergence of the postwar 'teenager'.[5]

Throughout the period, documentary sources provide evidence of this association between the years of youth and the pursuit of leisure. As a case study of local newspaper evidence will shortly demonstrate, the press often reflected upon youth through an assessment of leisure. Activity in this realm was regarded as constituting grounds for general assessments of young women's behaviour and their position within society. Elsewhere, the leisure experiences of young women attracted the attention of academic researchers. Within Manchester, the late 1930s and 1940s witnessed a series of investigations into leisure activity: James and Moore used the diary records of 535 Hulme adolescents, recorded in the summer of 1939, to examine leisure activities; Joan Harley used a combination of question-naires and interviews to access the leisure interests of elementary- and central-school-educated female wage-earners, aged between fourteen and nineteen, within central Manchester; Olive Morgan used similar methods to assess the impact of schooling upon the subsequent leisure 'occupa-tions' of 102 young women aged fourteen to eighteen in the East Man-chester district of Bradford.[6] Elsewhere, studies of Birmingham, London, Nottingham and Oxfordshire demonstrate a national preoccupation with the leisure of young people.[7] Within these studies, particular attention was paid to the 'rational' use of leisure amid concerns surrounding the influ-ence of commercial forms upon the young. As Harley asserted in justifi-cation of her own study: 'In view of the general increase in leisure which has been brought about in quite recent years by the regulation of the length of working hours, the question of its proper use has become of vital importance, since it affects the happiness of the individual, but also the well-being and stability of the community.'[8]

These writers, then, approached their subjects with a pre-defined no-tion of the 'proper use' of leisure; most were critical of the leisure choices made by adolescents. James and Moore, for example, condemned the apparent passivity of the activities they surveyed, noting: 'the cinema, the radio, the "pulps" are examples of this casual entertainment'.[9] Across the period, social investigators promoted an 'improving' use of leisure time through the evening school, youth organisation or club. However, in their studies they actually observed a tendency towards consumption which they perceived as destructive to a girl's well-being. Morgan's conclusions made her disapproval of the working girls' leisure choices clear:

> The function of wage-earning should be kept in proportion to the rest of life, and should not be the mainspring of leisure occupation, as it too often is. The attitude of most of the girls is that the more money they have, the more pleasure they can buy. The fact that they buy entertainment instead of making it for themselves robs them of much of the fullness of enjoyment.[10]

As the following discussion of local newspaper evidence will demonstrate, a characterisation of the young female worker as a reckless consumer was often used as a vehicle to express a more fundamental unease concerning changes in women's work and behaviour.

Young women's leisure: a site for fear and optimism?

Throughout the interwar period, the leisure activities of young women provoked a contradictory mixture of concern and approval among readers of and contributors to the *Manchester Evening News*. For example, leisure behaviour was used both to identify, and to condemn the flapper: a woman to whom the pursuit of personal pleasure was deemed more appealing than marriage and – crucially, at a time of birth-rate concern – child-bearing. In 1920, one article recorded the words of Dr R. Murray Leslie under the title 'Too Many Women. Is it the cause of social unrest?', expressing his concern at the prevalence of 'social butterflies' within society, and condemning the, 'frivolous, scantily-clad, jazzing flapper, irresponsible and undisciplined, to whom a new hat, a dance, or a man with a car are of more importance than the fate of the nation'.[11] Thus, a love of dancing and fashion was used to imply a recklessness with more serious repercussions for the nation. Similar concern at the leisure behaviour of the flapper was expressed by a male reader, later in the same decade, who claimed:

> a great number of flappers do swear and smoke. Two cafés, not a stone's throw away from where I live, are every Sunday evening simply packed with this type of girl, joking and sipping coffee in the company of boys, and unless you have an unseemly joke or tale to tell there, you are considered dull. The tap-room of a public-house, in many instances, is far more preferable.[12]

'The flapper' constituted one archetype of the interwar period – popularly, although not entirely accurately, perceived to be the unmarried, middle-class girl, with time and money to spare. Within Manchester, 'the mill girl' represented another image of young womanhood, identified as much by her leisure behaviour as by her employment. For example, an *Evening News* article at the start of the period expressed surprise, and an ill-disguised disapproval, of the leisure opportunities apparently enjoyed by this young worker. Under the somewhat sensational headline 'Dressy Mill Girls. Saturday Afternoon House Parties. Money to Burn. Chocolates, Cinema and the Hesitation Waltz', a Special Correspondent recorded the consequences of increased pay for the adolescent worker: 'A new type of factory girl has arisen since 1914. She can afford to entertain friends generously and she dances the hesitation waltz.'[13] Thus an underlying fear of the economically independent working-class woman was articulated with reference to her leisure behaviour.

However, in contrast to the national figure of the flapper, the mill girl was a particularly local character and, as such, could not be uniformly castigated. Indeed, the mill girl's treatment within the pages of the *Manchester Evening News* provides clear evidence of the complexity of attitudes towards young women's leisure at the local level. While some writers, as we have seen, viewed her behaviour with alarm, others adopted a more optimistic tone. One ex-mill worker, for example, wrote to the newspaper defending her increased earnings: 'Instead of being criticised a monument should be raised in her honour. She is a heroine emerging from slavery. The Lancashire mill-girl, God defend her, has feelings as keen, and as tender, as your proud city ladies.'[14] A decade later, a series entitled 'Girls we all know' provided a characterisation of the mill girl, referred to here as 'Lancashire's own girl'. As in the 'dressy mill girls' article, leisure choices were cited as evidence of her personality, but – significantly – that personality was regarded as 'shrewd, capable and self-reliant'; in effect, she was assigned the traits of the respectable working class. This very positive assessment of the mill girl both informed and had its basis in the writer's view of her leisure behaviour. As the reporter asserted: 'It is at Blackpool during her town's Wake Week that you see the Mill girl in all her glory. The clothes she wears she bought for Whit Sunday, for Whit Week is *the* week in Lancashire for new clothes, and she revels in their smartness. She has all the money saved up for this annual holiday and she does have a good time.'[15] Here, there is a clear sense of earned leisure; the mill girl had saved the money for this holiday, and the writer saw no reason why she should not enjoy it to the full. The article also points to the importance of appearance among young women of this period. As both Jerry White and Sally Alexander have demonstrated with reference to London case studies, clothes, make-up, hairstyles and jewellery, as well as the pursuit of leisure which allowed them to be seen, were indicative of a new femininity of glamour and – albeit short-lived – independence, evident in the interwar period.[16]

As the treatment meted out to the mill girl demonstrates, the *Manchester Evening News* did not speak with one voice on the subject of young women's leisure. While the activities of some could occasion concern, elsewhere leisure was treated as a barometer of progress. In 1920, it carried a eulogy to the modern girl of fiction: 'The new heroine has marched with the new girl of fact. She is confident. She is "all there". She fears neither mice nor men. She can combine the gentle gaze of the dove with the strategy of a field marshal. She can face facts. She has been to cinemas.'[17] The fact that the 'new girl' visited the cinema was presented as an integral part of her onward march, as well as an indication of her loss of innocence. Later in the same decade, the link between women's leisure activity and wider changes in their position within society was made explicit when a *Manchester Evening News* reporter went in search of what he called 'Miss 1926': 'She is still shingled but skirts are shorter, she continues to revel in her new-found freedom, and she is more charming than ever.'[18] The writer observed, in an approving tone, that this 'freedom' extended to the absence of chaperone and her presence at the dance unaccompanied. A *Manchester Evening News* editorial of 1930 catalogued the exploits of 'these modern girls': 'One of them won the King's Cup ... Another flew to Australia. Another won the King's prize at Bisley. More of them have broken motoring, exploring and mountaineering records, and they hardly bother to swim the Channel now. Before long we shall probably see a girl bowler dealing with Bradman.'[19] The achievements listed in this piece as evidence of the changing nature of womanhood were, without exception, rooted in the sphere of leisure. Specifically, sporting prowess was used as a vehicle for wider pronouncements concerning the role of women in society: an indication of both the increased visibility, and the continued novelty, of the British sportswoman within the interwar period.

Wartime led to a dislocation in the reporting of leisure within the *Manchester Evening News*. Certainly, this local source had other preoccupations during the war years, although the newspaper continued to provide general information concerning leisure opportunities within the Manchester area. The oral evidence presented later in this chapter will testify to the continuing importance of the cinema and dance hall within young women's lives during this period. Indeed, life-cycle stage continued to be the dominant factor in structuring women's access to leisure throughout these years. However, attitudes towards young women's leisure are less easy to detect in the press. The complex mixture of fear and optimism which pervaded writing on young women's leisure in the interwar period was superseded by the more pressing concerns of war.

In the postwar period, the young female at her leisure was regarded as neither threat nor anomaly. While youth became increasingly associated with the sphere of leisure, women's continued tendency to marry, at an ever earlier age, nullified the threat posed by economically independent females at their leisure. The attitude of the *Manchester Evening News* towards young women's leisure shifted from one which heralded their activities as remarkable, and therefore newsworthy, to one which viewed them as an accepted norm. While the young woman could still provoke disapproval, it was her appearance, and implicitly her sexual behaviour, rather than her leisure choices which captured the attention. In 1950, John Ryan criticised the appearance of a certain type of Manchester office worker, condemning: her walk, unshaven legs under sheer nylon tights, 'bizarre head scarf', bleached and unbrushed hair, smeared lipstick, 'the lumpy effect of inexpertly applied make-up on the lashes', bright-red varnish on her fingernails, and shrill voice.[20] Not surprisingly, the newspaper's readership responded with a storm of protest; one writer asserted: 'Maybe if he had finished his tour he would have found that this girl has brains.'[21]

Within the pages of the *Manchester Evening News* there was an assumption that young people of both sexes were, justifiably, interested in leisure activity of all types. Moreover, youth became ever more closely associated with the consumption of leisure commodities.[22] By the 1950s, the newspaper conducted quite wide-ranging surveys of teenage leisure behaviour, including 'Stepping Out With the Young Set in 1955.' which demonstrated the popularity of dancing among Manchester's youth.[23] When, in 1955, the newspaper began to break up into different sections aimed at different readerships, a regular 'teenagers' page' emerged, with items on clothes, music, dancing, fashion and sport. An example from January of that year included: a fashion piece entitled 'Girls! Look out for dazzling cottons, creamy tweeds'; a report on 'hairstyles that are band-box fresh'; a column concerned with male fashions which urged 'Go sporty young man'; and the regular item 'Placed on record', which dealt with the record industry.[24] Young people were no longer simply observed at their leisure; they constituted an established leisure class capable of making their own demands as part of the local newspaper's constituency – a fact that other leisure industries had recognised a generation earlier. Reader participation was thus encouraged, with answers solicited to questions such as 'Who is your number 1 teenager at the moment, the boy or girl you would put top of the list for fame and achievement?' and 'When should a girl get in of an evening?'[25] Overall, the newspaper strove to portray the average Manchester teenager as responsible and thoughtful, perhaps leaving the more sensational exposés of juvenile misdemeanour to those who could better afford to offend this section of society: the national press.

Youth culture, 1920–60

At the end of our period, Mark Abrams identified patterns of 'distinctive teenage spending for distinctive teenage ends in a distinctive teenage world'.[26] However, as David Fowler has demonstrated, 'youth culture' was not an invention of the postwar period, nor did the consumption of leisure goods, by which it was defined, emerge only after the Second World War.[27] The success of commercial entertainments such as the cinema and dance hall was, in large part, predicated upon the existence of a youthful clientele eager, and able, to assert their own leisure choices. Moreover, as Davies has demonstrated, the distinct identity of working-class youth was apparent in less formal leisure choices such as the Sunday-evening 'monkey parade'.[28] Representations of the youth–leisure relationship, outlined above, provide evidence of a distinct youth culture prior to the 1950s. For young women, this association was particularly acute; in later life many would look back on this period as a golden age of leisure. None the less, trends which were apparent in the interwar period intensified after the Second World War. As Osgerby writes: 'The post-war era saw a range of developments in labour markets, earning power, cultural provision and marketing which, together, served to accentuate considerably the profile of "youth" as an identifiable social category.'[29] Consumer culture became increasingly attractive to young people, who spent their money on a wide range of leisure goods and commercial entertainments. Moreover, girls in particular were less likely to be asked to contribute to the running of the home, thus adding to the time spent in pursuit of personal pleasures.[30] Newspaper evidence points to a deepening characterisation of youth as a leisured age, and an acceptance that adolescents of both sexes possessed the money with which to finance their pursuits. As Patrick Nicolson concluded his article 'Young people and their money. How do they spend it?': 'They expect high wages and they get high wages. And it never, never occurs to them that things will ever be any different.'[31] In the case of women, an intensified focus upon the years of 'youth' may have reflected the reality that these years of relative independence were becoming ever shorter, a consequence of the falling age at marriage in the postwar period.

Leisure experiences in youth

In her 1942 thesis, Olive Morgan observed: 'In my interviews with the girls … the most usual reply I received to my question "what do you do in your spare time?" was "I read, knit, go to the pictures and dance."'[32] In a book published in the same year, Pearl Jephcott used a chapter on leisure

to explore reading, dancing and the pictures, while James and Moore identified the chief leisure interests of working girls in Manchester as dancing,
cinema, reading, radio and 'talk', a category in which they included 'sex
activity'.[33] As I have already indicated, these and similar surveys from
across the country were critical of the extent to which young girls spent
their leisure time in 'escapist amusements', notably dancing, the cinema
and 'romantic stories'.[34]

Oral testimony also indicates that two forms of commercial leisure
were the most popular *activities* among young working women. In almost
all the interviews, women described either picture-going or dancing as the
pre-eminent leisure pursuit of their youth. Freda, referring to the 1920s,
recalled: 'Dancing was all the rage then, you see, dancing and pictures were
the two main ways of enjoying yourself.' Dorothy spoke of a later period:
'Well I was fifteen when the war started which was 1939, and our biggest
pleasure was dancing. It was very, very … you know, everybody danced,
yes and, erm, also the cinema.' Those women whose youth spanned the
postwar period similarly recalled the popularity of these two leisure activities.
Jean, who married in 1955 at the age of twenty-five, said: 'I mean you
would go to the local cinema you see, the cinema was very much the thing
in, in the thirties. And in the forties as well, with, even during the war.'
And Amy, who was born in 1936, remembered: 'I used to love going
dancing. It's the one thing now that I really, really miss. We used to go to
dances ever such a lot.'

Neither dancing nor visits to the pictures were entirely the preserve of
youth. Both forms of leisure, in fact, provide evidence of the way in which
the same activity could carry different meanings at distinct stages of the
life cycle. As such, we will revisit them in Chapter 5, when their role in
adult life will be explored. However, youth was usually the period in life
when most women enjoyed these activities to the full; in this chapter,
therefore, their particular attraction as leisure for young working girls will
be addressed.

The cinema and dance hall

In 1935, *The New Survey of London Life and Labour* observed that the 258
cinemas within the county of London were capable of accommodating a
quarter of the whole region's population on any one day.[35] Nationally,
there were 4,618 cinemas open in 1941, although this figure had dropped
substantially to 3,080 by 1960.[36] In their study of weekday leisure, James

and Moore concluded that for working girls between the ages of fourteen and twenty-one living in the Hulme district of Manchester, the cinema represented the most constant use of leisure time.[37] While the hours dedicated to reading and the radio, clubs, 'talk', and dancing either diminished or expanded over the age range, the cinema retained a constant attraction, accounting for between 14 and 17 per cent of their non-working hours.[38] In a subsequent report on weekend leisure, the authors did, however, note a decline in Saturday cinema attendance from the age of sixteen, as dancing, and particularly 'talk', increased in popularity.[39] The explanation for this – particularly female – shift in time use was said to lie in the growing importance of courting activity at weekends from the age of sixteen, a phenomenon which will be explored in the following chapter. Nevertheless, the popularity of the cinema as a leisure pursuit for young girls remains apparent. Of the 169 unselected girls and 95 club and evening school attenders surveyed by Joan Harley, 90 per cent went to the cinema at least once a week; in Olive Morgan's study the results were even more striking, with 84 per cent of the girls surveyed attending twice or more every week.[40] In 1942, Pearl Jephcott noted: 'It is not unusual to find a girl of fourteen who goes to the pictures nearly every night.'[41] Even in 1955, when cinema audiences had begun a national decline, a *Manchester Evening News* survey asserted that 98 per cent of Manchester's working boys and girls attended the cinema one or more times a week.[42] In their 1951 national study, based on indirect interviews, case histories and specialised enquiries, Rowntree and Lavers found that cinema audiences were composed of a disproportionate number of young people.[43]

Oral testimony supports documentary evidence as to the continued popularity of the cinema among young women across the period, although clear class differences in the experience of picture-going do emerge. A diary kept by one working-class respondent, Irene, testified to 141 cinema visits in the year 1941. Freda, who contributed just half of her wages to her lower-middle-class family economy, recalled attending the cinema every Monday, Wednesday and Friday. As she stated: 'My married sister insists that I went every night of the week, but I didn't, I think about three times, about three times a week we used to go.' In contrast, Ivy, whose upbringing in Ancoats was framed by poverty, recalled: 'we just went to the pictures on Saturday night. Well you only had enough spends to go once.' She remembered that the money her mother gave her was just sufficient to pay for this trip, a block of chocolate and her contribution to the church collection. At a basic level, therefore, economic circumstance dictated the frequency of visits to the cinema.

The cinema did, however, remain a predominantly working-class activity.[44] In a survey of the civilian cinema audience during World War Two, Louis Moss and Kathleen Box found that there was a higher proportion of frequent cinema-goers among those working-class families with an income of five pounds a week or less, although it should be added that this group also contained the highest proportion of those who did not go at all.[45] Within this group, it was young women wage-earners who were best represented among the 'cinema enthusiasts'.[46] Three years later, Box noted that the higher-paid sections of the working class attended with most frequency, paying an average price of one shilling and ninepence per cinema seat.[47]

Although cinema prices could be as high as the eight shillings and sixpence advertised by the Leicester Square Theatre in the 1930s,[48] the cinema was generally regarded as a cheap form of leisure. Local cinema prices in the middle of this period ranged from a few pence for the cheaper seats to just over a shilling for the more comfortable accommodation, and prices were reduced for matinée performances. Even in the 1950s, prices at inner-city picture houses such as the Crescent cinema in Hulme, which seated 1,000, remained in the range of tenpence to one shilling and sixpence.[49] In fact only one respondent, Ada, claimed that economic considerations prevented her from regularly attending the cinema. However, as she had possessed fourteen shillings and sixpence spends a week in the interwar period, a more likely explanation for her non-attendance would appear to have been her own leisure priorities, which included expensive weekly piano lessons.

Price of admission did, however, generally determine the type of cinema to which girls would go, thus maintaining class distinctions among the cinema-going public.[50] Irene, a particularly keen cinema-goer who claimed that she had known the programmes at every cinema in Manchester, recalled one Ardwick cinema, the Coliseum, which had prices as low as tuppence. Her description of its interior confirms the link between cost of admittance and quality of experience: 'It was a huge barn of a place and the doors opened straight out into the street and if − of course we used to get fog years ago and if it was foggy the fog'd come seeping in and you couldn't see. You couldn't see anything.' She also remembered usherettes spraying disinfectant in the air, and recalled: 'You could hardly see the screen for

The Paramount cinema and Plaza ballroom in Manchester, c.1930s.   **3**

cigarette smoke sometimes.' Similarly, Barbara remembered being unable to see the film at her local cinema, despite having 'gone mad' and paid ninepence to sit at the back of the stalls. She recalled that a seepage of fog into the cinema from outside prevented her from seeing Nelson Eddy and Jeanette MacDonald on the screen.

For those who were able to pay the slightly higher prices charged by city-centre picture houses, a world of glamour and luxury replaced the seeping fog and lingering disinfectant. The 'supercinemas' of this age were sumptuous evidence of the vitality of commercial entertainments, as the following description makes clear: 'These buildings, made mostly of concrete, have very "modernistic" decorations, and display many neon signs across their façades. Inside, the upholstery is most luxurious, the seats well sprung and covered with velvet, and there is much space, warmth and light.'[51] In periods of momentary affluence, a trip to the cinema allowed working-class girls access to a physical environment which differed markedly from their home experiences. As Irene explained:

> Well you see, erm, our homes weren't very comfortable. Er, just a two up and two down. We had no, er, no hot water and the outside toilet. Er, just gas

light and especially if you went to the Odeon, or the Paramount cinema, they were like palaces, so you could spend two or three hours just going inside, cos they were wonderful, especially the, erm, the Paramount. They were … they were just like palaces inside. And, er, you'd be taken out of your, well it was a bit of a miserable environment for two or three hours, go to this lovely palace and sit in a comfortable seat and see, er, well it … going to the pictures as it was called.

Jephcott recognised that a key attraction of the cinema was the 'escape' it represented from an uncomfortable or overcrowded home, and cited the example of one young cinema-goer, who shared a house with 'a blind father and eight other people' and visited the cinema for solitude and relief from household chores.[52] Like the bingo hall of later years, the cinema provided a relatively safe and respectable public leisure space for women, which could – in direct contrast to the dance hall or public house – be enjoyed alone.

Visits to the cinema constituted good value for money, providing a whole afternoon's or evening's entertainment which included forthcoming attractions, the news, cartoons, and a 'B' film as well as the main picture. The cinema also provided other forms of leisure that appealed to the young woman worker, although, once again, these attractions were subject to class differentiation, particularly in the interwar period. Mary, for example, remembered the social aspect of visits to the cinemas of Didsbury and Withington: 'all the picture houses they had cafés and you met your friends there and you had a coffee before you went into the pictures. First- and second-house pictures, picture houses everywhere.' The Piccadilly cinema in the city centre offered its patrons restaurant, café and dancing facilities, as well as a programme of films.[53] Other cinemas offered variety acts as part of the programme, music from the electric organ or even orchestral interludes. In Manchester, the Ardwick Coliseum – or 'bughut', as Irene called it – organised mid-programme talent shows for its working-class clientele: 'I don't think anybody paid, they used to go on the stage and just make a fool of themselves. But it were, it was wonderful.'

A trip to the cinema constituted a substantial night out for many of the women interviewed. As Margaret remembered:

Well it used to be a planned night out, love. You'd take enough money to go in, enough money to buy an ice cream or a chocolate and if it was out of Urmston, we used to walk to the Empress and the Palace, they're not there any more, but we used to get a bus if we went to Stretford or Manchester.

And you used to go out and it was an evening out. You'd go there to the cinema, in the interval you'd have your ice cream or your chocolate then you'd see the big film and then you'd come out and get the bus home or walk home.

The cinema was also a convenient place to meet boyfriends or friends away from parental supervision – a use which will be examined in Chapter 4. Others regarded it as a convenient, and cheap, sanctuary from the cold. For example, Amy used the Manchester News Theatre in the 1950s as a kind of shelter:

And you could go in there for a shilling or something, and if it was cold and wet and raining and you'd been in town all day and you were too tired to go back home before you went out at night, you could go in for a shilling and have a cup of coffee for sixpence and have a little sleep, because it was always warm and quiet and a nice rest and then you were ready for, you know, for the night.

Other girls viewed the films they saw as a window on changing fashions and behaviour.[54] Later in the period, girls, as well as boys, were to be found dancing in the cinema aisles at screenings of *Rock Around the Clock*, as film, dance and music came together in one explicitly 'teen' experience.[55]

Pre-eminent among the alternative commercial leisure forms vying for the time and money of young women during these years was dancing. In the interwar period, commentators observed a 'dance craze' founded upon the influence of modern jazz, which led one writer to pose the question: 'Dance Mania. Has it a degrading tendency?'[56] This report reflects a view in which dancing, and particularly jazz, were seen as 'symptomatic of social decay' in the years immediately following the First World War.[57] In particular, there was concern around working-class women's sexuality, a resentment of American influence and an undisguised racism concerning the adoption of black-influenced dance forms. As the period progressed, however, dancing itself met less overt disapproval from those who wrote on the subject. In 1925, the *Manchester Evening News* contended: 'Dancing is, undoubtedly, getting a firmer grip of the people every day. New dance halls are being opened everywhere, and old and young spend happy hours gliding around to the strains of syncopated melodies.'[58] None the less, each new trend – from the Charleston to the Lambeth Walk, the jitterbug to rock'n'roll was subjected to critical rigour and often observed with some distaste by teachers of ballroom dancing who sought to enforce uniformity in dance steps.[59]

As with the cinema, different dance halls carried different reputations and status, depending upon their location, admission price and clientele. Within interwar Manchester, the Piccadilly Dance Salon, part of the Piccadilly cinema and restaurant complex, offered both tea dances and evening dances at a cost of one shilling and sixpence. In contrast, the Belle Vue ballroom – which, according to one local survey, had a reputation of being 'common' and 'rowdy' – offered dances with an admission price of ninepence.[60] In the postwar years, dancing grew increasingly popular. In their 1951 study *English Life and Leisure*, Rowntree and Lavers estimated that there were 450 dance halls in the United Kingdom admitting three million – predominantly young – dancers per week, and charging admission fees that ranged from one shilling and sixpence to two shillings and sixpence.[61] The *Manchester Evening News* claimed in 1955: 'More people go dancing on a Saturday night than go to football matches in the afternoon.'[62]

Dancing, then, constituted an extremely popular form of leisure activity for young women throughout this period, although less so than the cinema in the interwar years and slightly more so by the late 1950s. Harley noted: 'Dance halls are not as popular with the girls as cinemas, but many girls spend a considerable part of their time dancing. Its attractions are obvious. The girls enjoy the lights, the colours and the band. They feel excited at the opportunity of dancing with the boys they meet and hope to find "romance".'[63] Mass-Observation found that 42 per cent of the 200 London girls they interviewed in 1949 enjoyed dancing in their spare time compared to the 36 per cent who favoured the cinema.[64] Oral testimony provides strong evidence of the popularity of dancing among women of both working-class and lower-middle-class backgrounds. Margaret, for example, said: 'I can't remember anything really except dancing from fourteen to twenty-one'; and Freda, remembering her youth in the 1920s, recalled: 'Dancing was all the rage then, you see, dancing and pictures were the two main ways of enjoying yourself.' For one interviewee, dances at the Sale Lido were the only pleasure available to her as she struggled to care for a seriously ill mother. Demonstrating considerable commitment in fitting her dancing into an otherwise exhausting schedule, she explained: 'When I went shopping on a Saturday, I'd go to the Saturday-afternoon tea dance even if I only stayed half an hour.' Tellingly, she referred to dancing as an 'escape' from an otherwise difficult lifestyle: 'I don't remember any regular pleasure except escaping now and again to dance. That was my main pleasure.'[65]

Inside the Ritz ballroom in Manchester, c.1930. **4**

Like the cinema, dancing did provide an element of escapism for young girls, allowing them access to a world of comfort and glamour which many normally had little opportunity to experience.[66] Harley noted that dancing lifted girls out of their everyday surroundings, and Morgan explained the attraction of the dance hall by reference to the bright lights and loud dance music which provided a contrast to conditions at home.[67] Morgan also observed that this activity enabled young women to show off new items of clothing, and allowed them access to potential boyfriends.[68] Indeed, Freda stressed the importance of dressing up for the dances she attended at the Chorlton Palais de Dance in the 1920s: 'Well it made the ev' ... well if you didn't get any partners, at least you knew you were looking nice.' One twenty-three-year-old typist from Liverpool told Mass-Observation in 1939: 'Preparing for a dance is half the fun to my mind. Getting one's frock ready. Wondering whether you shall have your hair done, or whether it'll stick up by itself, hoping it won't be wet, or cold, for that matter, for even if you go by car it's generally pretty draughty.'[69] Certainly Sally Alexander has noticed the 'insistent presence' of both dress and romance in London women's recollections of their youth.[70]

Dancing was, then, a complex leisure experience which transcended the dance venue itself: appearance, consumption, sexuality, and friendship as well as music and physical movement were aspects of the overall experience. However, access to the dance hall itself was more costly than visits to the cinema, and made more consistent demands upon a young girl in terms of appearance and skill. Harley recorded that entrance fees could range from threepence to two shillings, and Morgan noted the cost of attendant articles such as appropriate dress, cosmetics and dancing lessons.[71] One interviewee recalled that a trip to her local dance hall would have to constitute a whole week's leisure: 'You know, er, just probably had enough to go to a dance on a Saturday and that was it for, er, you know, the rest of the week you had to stay in.'[72]

Those who could afford regular visits to the dance hall remembered them vividly and with great affection. Many still regarded dancing as a favourite activity, even if they rarely found the opportunity to dance after marriage. As Jane remarked: 'Dancing has really always been my major, er, leisure activity'; and Dorothy remembered dancing at 'every opportunity, mostly every night'. Several women, particularly those whose dancing years spanned the prewar and wartime years, had fond memories of trips to the Mecca-owned Ritz and Plaza dance halls in Manchester city centre. Margaret, for example, recalled nights spent at the Ritz in Whitworth Street:

> Where they had a turntable bandstand. And one band used to play for half and then it would turn round and another band would play. That's where we used to meet the fellas. *What kind of music was it there?* Ah! We used to dance in those days. Waltz, foxtrot, quickstep, one-step, tango, mmm. Oh yes! … I used to love going to the Ritz. We used to sit at tables and fellas used to come up and say 'May I have this dance?'

She remembered that a visit to the fish-and-chip shop after the dance would provide an end to the evening's entertainment. Another respondent, who worked on munitions during the war, asserted that 'everybody danced, it was you know, erm, really, even during the war when, you know, people were … were worried and that, they still danced.'[73] Indeed, even when she was working nights, Dorothy would get up in the middle of the day to dance every other afternoon: 'And, erm, I'd have a quick bath and, er, go to bed and then she'd [her mother] shout me about one o'clock ... And erm, you know, dance all afternoon.' Dance halls such as these would often provide trained staff with whom to dance and improve your own dancing ability, or adapt to new genres of dance. As Davies has argued, dancing thus offered those working-class youths who could afford it, an important opportunity to develop skills.[74] The postwar period did, however, witness the decline of the professional partner.[75]

While many of the women interviewed attended public dance halls, other venues for dancing were available and catered for women of different social backgrounds. As Morgan explained, Sunday-school socials, works dances and private parties also offered opportunities to dance.[76] Those predominantly middle-class young women who replied to the Mass-Observation directive of January 1939 mentioned private dances given by friends or club, hotel and restaurant dances, college dances and private charity dances.[77] Among the lower middle-class Manchester interviewees, Mary recalled that in the 1920s: 'There were dances everywhere. Everybody, every Saturday there were tennis club dances and, er, hockey club dances, erm, Conservative people had dances, everybody either danced or went to the pictures on Saturday.' Freda remembered tennis club dances, Joyce frequented dances at the Boys' Brigade and Kate recalled going to dances at the local Scout hut. In the 1950s, Amy danced at the students' union as well as jazz clubs, such as the Bodega, in the city centre.

Manchester women of contrasting class backgrounds found opportunities to dance in their membership of one of the two Gaelic Leagues that were in existence until the mid 1960s – an indication that ethnicity could operate as a cross-class force in leisure. Ivy, for example, who had originally learnt to dance by watching older girls on the streets of Ancoats, and had later taken lessons at the Jimmy Winters dancing academy, was a committed member of the *Craobh na Laimhe Deirge* branch in Dickinson Street. She explained that she was drawn to the league by her fascination for Ceilidh dancing, sparked by her Irish Catholic background, and recalled: 'Up till I got married, I really, I went Ceilidh dancing ... And, er, we never stopped going, you know, we kept on going, you know, we kept on going there Wednesday and Sunday.' Alice, another woman who took dancing lessons in her youth, and had Irish Catholic roots, also attended this branch of the League; while Joyce, a lower-middle-class, second-generation Irish Catholic, was a member of the rival, and more established, Cross Street organisation, *Craobh Oisin,* and used to go dancing there every Sunday night. As she observed: 'So as I say, that ... that was my main social life then with the, with the Gaelic League, erm really.'

As Morgan observed, some parents did in fact forbid their daughters to attend public dance halls, especially where these were licensed, on the grounds of 'respectability'.[78] Evidence for this type of parental control comes from women of all backgrounds, and supports Davies' understanding of respectability as 'a complex and multi-layered category'.[79] For example, Jessie's working-class father exercised a strict control over her movements, particularly after her mother's death when she was just fourteen: 'then he would only let me go to a dance if it was down at church. And er, I couldn't go to dances anywhere else ... he didn't want me to go into bad company.' Joan noted that her parents restricted her dancing to ticketed affairs:

> You couldn't go to a public dance, my mother and father wouldn't let you. Now that was a dance where you can just go in, and, erm, pay money and go in. They would only let you go to a dance that had tickets. Church dance or ... a charity dance or something like that you know. Because of who you'd meet. Places like the Ritz, which ... but there was, there were local places like that, it didn't have to be in town. But those places, no way. *Why, what was th'?* they thought you'd meet the wrong type of person there. *What, rough or...?* Rough and perhaps dangerous, you know.

Similarly Celia, who remembered her father as an excessive drinker, was warned not to attend the Ritz during the war years because of its reputation as a 'picking-up place'. In a study of 103 girls aged between seventeen and twenty-one, conducted in March 1945, Jephcott claimed that girls were generally aware of the kind of company to be found at different dance halls.[80] Certainly, Jane was aware of the reputations carried by particular halls, noting that Friday night at Finnigans on Queens Road and Saturdays at the Devonshire Street Ballroom in Cheetham Hill were commonly regarded as the fighting nights. In fact, she recalled that the Devonshire was known as 'the blood bath' on that particular night.[81] Mass-Observation directive replies from July 1939 provide evidence of middle-class views of public dance halls. For example, one twenty-four-year-old single BBC employee stated: 'I've never been in a dance hall – if by that you mean the shady-looking places usually in the neighbourhood of Charing Cross Road and thereabouts where you can go and dance. Or more local Palais de Danse halls, like the one in Hammersmith. I think of them as haunts of the less desirable sections of the lower classes.'[82] A thirty-seven-year-old housewife from London said: '[I] have never been in a dance hall. I think they are all right for the lonely person who is keen on dancing or the working-class girl or fellow who has no other opportunities of meeting the opposite sex.' [83] Certainly few of the respondents to either the January or the July directive admitted to frequenting public dance halls themselves.

Social researchers of the period uniformly emphasised the attraction of the dance, regardless of venue, as an arena for meeting boys. Harley, for example, observed that: 'It is generally more popular with girls of sixteen or over than with younger girls since the former have a much more clearly defined interest in boys. While it is difficult to estimate with accuracy the extent of interest in boys, it is safe to say that they loom fairly large from the age of fifteen onwards.'[84] Morgan claimed that 'The whole question of dancing is intimately bound up with the sexual development of the girls'; while James and Moore equated an increase in dancing from the age of sixteen with an increased interest in 'heterosexual activity'.[85] A *Manchester Evening News* survey of 1955 asserted: 'It is the easy opportunities of meeting members of the opposite sex that makes the dance hall such a popular rendezvous.'[86] This aspect of dance-hall culture appears to have become particularly pronounced in the postwar era, as traditional methods of 'picking up', primarily the Sunday-evening 'monkey walk', began to die out.

Certainly some of the respondents did meet future husbands at dances, and many others recalled boys they had met at a dancing venue. The role of the dance hall as an arena for courting will be explored further in Chapter 4. Normally, women were not expected to ask a man to dance; they simply waited to be asked. However, 'excuse me' or 'buzz-off' dances did provide an opportunity for girls to choose their partners. Margaret recalled: 'They used to have a ladies' excuse me, we weren't as forward as you lot ... er, no, we were very hopeful, we'd think oh I like him over there, you know, you would never dream of, er, never dream of going. They used to stand, the fellas ogling and then they'd amble over, and some of them were very nice.' Oral evidence does not, however, support a notion of women dancing only to gain contact with the opposite sex. Indeed, as Jephcott observed: 'Girls generally go dancing in twos and are often quite content to dance with each other, as well as with a boy partner.'[87] Mass-Observation observed that at a large open-air dance in Camberwell in 1938, 'there were about equal numbers of men-and-girl and girl-and-girl couples'.[88] Kathleen confirmed this point: 'Well usually, girls used to go together you see. And the girls'd dance together. And if ... if a boy didn't, er, kind of fancy you and ask you to dance, er, you danced together, you see.' As Abendstern has argued, the dance hall thus represented 'one of the few mixed leisure environments where men were not necessary to women's enjoyment, though women were vital to men's'.[89] Moreover, as Kerr observed of her study of sixty-one families living in 'a typical slum' area of central Liverpool, which she conducted by home visiting between 1950 and 1955: 'for the adolescent girls dancing is a pleasurable activity for its own sake and steps are tried out and practised with mates and a high standard of proficiency is reached'.[90] McKibbin suggests that this love of dancing well might help to explain the popularity of jitterbug-literate American soldiers, as partners in wartime dance halls.[91] Quite simply, they were better dancers than the average Englishman.

While the absence of a male partner did not preclude women from entry to the dance floor, the association of this particular leisure form with the act of finding a partner did control access to the dance hall itself. Jephcott recorded:

> As a matter of principle some stop dancing when they get engaged (if their boy is away that is). If they do not stop altogether they go very much less, and say that somehow they are not interested in dancing now. Marriage in the case of most of the girls of this study puts an end to their dancing, anyhow for the time being.[92]

Kerr noted simply that 'dancing is extremely popular with the girls until marriage, when it is dropped at once'.[93] Oral testimony provides much evidence of the movement away from dancing upon serious courtship or marriage. Certainly, courting could have a disruptive impact upon young women's leisure patterns, as we shall shortly see.

Young women and pub culture

When interviewees recall the leisure of their youth, cinema-going and dancing dominate their recollections. In contrast, visits to pubs are largely absent from their accounts. Yet surveys from across the period, and country, demonstrate that if pub culture was undeniably masculine in character, women were not excluded entirely from this particular leisure venue. As Chapter 5 will demonstrate, visits to the pub sometimes constituted a form of shared leisure for wives and husbands; they also provided some women with an opportunity to escape the demands of home alone. In this chapter, however, the focus is upon the role played by the pub in young women's leisure patterns.

The oral history evidence presented here paints – initially, at least – a fairly uniform picture of female drinking habits. There was an oft-repeated assertion that young, unmarried women rarely viewed the pub as a leisure venue. Indeed, middle-class views on young female drinkers were pronounced. As Ada recalled: 'Oh women didn't. If you went to a pub you were a prostitute … In those days, nice women didn't go. You might go to a country pub on a holiday or walking tour, you know that sort of thing, but not a town pub down a side street.' Recalling her years as a student in the last decade of this study, Amy asserted: 'Going in pubs, was … was, erm, it sounds awful, but it was a working men's thing.' Working-class women concurred that, quite simply, 'women didn't'. Yet beyond this blanket assertion came glimpses of country pubs visited, drinking intervals at dances and Saturday nights spent with friends or boyfriends: an indication that attitudes towards, and experiences of, female drinking were more complex than many at first professed.

Documentary evidence is more forthcoming on this subject, yet complexity is not absent from the picture it paints. Certainly, it is difficult to assert with confidence the key trends in female drinking across the period. In 1935, the *New Survey of London Life and Labour* claimed that a general decline in the volume of working-class drinking in London pubs since the beginning of the century was most pronounced among women and the young.[94] In contrast, Rowntree's *Poverty and Progress: A Second Social Survey of York,* conducted between 1938 and 1939, asserted that within the same decade, the number of women, especially young women, who visited pubs was increasing. Moreover, Rowntree stated: 'there is not the old hesitation in entering public houses, especially those which have been improved in recent years'.[95] Does this suggest clear regional differences? I suspect not. Rather, it seems that Rowntree's findings relate to the better-class drinking establishment, the hotel bar, more likely to be frequented by those middle-classes women who readily admitted to frequenting country pubs. Certainly, Rowntree's evidence for type one pubs (the 'old fashioned' working-class establishment) suggests that less than 10 per cent of those women frequenting these establishments were under twenty-five.[96]

While it is difficult to come to any firm national conclusions concerning the extent of female drinking in the interwar period, wartime does appear to signal a significant shift in leisure patterns. There is certainly a real perception amongst the interviewees that war brought a changing attitudes. As Alice asserted:

> I think like I say it was after the war and I think women came more into their own. Girls came more into being what they wanted to be. Now I'm not talking sexually, but I'm talking in, in a way, because girls er were looked down upon before that. Just as they were about going in pubs, I mean I never dreamt of going in a pub when I was a young girl but after the war it was nothing.

For some women, life in the services presented different opportunities for leisure, such as regular pub-going, as Margaret observed: 'Going into the air force opened my eyes to a different world altogether. When we weren't fighting the Germans or were having a night off, it was either swimming for the air force or rather the pictures, or we'd go in a gang to a pub.'

The Mass-Observation Archive provides plentiful evidence of this perceived shift; the organisation conducted numerous enquiries and produced a series of reports on the subject of young female pub-going, the underlying rationale being that a change with far-reaching repercussions was afoot. Surveys of London, Portsmouth and Bolton all seemed to confirm that 'The war has made revolutionary changes in both the age and sex distribution of public house drinkers.'[97] So what were these changes? First, it appeared that the social composition of the pub changed. In a study of one south-west London borough, it was found that 45 per cent of women under thirty claimed that they were visiting pubs more often since the war began, while only 7 per cent were going less frequently.[98] Nearly three-fifths of the women surveyed claimed to visit pubs sometimes.[99] Secondly, Mass-Observation found evidence of a 'softening' in attitudes towards these female drinkers. Nearly half of those under thirty questioned in one survey professed a favourable opinion about female pub-going. Older people, and particularly older men, remained, however, significantly more antagonistic to the idea, objecting to female pub-going on the grounds of 'respectability and morality'.[100] Moreover, despite the changes identified by Mass-Observation during wartime, the cinema and dance hall remained the pre-eminent leisure attractions for the young, and the chief motive for pub-going was social rather than an interest in drinking itself.[101]

Despite an apparent shift in pub popularity during the war, the public house remained, in essence, a male institution up to the end of our period. The entry of women was subject to spatial restrictions and behavioural dictates. On the whole, young women looked for the sociability of the pub in alternative settings, as we shall see shortly. Yet the sources do indicate that female pub-going increased steadily as the period progressed, and suggest that regional differences were apparent, most notably between North and South. In a study conducted in 1945, Pearl Jephcott explored the leisure experiences of girls in three areas of England: a number of streets within a mile of Piccadilly, London; a northern industrial town notable for its armaments and shipbuilding; and a pit village in County Durham.[102] Among her London sample, pub-going was an accepted part of a young women's leisure. As she wrote: 'Pub-going is one of the recognised ways of enjoying your free time to many of the London girls.'[103] The girls from Northern England, however, were less likely to frequent pubs, and attitudes towards female pub-going were more antagonistic, although she admitted that attitudes here were changing too. A questionnaire-based study of 1,000 Birmingham youths aged between fourteen and twenty, undertaken at the end of the 1940s, concluded that very few of the youths surveyed visited a public house in their leisure time, or spent money weekly on drink.[104] Overall, it seems that the picture of young female pub-going which emerges is one of measured historical change, but that even at the end of our period it would be inaccurate to characterise the pub as the preferred leisure venue for more than a minority of young women. In 1959, less than 10 per cent of young women admitted to drinking alcohol at least once a week.[105]Another decade was to pass before the pub began to make real inroads into young women's cultural lives.[106]

Organisations and clubs for young women

Despite the overwhelming popularity of dancing and cinema as leisure for young women of contrasting social backgrounds, and the ambiguities surrounding the role of the pub in their lives, oral testimony provides evidence of a wide range of alternative leisure enjoyed in youth, both inside and outside the home. Many of these alternative pleasures were of a type to solicit the approval of those contemporary middle-class commentators who so disapproved of the recourse to commercial forms alone. For example, some women had memories of the more formal, organised leisure associated with club, night school or church. Hannah stated that her role as a Sunday-school teacher occupied a great deal of her time as a young woman. Doris enjoyed church activities until her marriage in 1940, attending missionary meetings on a Thursday and Sunday-school classes every week. Annie recalled: 'From being very small, we were always taken to church, regularly, and our whole life was bound up with the church.' Indeed, she would visit the cinema only when there were no activities

available at the Hulme Methodist church she attended. Others remembered weekly church socials, and whist and beetle drives. Ivy spent a great
deal of her spare time doing errands for the local Catholic church: 'We
were a very Catholic family, although we were in the slums, we were
brought up really properly, you know. And, er, so mainly it was church
activities from … I, I left school and I had three sisters younger than
myself. And of course the priest got hold of us, and we did all the running
round for the priest, you know.' For many others, however, involvement in
the church failed to outlive their school days. Irene recalled: 'I stopped
going to Sunday school when, er, after I started work, I didn't go any
more.' This is a trend identified by all the major leisure studies of the
period. Morgan believed that 'Once the girls become workers they put
away things which they consider childish, and, having been accounted old
enough to leave the day school they consider themselves freed from Sunday
School attendance also.'[107] Jephcott observed: 'Few of the girls of this
study look to the churches for their social life.[108] Indeed, the association
of some youth organisations with organised religion could act as a real
turn-off for young people.[109] Certainly, oral evidence suports a view of
church-based leisure as an important part of childhood and adulthood,
rather than youth.

Contemporary observers noted a similar lack of interest in night-school
activities. Harley asserted, with some regret: 'Home, clubs, cinemas, dance
halls, variety entertainments, boys, gossip and walks with friends, lighted
shops, anything that is new or exciting are all strong counter-attractions to
evening schools.'[110] Jephcott believed that girls avoided night schools because they preferred leisure which brought them into contact with boys.[111]
Oral testimony reveals some limited evidence of night-school attendance.
However, this was attendance related to vocational training and was, therefore, rarely viewed as leisure activity. One lower-middle-class woman, Mary,
did, however, recall the fun she had attempting to learn cookery before
her marriage in 1939: 'I went to night school when I was engaged. I went
with a girl from the office. And we did nothing but fool around and laugh.
I never learnt a thing … we thought we ought to be able to cook and
make pastry and (laughs) we had some most peculiar results.' Elsewhere,
Hannah viewed her attendance at English night classes as an enjoyable
form of leisure, and recalled that these classes led her to become involved
in the 'poetry in pubs' movement which began in June 1937 and continued
into the postwar period.[112] Here, both poetry and prose was recited to

drinkers in public houses such as the Blue Bell Hotel, Moston. As Hannah recalled: 'It was a bit of a change from "Nelly Dean" round the piano.'

Like the evening class, the club was perceived by middle-class commentators of the period as an improving form of leisure for young people, and one that should be actively encouraged. Articles in, and letters to, *The Times* demonstrate a middle-class preoccupation with the 'clubbability' of young boys and girls.[113] As Tinkler has demonstrated, this interest was heightened during wartime: the Board of Education's Service of Youth scheme was introduced in November 1939, and the 1944 Education Act made every Local Education Authority responsible for the provision of adequate leisure facilities for young people.[114] Social surveys were often driven by a desire to explain the inability of clubs to attract young people. In the 1950s, for example, two major studies explored this question in detail.[115] Certainly, Rowntree was perturbed by the existence of only one club each for boys and girls in the city of York before the Second World War: 'The fact that the provision for the social needs of boys and girls under eighteen is so scanty is greatly to be regretted, for it is just when young people leave school and go to work that they stand most in need of the kind of help which a good social club can give.'[116] Organisations such as the Girl Guide Association, Girls' Friendly Society and Girls' Life Brigade, and the umbrella organisation the National Council of Girls' Clubs, sought to attract young women of all ages into their ranks.[117] In contrast, specific hobby groups such as amateur dramatics societies appealed to predominantly middle-class women, despite the *New Survey of London Life and Labour's* claim that 'Acting has become a "hobby" for all classes.'[118]

Yet, despite the range of club activity available, Morgan discovered that only a very small proportion of the girls she surveyed attended recreational clubs, and Harley recorded a leakage of members from clubs at the age of sixteen.[119] Between 1950 and 1952, the King's Jubilee Trust sponsored a study of 939 boys and girls aged fourteen to seventeen in two districts of central London, an industrial quarter of Nottingham and four villages within twenty miles of Oxford. The survey found that only one in three adolescents joined youth organisations, and that among girls the figure was even lower.[120] Indeed, the *Manchester Evening News* reported that youth leaders themselves were particularly concerned by the patterns of club attendance among young girls:

> Youth leaders all over Britain are seriously worried by the lack of interest girls show in youth clubs once they have passed the age of 16. The older they

grow the more readily they drop out, and leaders are at a loss to find any concrete reason for it … One Manchester youth leader told me: 'Girls grow up more quickly than boys. At 16 they are beginning to lose interest in club games, and look for older companionship. They start courting and then giving a lot of attention to their clothes and appearance. Their mothers, who are only too glad to send clumsy boys off to the club, ask the girls to help in the house.'[121]

In adolescence, other forms of leisure fitted in with the interests and self-perception of girls more comfortably than membership of a club. Often seen as symbolic of childhood interests, clubs found it difficult to compete with commercial pleasures and the distractions of courting activity. Moreover, as a number of surveys indicated, there was a perception of clubs as being 'old-fashioned' and failing to respond to the 'modern tastes' of youth.[122]

As our period ends, however, there is evidence that youth clubs were undergoing a transformation. In response to the criticisms of both young people and social commentators, their very nature began to change with a burgeoning of club activity, often related to the workplace. These were clubs of a very different type to those of the earlier period, and they attempted to respond more directly to the interests of the young. For example, one *Manchester Evening News* report drew attention to Manchester's 'first teenage night club', La Ronde in Cheetham Hill Road, where: 'Cliff Richard's voice boomed from the juke box; conventionally dressed young-sters started to jive; crowds gathered around the bowling alleys and pin-tables; and groups sat chatting over soft drinks and sandwiches.'[123] Even the National Association of Mixed Clubs and Girls' Clubs felt compelled to open 'teenage' coffee bars, the first of which was based in Sheffield, which would 'seek to attract young people between the ages of 15 and 18 to come and drink coffee, to talk and perhaps to make music and dance'.[124] There is clear evidence, then, of change over time. In the first part of this period, clubs for the young remained linked to the ideology of 'rational recreation': a venue for control and personal development. By the end, the very nature of the youth club had changed, as it became, simply, somewhere to go. The rationale may well have continued to be that of control – in the 1960s they provided an alternative to the pub, but they sought to appeal to the young on their own terms.

Sport and physical exercise

In 1935, an editorial in *The Times* noted that despite the best efforts of youth leaders and middle-class opinion-formers, open-air amusements such as rambling, cycling and camping were considerably more popular among girls and young women than more formal attempts to organise their leisure hours.[125] While *The New Survey of London Life and Labour* cautioned that the popularity of hiking might be a 'temporary craze', a Mass-Observation report of 1947 emphasised the continued popularity of hiking, biking and camping into the postwar period.[126] As Hargreaves has demonstrated, life-cycle stage was a significant determinant of both participation in physical activity and spectatorship of organised sport.[127]

Rambling appears to have been one of the more popular forms of physical activity pursued by young women: by the mid 1930s the *Manchester Evening News* provided a regular column entitled 'The Rambler', and one study estimates that there were half a million ramblers and hikers in this decade.[128] Morgan found that half of the girls she surveyed enjoyed country rambles, at least occasionally, and oral testimony provides further evidence of the popularity of rambling, both organised and informally pursued, as a leisure activity for the young.[129] The sisters Ada and Freda, for example, were both members of a Fallowfield rambling club. Those who were members of Manchester's Gaelic League regularly spent their Sunday after-noons rambling and hiking in the local countryside.[130] As Mary recalled: 'Everybody went out at Easter and Whitsun, everybody went out rambling as they called it. We used to go right into Derbyshire. You'd go with a crowd, walking.' Jean remembered that 'when the weather was better, erm, you would like to go ram … rambling in the country, and of course you see, once again there were plenty of buses and trains, and you would go out to Marple and Hayfield and, erm, Buxton, you know, areas like that and take your sandwiches.' Indeed, Ada and Freda pursued this interest in rambling at holiday time, taking annual breaks with the Co-operative Holidays Association, one of a number of organisations which organised hostel accommodation for walking holidays: 'We used to pay two pound ten … the, the posh centres were two pound ten. The ordinary ones were two pound five. And the primitive ones were two guineas. And then you had your railway fare.'[131] However, few of the working-class respondents had the spends to devote to such an undertaking. For these women, rambling expeditions were enjoyed within stricter geographical parameters dictated by the cost of travel. As the *Social Survey of Merseyside* concluded in 1934: 'among the poorer workers the institution of rambling in the country is virtually unknown'.[132] Certainly, Rowntree found that the membership of rambling clubs in York was disproportionately composed of black-coated

5   Rambling was one of the more popular forms of leisure activity pursued by young women in the interwar period, although economic circumstance would dictate the scope of expeditions.

workers, able to afford the two shillings or more charged for weekly rambles in the Yorkshire countryside.[133]

For those who found the costs involved in rambling prohibitive, cycling could provide an alternative form of physical exercise. Moreover, once the initial financial outlay for purchasing a bicycle had been found, or a suitable instalment plan had been agreed to, cycling constituted a relatively cheap form of transport: 1.6 million bicycles were sold in 1935.[134] Between 1918 and 1933, the total membership of the Cyclists' Touring Club rose from 8,500 to 30,000; in 1949, 18 per cent of those London girls surveyed by Mass-Observation cited cycling as a major leisure interest.[135] At the time of the King's Jubilee Trust survey of youth, there was even a 'cycling craze'.[136] Oral testimony provides much evidence of the enjoyment of cycling as a leisure activity in itself. For example, Barbara remembered cycling from her home in Hulme down to Wythenshawe in the 1930s: 'We did a lot of cycling in those days, cos, it was safe you see.' In the late 1940s Joyce also had a bicycle, and recalled joining a local cycling club on their trips out of Manchester:

6

My friend down the road, who was Church of England, and her parents had a chemist's shop, she joined, er, a cycling club, and she had the racing bike with the drop handlebars and they used to meet in Didsbury, honestly the things you forget, er, sometimes, er, I'd go out with them, in my school, my holidays from college, I would go out with them. And of course so with my sit-up-and-beg bike (laughs) and the fellas used to help me up the hills (laughs). So I used to do quite a bit of cycling, I used to love it.

Chief among the other popular forms of sporting activity for girls were swimming and tennis. Morgan found that half of the girls she surveyed swam in their leisure time,[137] while Mass-Observation found that about half of the girls interviewed in 1949 devoted their spare time – in summer, at least – to these two sports.[138] The provision of public swimming pools, where swimming instruction was sometimes given free, encouraged the participation of young working-class girls; in the winter months baths were often used as dance halls. Swimming was a cheap and accessible activity for girls across the period. Bowker notes that admission prices to interwar Ashton-under-Lyne pools ranged from the concessionary rate of one penny to sixpence, depending on age and facilities.[139] Tennis, also, seems to have attracted large numbers of women from different class backgrounds, despite its image as a sport of the middle classes. In a study of working-class leisure in 1930s Liverpool, Middleton observed the growing popularity of the sport prompted by the provision of public courts.[140] In 1930 alone, 100,200 players used the public courts.[141] As Mary noted: 'Wherever you went you went and played tennis. You know if you went and stayed with a friend, it was the thing to do, to go and play tennis.' Margaret expressed her preference for active forms of leisure: 'And I used to go playing tennis, I used to go playing table tennis, I used to go dancing like you say, but er, I never liked dressing up, I preferred sports to being ... dressed up.' Tennis was not the cheapest of leisure activities, but the provision of public courts, and those sponsored by industrial companies for their workers, did increase its accessibility as our period progressed. At least in the first part, however, there remained a suspicion of those girls who took the game too seriously and treated it competitively rather than as an opportunity for socialising. In 1925, one journalist warned young Manchester girls against 'tennis intemperance' and advised that 'much of the lasting happiness of social games arises out of the companionship and conversation to be had in between games'.[142]

Rambling, cycling and tennis were forms of sporting activity which fitted – or could be made to fit – dominant constructions of adolescent femininity. Ice-skating, too, fitted this mould: graceful, non-aggressive and non-competitive. Several of the Manchester women recalled visits to the Ice Palace on Derby Street; in 1930 the *Manchester Evening News* recommended ice-skating to young women in the following terms: 'Ice skating is one of the most health-giving, fascinating, and invigorating sports. It gives poise and grace, and for those reasons alone every woman should go in for it.'[143] However, the relative expense of skate hire and lessons proved too much for some – even those who, like Mary, came from better-off families. As she explained: 'I found that it was costing me too much, although I did, dearly wanted to learn to skate, but I felt I, I couldn't afford it at the time.' Skating at a public rink could cost as much as two shillings for entry and a further two shillings for skate hire. As *The New Survey of London Life and Labour* admitted: 'Skating is a fairly expensive pursuit and is not, therefore, very popular amongst any but the middle and richer classes.[144]

Swimming was a cheap and accessible activity for women across the period –   **7**
as well as an arena for childcare, as this photograph of a 1930s swimming club
picnic demonstrates.

Young women from the social backgrounds described here were less likely than their middle-class counterparts to engage in more organised team sports, either at school or during their working lives. Lack of facilities, and a fluctuating antagonism towards girls' involvement articulated by entrenched interest groups, militated against participation in so-called 'national' sports such as football and cricket. The example of women's football is instructive here. At the beginning of our period, women's football was a popular game, which had grown considerably during the First World War, and boasted domestic and international fixtures. In Spring 1920, for example, Dick Kerr's Ladies of Preston, the 'unofficial England team', played four matches against the French women's national side watched by a series total of 61,000 spectators.[145] A year later a match between the Kerr's team and St Helens AFC, at Goodison Park, attracted a crowd of 53,000.[146] By 1921, there were approximately 150 women's football teams, including a Lyons Tea girls' team.[147] In 1921, however, the Football Association banned the women's game from its grounds on the pretext of the misappropriation of gate receipts from charity matches.[148] As Melling observes: 'The ban appeared to be just another of many attempts to subjugate a sport that was competing strongly with male football in terms of skill, crowds and gate receipts.'[149] Certainly, there is clear evidence that the FA felt that football was an unsuitable game for women.[150] Women's football fell into a dramatic decline, not to be seriously arrested until the World Cup final of 1966 added a new impetus.

Nevertheless, despite such weighty and institutionalised opposition, working-class girls and women continued to find opportunities for organised sport. Drawing upon a series of oral history interviews with cotton-workers, Liz Oliver has uncovered the considerable popularity of rounders as a game organised through the workplace and through Sunday schools, and enjoyed by single and married women alike.[151] Women's rounders was, as she writes, 'a well-established and very well-supported sport. It was a unique and important part of local working-class culture.'[152] Middleton also observed the particular popularity of rounders among working-class girls in Liverpool.[153]

Young women were not absent from the ranks of sports spectatorship, either. Football and speedway were particularly popular with the women interviewed here.[154] The *Manchester Evening News* identified female spectators at a number of sporting events in the interwar period. In 1925, for example, women were spotted at Lancashire County's first cricket match of the season.[155] Also in that year the *Evening News* reported the presence of women supporters at the Manchester football derby, publishing a photograph of 'two of the first of many hundreds who made Maine Road football ground their Mecca today'. The newspaper observed: 'There were many ladies among the throng, and some of them had shown their partisanship in spirited fashion by wearing big adornments of club colours.'[156] Press reports of the 1935 Cup Final noted: 'There seemed as many women as men.'[157] In the postwar years, however, the press seemed to lose interest in the spectacle of women either watching or participating in sport. By 1960, women's sport was certainly virtually invisible within the *Manchester Evening News*. The most notable item concerning women and sport in 1955 consisted of an interview with 'Cricketers' Wives'.[158] None the less, women remained an – albeit minority – presence at sporting events. A series of football and rugby counts conducted by Mass-Observation in April/May 1947 found that between 2 and 24 per cent of the sampled crowds were female.[159] The highest total was evident at a Saturday-afternoon match at Fulham's ground, while the lowest was also a Saturday match at Aston Villa's ground. At the two football grounds where Saturday attendance can be compared to Wednesday weekday attendance, the latter saw significantly lower female attendance. Moreover, where women did attend they did so largely as part of a male–female couple.

Friendship and social life

Most of the activities indulged in by young women were founded upon the opportunities they provided for socialising and friendship – an aspect of leisure experience all too frequently overlooked by historians whose focus has been 'leisure' in its activity-defined form.[160] Ada, for example, recalled evening visits to the home of a wealthy school friend: 'And she used to arrange evenings, boys and ... included us, very good of her, because we were nothing to write home about.' This particular friendship seems to have allowed Ada and her sisters access to a middle-class social world to which she felt that their lower-middle-class status would otherwise have denied them entry. Jean explained the importance of 'high tea' to young people of her – younger – generation:

> Go back to the forties then, so, with this build-up, erm, of friends, erm, I
> think nowadays, you see young people do more late-evening things, don't
> they, erm, whereas with us you were invited to high tea. I quite miss this now,
> but when I think that, erm, food was still very short you know, because it ...

it went on being rationed until 1953. And, erm, but people would always endeavour to put this high tea on. And most weeks, you know, you would be invit' … you were invited somewhere, you know, even if you had to go on two trams or something like that, you know.

She remembered visiting work friends and boyfriends' relatives in this manner. Others remembered the importance of visiting relatives, particularly for the holidays, which would otherwise have proved too costly. The postwar survey of Birmingham noted that visiting relatives and prospective 'in-laws' accounted for a considerable amount of young girls' leisure time.[161]

Some women spoke with great fondness of individual friendships which persisted throughout their youth. Margaret talked about one particular friend with whom she lost contact during the war: 'I loved her really. We were good mates. We fell out, we did this we did that, we separated and that was it.' Jane remembered her own best friend: 'We were always friends and we used to go everywhere together, but we always used to fight over boyfriends and be jealous over them, you know.' Kate recalled a woman who remains a close friend: 'We've partnered up all that time from teenage years onwards.' Certainly Jephcott identified the importance of 'my mate' as a companion for leisure activity.[162] Having a partner for leisure was often of great importance to young girls. Kathleen, for example, developed her smoking habit in association with her best friend Jane:

> We were both little smokers a little bit and we used to, you know, (laughs) get in odd corners and have a little smoke and I remember sitting in … in Jane's upstairs, they had an upstairs sitting-room, and she used to take the fireguard down because there wasn't a fire in, and we used to sit, we used to share my gloves, cos I'd come in, in gloves and we used to sit at one side of the fire blowing smoke up the chimney.

While smoking could intensify feelings of comradeship in youth, in adulthood it could represent a means of taking time out for momentary relaxation.[163] The best friend was also a vital companion for other leisure activities. Kathleen recalled trips into the city centre with hers: 'We used to go down to Manchester, Saturday afternoon and have a walk round the shops and look at the shops and things like that.' For Amy, a major part of such activity, was time spent in conversation in Manchester's many coffee bars in the 1950s: 'You could sit and put the world to rights over a cup of coffee which cost you sixpence and you could stay there all day.' The café was not a postwar innovation, and McKibbin shows that cafés were com-

Friendship provided a crucial context for leisure activity for young and adult   **8**
women, as this photograph taken in Scarborough in 1960 indicates.

mon in working-class districts throughout the interwar period.[164] However, the postwar coffee bar was more explicitly founded upon a youthful clientele. As Bill Osgerby writes, it was 'the pre-eminent focal point to British teenage life … a place where youngsters could gather and freely chat amongst themselves or dance to their favourite records on the juke box'.[165] For young women, the coffee bar and its rival, the 'milk bar', constituted a public space for socialising which was cheap and accessible.

Leisure in the home

Throughout this period, leisure was not experienced only outside the home; a variety of activities also took place within it, although the housing conditions of some working-class women in the interwar period largely precluded such home-based leisure.[166] Morgan detailed the popularity of reading as a cheap form of leisure for girls, as well as a form of romantic

escapism; and Mass-Observation found that 18 per cent of the girls interviewed in 1949 cited reading as their prime leisure interest.[167] Distinct
girls' magazines, sometimes referred to as 'books' – such as the mill-girl
magazine *Peg's Paper* (1919), and the racier publications *Oracle* (1933) and
Glamour (1938) – catered for the young consumer of different ages.[168]
David Fowler argues that the vibrancy of the magazine market adds fuel
to his thesis that the interwar period saw the emergence of the 'first teenagers' explicitly targeted as such by leisure entrepreneurs.[169] Described by
one middle-class commentator as 'erotic magazines',[170] reading of this type
constituted an enjoyable form of leisure, as well as a source of what
Jephcott termed 'informal education' for their audience.[171] It was also a
fairly cheap pleasure; out-of-date copies could be purchased from some
newsagents, bookshops and market stalls.[172] In the 1950s, the range of
magazines targeted specifically at young women expanded with the launch
of titles such as *Marilyn* (1955), *Valentine* (1957) and *Boyfriend* (1959) While
the staple of girls' magazines across the period was 'romance', specialist
magazines did cater for more specific leisure interests. For example, Irene
took two magazines every week: *Picturegoer* and *Picture Show*: 'Cos I was film
mad, so I'd read these religiously.' Ada, too, said that her great interest was
reading, an activity she pursued both inside and outside the home, particularly in the snatches of leisure time she found on her tram journey to
work: 'I had Milton's *Paradise Lost* and I read it going down on the tram.
Lost to the world in Milton's Paradise, I've always read a lot. Erm, the
world didn't matter, it was what I was reading that mattered.' Ivy confined
her reading to the house or public library: 'But mainly in the house, I was
reading. I was always in trouble for reading. "Get your nose out of that
book! Put some coal on the fire." (laughs) "Get your nose out of that
book." I was always in trouble for reading.' In fact she recalled the luxury
of visits to the library: 'Oh it used to be lovely, a full hour, you know,
undisturbed reading.'

Very often, for those spending time in the home, the radio provided an
accompaniment for other activities such as reading – or, in the case of
Kathleen, the ironing, which she did as part of her chores. For many,
Radio Luxembourg, established in 1933 and dedicated to the provision of
dance-band music, provided a more youthful alternative to the Reithian
BBC, while the advent of the seven-inch single in the 1950s allowed teen-
age girls to express their individual musical preference more explicitly.
Abrams estimated that in 1959, those aged fifteen to twenty-five accounted

for 42.5 per cent of total national spending on records and record players.[173] Other – generally lower-middle-class – women created their own musical accompaniment. Ada recalled that piano lessons were her main leisure interest, and that her parents owned a piano: 'Oh I loved it, I loved it, erm, when I was unhappy I used to go and play the piano.' Kate also played the piano and the cello. Working-class women were, however, less likely to have such opportunities, and for them the radio provided their primary access to music in the home. As Hannah stated: 'I used to long for a piano but I never got one.' None the less, music-playing was not exclusive to the middle classes. Middleton found that in his study of working-class leisure in Liverpool, a little less than a third of the women surveyed pursued this interest, mostly in the form of piano-playing.[174]

Some girls found enjoyment in activities more generally associated with housework. Morgan noted: 'Household duties as a form of leisure occupation for older girls are not usually done for pleasure, but from a sense of duty. There are, however, some forms of housecraft in which the girls can find the satisfaction of enjoyment, and which they will do voluntarily if allowed. Cookery is the most popular of these forms.'[175] As we saw in Chapter 2, the absence of compulsion in youth could enable girls to look upon cooking and baking as pleasurable activities. Others found enjoyment in needlecraft, particularly knitting. Morgan recorded that knitting was considered a pastime by two out of three of the girls she surveyed, while approximately the same numbers sewed.[176] Freda described her own knitting activity: 'I knitted about three bathing suits. I knitted one for my friend and it was a blackberry pattern and she (laughs) went on her honeymoon in it as soon as she got in the water (laughs) it went to pieces (laughs) she had to drag it … on her (uncontrollable laughter).' Jean combined her knitting with family visiting in the 1940s: 'and then, er, when we used to go to visit, when, all the time, before you like, when I was engaged, and afterwards, er, when you, when you went to visit, particularly if you went to visit, erm, older relatives, I always used to take knitting or … or embroidering, you know.' Dorothy enjoyed patchwork, an activity which the *Manchester Evening News* identified as particularly popular in 1930:

It would appear that quilting is quite the needlework of the moment, in fact there are symptoms of a quilting craze. Youthful matrons are industriously quilting cot and pram covers, debutantes are exercising their talents on three-quarter length coats, and cushions and bedcovers galore are being produced.

It is the kind of work one can do on winter evenings, as it involves no tiresome matching of colours, and isn't fine enough to strain valuable eyes.[177]

Dorothy also made her own clothes during the war: 'Yeah, I'm still a home-bird really, I love, erm … You know, even tho' I was, kind of, you know, eager to go dancing and rambling and that, erm, clothes were rationed when I was in my teens and, erm, I used to attempt to make dresses, that turned out, that you could tell they'd been made by me (laughs).'

So far, this chapter has demonstrated the remarkable variety of leisure experienced by working girls across the period 1920 to 1960. Women re-called dancing, rambling, cycling, swimming and reading their way through their youth, within the context of close friendships and sociability. The cinema, in particular, constituted an ever-present interest throughout the period. However, youth was rarely a period of unbridled leisure for women, despite their status as wage-earners. As Pearl Jephcott asserted:

> The status gained by working, or rather by earning, carries the right to spend your non-working hours more or less as you like, and not as your mother dictates. That is the theory. In practice the girls' own good nature, pressing family needs and in some cases very definite parental control, mean that many are not nearly so free to come and go in their non-working hours as might be supposed from the hair-raising time-tables of an occasional one or two.[178]

The final section of this chapter directs attention to those factors which limited and determined the nature of freedom and independence in youthful leisure.

Constraints upon leisure in youth

Throughout this period there were two main limitations upon the free expression of leisure choices among young women: the resources of money and time available to them. Leisure experience was framed by a number of considerations: the age when work started, the level of wages, conventions around tipping up and the amount given in spends, the hours of work, the issue of chores and family duty, and parental discipline and control. These factors were not static across the life stage or the historical moment, or even among classes. Indeed, apparently insignificant factors, such as position in the family, could affect experiences to an enormous extent. Other women found that the death or illness of a parent had profound implications for their pursuit of leisure. However, these were all factors which regulated personal leisure; as such, their examination provides a necessary caution to any notion of leisure in youth as inevitably rooted in freedom and independence.

Time and leisure

The amount of leisure time available to young women was dependent upon both the nature and hours of their paid work and the demands of their family concerning household chores and childcare. As Harley observed:

> A working day which leaves a girl with energy to spend her evening actively, and fixed and ample free time, which coincides with the leisure of friends or with sessions of evening schools, clubs and other leisure organisations, are essential before a girl can be reasonably expected to take advantage of opportunities for further education or to make a wise as well as an enjoyable use of her spare time.[179]

In her study of 1,250 working-class wives, based on information collected by the Women's Health Enquiry Committee, Spring Rice indicated that the health problems evident among the married women she surveyed were not absent from the lives of young, single women, engaged in paid labour. As one woman wrote:

> There are many girls who work (especially piece workers) when obviously a few days off would put them right. Then again plenty of people value money more than health. Speed is the great thing in industry … It plays havoc with most people's lives … In the winter we often work over (overtime) one hour a day, and it makes a tremendous difference to many girls, one feels like going to bed of an evening instead of doing something interesting.[180]

The snapshot representation of occupational patterns provided by printed census reports shows that while the broad category 'makers of textile goods and articles of dress' remained the largest employer of Manchester women in the fourteen-to-twenty age group in 1931, by 1951 this category had been superseded by that of clerks and typists.[181] The most dramatic national shift in young female occupation patterns, however, related to domestic service. In 1931, 31.1 per cent of the female workforce aged between fourteen and twenty was engaged in 'personal service'.[182] Domestic servants often worked long, exhausting hours with little free time. Parratt cites the example of one interwar domestic expected to work from 6 a.m. until 8 p.m. or 9 p.m. with only one free weekend a month.[183]. During the

Second World War, however, private domestic service declined dramatically, never to recover, replaced by areas such as light industry and the service sector, which continued their interwar expansion. Most of the women interviewed here were engaged in office employment, reflecting the change in female occupational structure which occurred over our period. All those lower-middle-class women who did not attend college in their youth were so engaged, and two-thirds of the working-class women were also employed in offices, leaving only a minority in factory occupations. However, as Tinkler points out, office work 'implied different things for girls who entered at 14 as opposed to 16'.[184] Elementary-school-educated girls were generally employed in the 'dead-end' post of general office worker.

While few of the women interviewed for this study believed that their hours of work restricted their leisure greatly, some did find their hours of work unduly long. For example, a lower-middle-class woman who started work in 1933 recalled the extended hours which she and her fellow office staff were obliged to work:

> *What was your first job?* Erm, I was, erm, shorthand typist come, erm, we used to erm, it was in a cotton manufacturers' office in Tariff Street in Manchester, Platt Howarths it was called … trouble is, we worked sometimes till seven at night, because the boss used to go on what they called the 'change' it was the exchange, cotton exchange. Well, they didn't come off the exchange till about four o'clock or half-past four, then you had to start, they started dictating letters, so in the end, we got so, erm, fed up with this that, erm, they started a scheme where one of us could go, have an early night, and that was quarter to six. That was considered early.[185]

Kathleen, a working class woman who started her working life a decade later, remembered that she worked from 8.30 till 5.30 on weekdays and until midday on a Saturday:

> Well you didn't have an awful lot of spare time. Because, I mean, I worked Saturday mornings, I mean, it wasn't until after the war, I think, that, well after the war that you stopped working Saturday mornings. So apart from people with shops, worked in shops and jobs like that, factory workers and office workers worked Saturday mornings. You know, so that you didn't really have as much leisure.

In the first half of our period, many shop assistants worked forty-eight to sixty-hour weeks;[186] Fowler observes that cinema usherettes, in particular, worked very long hours.[187] More generally, however, hours of work did not preclude leisure time. In her own research, Morgan concluded that 'the majority of the girls are free for leisure occupations from 7 to 7.30 p.m. each evening in the week, from about 1.30 to 2 p.m. on Saturday and all day Sunday'.[188] Harley noted: 'The approximate average length of working day is ten hours, allowing in most cases at least four hours' leisure in the evening.'[189]

The effect of wartime upon leisure patterns has been alluded to already with reference to public-house usage. Here, however, it should be noted that for those who experienced their youth during the war, conscription into wartime occupations does not seem to have substantially restricted their leisure choices, although it might have upset previously established social networks. For example, both of those women who switched to munitions continued to enjoy their preferred leisure activities, even when they were working nights. Dorothy continued to dance, during the day when necessary, and Irene similarly restructured her cinema-going to accommodate those months when she worked nights. As she recalled: 'Working nights, coming home in the morning and, er, you just seemed to adjust, you just spent a few hours in the morning doing whatever or perhaps, er, going to the pictures, and then, perhaps, having another hour's sleep before you went on in the evening.' Elsewhere, however, war work could leave girls too tired in the evenings to do anything other than rest. As one twenty-year-old munitions worker told Mass-Observation in 1943: 'I come home so tired and I have to be up so early for work, that its not worth going out.[190] Moreover, younger women did perhaps feel the restrictions of war more acutely. Jane, who was ten when war began, said:

> There again you've got to remember we did have the war intervening be-
> tween 1939 and 1945. So there was not a lot, well there wasn't any, er, evening
> entertainment really because there was nearly always raids ... In fact I, I, erm,
> honestly think during 1939 to 45 we didn't really, erm, go out, I can't remem-
> ber going out at all. Erm, in leisure pursuits, certainly not in the evenings.

While paid work could act as a restriction upon the hours available for leisure activity, it could also act as an arena for social activity. 'Work' could include elements of 'leisure' for the young woman worker. As Jephcott noted: 'Workrooms are generally highly "matey" worlds. Crowds of young people, bursting with vitality, give the place the camaradie, without the primness, of a school.'[191] Mass-Observation reported that 'pleasant company' was as important as the nature of the job itself in determining whether a girl enjoyed her work, giving the following as a 'typical reply': 'I work in an office. Yes I'm happy, my friend and I work in the same firm and we have fun. (16 years old).'[192] Certainly oral testimony suggests that for some, the workplace provided such an arena for leisure. Joan described her workplace, the Co-operative biscuit-packing factory at which she worked until her marriage in 1940, in the following terms: 'It was like a little club. We all began. We were all fourteen at the same time and so we all sort of stuck together. As a class would, you know.' Another factory worker, Edith, spoke of her experiences at the foundry where she spent all her working days: 'I think everybody enjoyed it. Well, in the room that I was, the girls' core-making shop, there was six sisters out of one house alone. Six sisters, er, they all worked, er, we all worked behind each other. And we used to, you know, chat and that.'

Moreover, works outings could provide an opportunity for travel that was not generally available to some young women. Edith recalled that in the 1930s, the centenary of her workplace was celebrated by a trip to the Belle Vue complex in East Manchester: 'But it was absolutely out of this world. Everybody enjoyed [themselves]. There was buses that took us there and the food was absolutely marvellous, you know.' Doris recalled an outing further afield later in that decade: 'Well, erm, the son married one of the girls from the office, and er, we didn't go to the wedding, because … didn't have a big wedding … so instead of inviting us to the wedding, he took us all to the Scottish Exhibition, erm, we went overnight by train, we had a lovely time. And we could take our respective boyfriend or whatever, you know, with you.' For others, the workplace itself provided recreational facilities – as did Sunlight House, the building where Freda worked as a civil servant, which had a swimming pool and other games facilities which could be used in the lunch hour. Elsewhere, tennis clubs, rambling societies, social clubs and – as Oliver demonstrates – even facilities for team games such as rounders were provided by employers eager to engender goodwill and stimulate efficiency.[193] Middleton describes the facilities provided by one large Liverpool firm, which included a recreational ground where young women played hockey and tennis, and performed gymnastics.[194] As we have already seen, the 1950s witnessed an increase in the numbers of social clubs aimed specifically at younger employees.

The types of paid occupation engaged in by women had an impact upon the time, money and energy available to them for leisure. Indeed, contemporaries made a direct link between the decline of live-in domestic service and a demand among young women for clearly defined spare time in which to attend the cinema and dance hall.[195] While this book contends that life-cycle stage, rather than occupational status, was the most significant factor in structuring female leisure patterns, occupational factors could influence cultural expectations and the types of leisure pursued. In particular, the expansion of white-collar employment introduced young working-class women to forms of leisure activity which were different from those pursued by both their mothers and their blue-collar counterparts. For example, Jean's experience of office work in the late 1940s and early 1950s influenced the leisure choices she made:

> I was first introduced to Gilbert and Sullivan through this, you know, I probably hadn't heard of Gilbert and Sullivan, erm, and er, someone said oh you know this is being put on somewhere in the Stockport area, and erm. So, you know, your ... your culture was erm, was building up, you know, because ... because my mother wasn't sort of too keen on anything you know, like that, so, so I was being introduced, you know, erm, to other interests. *Was that with people from work?* Yes, yes, yes, you see sort of erm, you know, old, older girls, you see, would say er well why don't you try this.

Oral evidence makes it clear, however, that the workplace acted as an arena for social activity for young women regardless of occupational type. Moreover, the most popular activities among young women, the cinema and dance hall, were pursued across occupational categories. Here it was levels of spends and parental control, rather than wages rates or work type alone, which dictated the precise nature of the activity.

The hours and nature of paid employment were not, then, the only factors which influenced the leisure hours of youth. The family could also place demands upon a young worker which curtailed her spare time, although the demands of the home had generally declined by the end of this period.[196] In 1940, James and Moore argued that while entry into the workplace generally signified the end of family demands for boys, starting paid work did not carry the same significance for young women. In their analysis of adolescent diaries, they found: 'It is only from sixteen onwards that the real release from family claims, the real achievement of independence and freedom from supervision begins.' As they pointed out, this decrease in family demands and increase in the time spent on dancing and 'talk' coincided with an interest in the opposite sex.[197] In their analysis of weekend leisure, the same writers acknowledged that the reduction in household duties was never complete for adolescent girls.[198] Morgan stated simply: 'Most of the girls help with housework';[199] Middleton found that nearly three-quarters of the wage-earning women he surveyed helped in the home, while only a third of men did so.[200]

Oral testimony, too, provides evidence that young women, of different social backgrounds, regularly performed housework and other family duties. Indeed, only two of the women interviewed remembered making no contribution to the running of the home. The first, a working-class woman, believed that this was because of her position in the family as the youngest of three daughters. As she explained: 'Needless to say I didn't do much in the way of housework with my mother because I had two older sisters, so I was able to do most of the things I wanted to do, except, you know, what my father laid down the law about, you know.'[201] The second woman was an only child from a lower-middle-class background. As she recalled, until her wedding day in 1939, she had little knowledge of domestic work: 'I didn't know a thing about baking. Mother had never allowed me in the kitchen … No, she didn't like me in the kitchen. *Did she like you to help elsewhere in the home?* Not really. No, it was all done when I got home. So I didn't. So when I got married it was a bit of a shock because I'd got to start cooking.'[202]

The majority of women did, however, spend time working in the home. Ada, who was born in 1907, was trained in domestic work from an early age in a manner befitting her lower-middle-class status: 'We were trained to do housework very young. My mother was very capable, very efficient. And she said, whatever your circumstances in life, even if you have a (pause) staff, you should know how things should be done. And she used to stand over us, and make us do things properly.' The illness and subsequent death of her mother in 1922 meant an expansion of this role, as she remembered: 'And I did all the housework. I more or less ran the house, of course, Mother was in bed most of the time.' Other women, whose youth also spanned the interwar years, had particular jobs to do in the home. Ivy, for example, did the ironing, stoning and Sunday baking from the age of eleven; and Doris also had responsibility for the stoning, a chore which she professed to have enjoyed: 'Oh! I used to, er, oh I'd go and stone anybody's steps if they asked me.' Jephcott observed that many of the girls she surveyed during the war had particular responsibility for younger siblings, and oral history interviews offer evidence of young women spending their spare time looking after younger children and babies.[203] At the start of this period Edith informally looked after a neighbour's child while its mother was at work, and Irene was expected to care for her younger sister while her mother went out to work in a city-centre public house.

While childcare was unlikely to be a duty expected of young working men, housework, too, was rarely performed by wage-earning boys. James and Moore found that the category 'duties' was absent from their records of the use of leisure time among working boys. Yet working girls as old as twenty-one dedicated more than one of the nine Saturday hours not accounted for by meals and travel to duties.[204] At the age of fourteen, such tasks could account for approximately 33 per cent of their Saturday hours.[205] This gender inequality was articulated by Margaret, who recalled that her brother was obliged to do none of the chores performed by herself and sister: '*Was there a difference between what boys were expected to do and girls were expected to do?* Oh definitely. *In what ways?* Well, a girl was supposed to be in the kitchen, put it that way. A boy didn't have to wash up, or do things like that, that was unmanly.' Friday night, in particular, was often a time when girls stayed in to attend to chores of different types while boys went out. As Celia recalled: 'Friday night was bucket night. We had to blacklead the grate. And that was my job on a Friday, I had to do all that.'

As the interwar period progressed, however, Friday night in Manchester ceased to be viewed exclusively as a cleaning night. Very often young women spent it in more personal pursuits. Oral testimony reveals frequent reference to Friday night as 'Amami night', the advertising catch-phrase of a shampoo and setting lotion. As Margaret explained, Friday bath night was an exclusively female preserve: 'But we lived in this terraced house, it was a backyard with a toilet at the end and we used to have a bath in a tin bath every Friday night. My dad and my brother had to go out while we three girls had a bath. And that's what became known as Amami night.' Similarly, Doris remembered Amami night as a preparation for the weekend:

> Used to be Friday night is Amami night, you see, that was a saying when I was young, Friday night is Amami night. Cos you washed your hair, you only washed it once a week in those days, or most people only washed it, some didn't wash it once a week. And you always washed it Friday night. Ready for Saturday, you see, Saturday and Sunday. It was always, oh! Friday night Amami night, you couldn't go out Friday night. Amami night. *So girls never went out on Friday nights then?* Very rarely, oh yes, you stayed in and washed your hair and

did your nails and did everything, you know, ready. *Ready for the weekend?* Yeah, but we, we worked Saturdays, you know, I mean, most people worked Saturday morning.

As Davies has argued, the gendered demarcation of time evident in customs such as bucket night and Amami night left Friday-night leisure, outside the home, very much the preserve of men.[206]

While for most young women, across our period, family duties took up just a portion of their spare time, some girls found themselves burdened with the role of household manager, notably upon their mother's death or worsening illness. Joan's elder sister did most of the housework, since her mother suffered from ill-health, and she recalled that her father kept her off work for this very purpose: 'He kept her, she worked at Lewis's at the weekend only and he kept her off work the rest of the week. And, erm, she had to, she did everything and she used to make all the clothes.' Elsie had responsibility not only for the upkeep of the household but for the care of a mother suffering from what was then described as 'early senility', and a brother unable to come to terms with this illness. As she explained, her duties were all-encompassing:

> Before I went to work in the morning, I used to have to scrub my mother, all her cuts and wounds and so on, and I used to leave the bedpan on the chair beside one side of the bed. And on the little table, the other side of the bed, I would put – a cold cooked sausage, a cold cream bowl of rice, then bread and butter. You name it, fill it with drinks and food for the day, for her, you see. And try and shop on my way home at night. And I'd have to empty the bedpan, when I got home from work and all that sort of thing, you know, all the dirty pots and get her another meal ready. Er, because my father'd buggered off, you see.

For this woman, an occasional Saturday-afternoon tea dance was regarded as an 'escape', and her only real opportunity to take time for herself.

Even for those girls with time on their hands in which to pursue leisure, parental control and discipline could act as a constraint upon the choices they were able to make. As the study of dancing has shown, certain girls were forbidden by their parents to frequent particular dance halls. Parental control was, perhaps, most evident in the rules governing the time at which young girls came in at night. As the King George's Jubilee Trust survey observed in 1954: 'Parental rulings were still surprisingly strict in many homes, especially as to the hour a daughter had to be home at night.'[207] Most of the women interviewed here were expected to return home after an evening out at a set time, and as Kate asserted, there tended to be a discrepancy between the time girls were expected in and that demanded of boys. Certainly, Celia remembered having to leave dances before they finished in order to return home on time in the years immediately following the Second World War:

> Er, and even when I used to go when I got to sixteen and seventeen and we used to go to dances, local dances, I always had to leave before the end, you know. I could never, my mother used to be waiting on the, er, you know, but she, if she was alive now she certainly would be waiting but er, she always worried, you know. She was … and I knew she was worried so I always used to leave before the end.

Other women were expected home either at a fixed time or at one pre-arranged to coincide with the end of a particular activity. Mass-Observation found that in 1949, over half of the girls interviewed had to be in between ten and eleven o'clock.[208] For one woman the return of her father from military service in India in 1947 disrupted a well-established social routine. As she remembered, he began to impose his own authority by closing the door at nine o'clock: 'Well there was no way that I was going to come home at nine o'clock, you know. So, I would knock on the door and he would've gone to bed, you know, but he would come and open the door and we'd have a few … we'd have a few words.'[209] For some, parental restrictions lasted right up until their wedding day, as Jane recalled: 'I mean, I had to be in, it was half-past ten during the week, I had to be in at eleven o'clock on Saturday and half-past nine on Sunday. And even up to the day, the week I got married, the day before I got married, the … I still had to be in at those times.' She eventually married in 1952. For those, like Freda, who did not marry, the rule of a parent could extend into their thirties:

> *What time did you have…?* Oh well I used to be, had to be in at half-past nine at night and I said can I stay out till ten o'clock at night? And Dad used to be prowling down the entry at the back of Tatton View. I think he thought we were in danger or something. *How old were you then?* Oh! In my twenties, thirties. *Did you ever resent that?* Oh, I had plenty of freedom.

As Freda's words demonstrate, freedom in youth was an ambiguous concept which gained meaning through personal expectation.

For other women, parental restrictions could have an impact upon the types of activity they engaged in. Alice recalled that her eldest sister applied make-up in the lobby of their home during the 1920s: 'She … she darn't put it on if my mam saw her you see in those days, to go out to the dances.' For Jessie, make-up was only one of the things forbidden by her father a decade later: 'Erm, well, with my mother dying when I was fourteen my father was very protective. And, er, he wouldn't let me go, he wouldn't let me wear make-up, that was one thing. I couldn't wear make-up. Erm, then he would only let me go to a dance if it was down at church.' Dorothy was warned by her father not to be seen with American servicemen – a demand she partly acquiesced to by dancing with, but not being taken home by, such men. Jane believed that her father had been particularly strict with her in her youth:

> But there again, er, my father was very strict because if he came in, you were listening to a programme and did not think it was fit he would just switch it off. And say you're not listening to that. Off it goes. And erm, er, as I say when I … when I met my husband and he used to listen to, he, we were both very involved in music, he played in a band and he was a singer in a band. And he used to go home and listen to, erm, Doris Day and Teddy Johnson and Pearl Carr on erm, Luxembourg, Radio Luxembourg, and he used to tell me about them and he used to say oh! you should have heard it last night, it was really good … And I wasn't allowed to listen to it.

Finally, the constraints of parental control actually led one woman to conduct a secret courtship of her future husband which spanned four years, until the death of her father at the beginning of the war. As she explained: 'None of, none of, er, er, the … lads were any good for his, any of his daughters.'[210]

Those women who pursued further education of different types were not free from control over their leisure activities either. In a study of the years 1914 to 1945, Elizabeth Edwards has explored the experiences of young women at teacher training colleges such as Homerton in Cambridge.[211] She notes that relationships with men 'were made as difficult as possible', through a series of restrictions concerning where and when girls could meet their men friends.[212] One of the Manchester interviewees recalled that institutional control could be greater than that exerted by the family. Joyce attended the Catholic teacher training college at Sedgely Park, Manchester, at the end of the 1940s. Here she experienced a degree of constraint upon her behaviour which she had not previously encountered. As she explained: 'The two years in college when nobody would believe, er, the restrictions, you had to be in at nine o'clock on a Saturday night and, er, if you weren't you had to be in at … you had to be in at four the next Saturday, you see, so your, er, social activities were very much limited to what you did in college really, and it was an all-women's college.' Such restrictions seem to have caused difficulties for the girl of eighteen engaged in courting activities: 'And the odd boyfriend you did have I mean, er, you know they wouldn't believe it, they'd think you had another date if you said you had to be back, back for nine, nine o'clock.' Amy, who attended the Domestic Science College on Upper Brook Street in the period 1954 to 1956, and lived in college residencies in Chorlton-Cum-Hardy, experienced a similar degree of institutional control. She did, however, point to the ways in which regulations were challenged or, indeed, simply evaded:

> There were only twelve of us in it. But we all ate in the dining-room and there was a cook and, er, you know, bells to wake you up in the morning and, erm, you'd to be up in the morning and, erm, you'd to be in by, I don't know, I can't remember, ten o'clock I suppose or something. And you, y'know, you'd to, you were allowed a late pass out under duress once or twice and you'd to sign out and sign in and oh goodness me. Not that it stopped us climbing through the loo window and all the rest of it, you know, but, in a way, I think it was rather more fun than … than they are now really. Because if there's no rules to break it's no fun breaking them.

Once again, a notion of freedom defined through constraint is apparent.

Leisure and money

By examining the issues of paid work, unpaid chores and parental or institutional control, this chapter has addressed some of the factors which acted as a break upon unmitigated personal freedom in leisure among young working women. However, the issue of wages – and, more pertinently, spends – must also be considered in any analysis of such constraints. In her study of young wage-earners, Morgan concluded that girls showed a preference for commercial leisure: 'The attitude of most of the girls is that the more money they have, the more pleasure they can buy', and an analysis of leisure activity earlier in this chapter attests to the popularity of cinema and dance hall among young girls throughout the period.[213] Clearly, the extent to which women had money to spend on these leisure forms must be explored.

In the mid 1930s, Harley identified an average wage of fourteen shillings for the manual and white-blouse workers she surveyed; a few years later, Morgan noted that the average wage for the machinists she studied was fifteen shillings and sixpence.[214] Oral testimony points to some divergence among women in the wages earned in youth over the period 1920 to 1960. Primarily, women from lower-middle-class backgrounds earned substantially more upon starting work than those from working-class parentage. The two sisters Ada and Freda, who began work in the 1920s, both started their first office jobs on a pound a week. As Ada put it: 'Everybody began [at] a pound a week in those days in offices.' In the postwar period, Kate, who left school in 1948, received a wage of two pounds per week in the town hall health department. Other clerical workers, however, received lower starting wages, because they began work at fourteen rather than sixteen or eighteen. Elsie, for example, received an initial wage of ten shillings per week in the 1930s, a wage which rose to two pounds over the course of her employment; while Irene received seven shillings and six-pence for her clerical work, a sum much exceeded when she was obliged to go on to munitions in 1942: 'My wage went up, oh dear, the first week's wages, I couldn't believe it, I didn't like the work, but the money was good.' Those engaged in factory work earned sums similar to those cited by Harley and Morgan.[215] Young girls starting work in the 1950s, however, were beneficiaries of a postwar increase of up to 400 per cent in young workers' wages from their prewar levels.[216] In the 1950s, Jephcott recorded average clerical wages of twenty-eight shillings at age fourteen rising to sixty-three shillings at age eighteen. Wages for girl machinists in the areas she surveyed were higher: thirty-seven shillings and sixpence at fifteen and eighty shillings at seventeen.[217] The average wage for female manual workers aged eighteen or under at the end of our period stood at four pounds fifteen shillings.[218] For young girls across the period, wages would increase automatically and frequently as working life progressed.

While the level of wages would clearly be of some importance to the young woman worker and her family, of more direct importance to the girl herself was the level of pocket money (spends), which was her designated share of that wage. As Jephcott observed: 'Wages, to the girl of fifteen mean pocket money and a regular amount to spend on pictures, dancing, cigarettes and bus fares. Pocket money, in its turn, depends on home circumstances and may vary widely among girls who are earning identical wages.'[219] Harley found that the sums given in pocket money to the girls she surveyed varied from sixpence to five shillings, with an average amount of two shillings and sixpence (elsewhere she put the figure at two shillings): 'Most girls seem to spend their money on amusements, cosmetics and hairdressing. The majority go to the cinema and buy magazines. One or two may occasionally buy themselves a pair of stockings, a scarf or a handbag, but as a general rule, the arrangement is that their parents pay their travelling expenses to work and provide their clothes.'[220] The King George's Jubilee Trust survey found that in the early 1950s, girls continued to hand over their wages, less the week's pocket money, to their mothers, who provided them with essentials such as clothes, shoes, holidays and bus fares.[221] The money the girls retained was purely for personal pleasures. Another study found that even if a girl was working in a different town, she was expected to send something home to her mother.[222]

Most of the women interviewed for this study remembered tipping up their wages to their parents and receiving an amount of spends back. Amongst this number were women of both class backgrounds, and women earning very different wages. For example, Doris and Kate, both lower-middle-class women who experienced their youth either side of the war, handed their wages over to their mothers in this manner. As the former recalled:

> I know one time, I got half a crown a week, spends. I think, erm, don't know when that was, before ... before my mother died or after. But, I mean half a crown, I had to pay my bus fares out of that, and buy stockings and things. But I think my mother bought my clothes. *Right, so what would you spend the rest of your spends on then?* Oh, odd things, you know, powder and you know, cream and stuff like that, toiletries, and erm, save up for birthday presents, you know.

Kate remembered that she was permitted to keep her first week's wages in 1948, but that after this her wage packet went to her mother. Both remembered that their mothers would buy their clothes.

Working-class women, too, remembered tipping up their wages and receiving spends back. Very often the pay packet was given unopened, as Joan explained:

> *And did you tip your money up to your mother?* Oh yes, of course, unopened. And I remember in the end, towards the end, she gave me, er, I don't know whether it was, when the war had already broken out, no. I think it was about 1938, erm, she said you can keep yourself now. So she gave me five shillings a week ... But I kept within the five shillings and I, I was so proud of it, you know, to know that I'd got five shillings to myself and I could manage on it in my own way, you know. It was wonderful that.

Ivy, who spent her youth in Ancoats, similarly handed over her wages: 'The packet unopened, you know', receiving back one shilling and six-pence, which she spent on a weekly trip to the cinema. As she observed, spends would increase with age, but so would the financial responsibilities of a working woman: 'Er, and then when you earned a bit more, you got a bit more spends, but then you had to buy your own stockings then (laughs). So you didn't really gain (laughs). But your mother bought your clothes, you know, obviously.'

While boys more often paid board to their mothers rather than tipping up the whole wage, girls might continue to hand over their wages, some-times even up to their wedding day. Joan recalled that her brother, who sometimes earned more money than her father, paid 'keep', rather than handing over his wages. In her interwar study of leisure in Rochdale, Michelle Abendstern discovered that boys were more likely to pay board than girls, and that even those who received spends generally received more than girls because their wages were higher to begin with.[223] Certainly Irene, who received a shilling a week spends out of an initial wage of seven shillings and sixpence, continued to hand over her wage packet until the age of thirty: '*You didn't get married until you were thirty. Did ... did you continue to hand your wages over to your mother?* Oh no. Right up till I was, yes till I left home ... but until I got married I gave my mother my wage packet. Right till being thirty. I don't think that was usual, but it was, it was, er, usual with my mother (laughs).' However, spends would increase as the girl got older and her wages increased. Moreover, as Andrew Davies has argued, care must be taken when using oral testimony to access levels of spends. He found that respondents tended to describe arrangements when they first started work, when their relative contribution to the family economy was greatest, and were less forthcoming about how these changed as they grew up.[224]

The oral evidence presented here does indicate that arrangements for spends changed over the course of youth. Kathleen found that her engage-ment prompted her mother to ask for board rather than the wage packet:

And I think I was very ... privileged, with very little money, cos I ... I only got five shillings a week when I got engaged. I got five shillings a week. And when I got engaged my mother said well you can start to, you can start to give me something instead. Cos you'll want to start saving up to get married you see. But I mean it's amazing, isn't it? But I never felt deprived. Never.

Moreover, some women paid board throughout their youth, rather than tipping up. The lower-middle-class sisters Ada and Freda, for example, were asked to contribute half of their wage to the family housekeeping, leaving them with as much as fifteen shillings spends. Out of this money, however, they were expected to purchase clothes. In her study of working-class women in the period 1890 to 1940, Elizabeth Roberts found that a small minority of working-class girls, from better-off families, were allowed to board even before the Second World War. [225] Her more recent study of the later period points to a clear shift towards 'boarding' by the 1960s. [226] There is evidence of this shift in the sources consulted here. For example, the King George's Jubilee Trust survey found that wage-earners in London tended to go 'on-board' soon after leaving school.[227] However, it was suggested that – at least in the early 1950s – the London pattern was an exception to a perceived national norm. Other women were themselves responsible for the household budget, a responsibility which invariably brought with it an absence of money for personal spending. One such woman was Elsie, who had a particularly difficult family background: 'I gave the money into housekeeping, just took enough out for my fare to work and perhaps the odd pair of stockings now and again that's all.' Overall, however, few of the women interviewed felt that their leisure choices were unduly constrained by their wage levels and spends. Yet material circumstances did structure those choices. Levels of spends determined – among other things – the types of cinemas and dance halls they could visit, the frequency of their visits, the extent to which they could follow fashion, the geographical scope of rambling excursions and their ability to learn a musical instrument.

In his recent study of interwar teenagers, David Fowler has claimed: 'Outside the workplace, young wage-earners were relatively free from constraints of any kind.'[228] Refuting the findings of Elizabeth Roberts in particular, he argues that young workers did not hand over the majority of their wages to their mothers, nor were they particularly limited by the moral authority of their parents. The evidence presented here suggests that Fowler's case is overstated. Certainly, young women workers enjoyed significant opportunities for leisure, and pursued it in a variety of commercial and non-commercial arenas, across this period. Within interviews, youth was characterised as a period of freedom and independence in leisure, particularly compared to the experience of adulthood which followed.

However, independence in leisure had its limits. The available resources of time and money provided a framework within which the leisure experiences of young women should be understood.

Notes

1 R. Hoggart, *The Uses of Literacy* (1957; Penguin, London, 1992), p. 51.
2 P. Jephcott, *Girls Growing Up* (Faber & Faber, London, 1942), p. 56. Jephcott distributed her questionnaire throughout England and Wales between September 1941 and March 1942.
3 A. Davies, *Leisure, Gender and Poverty: Working-Class Culture in Salford and Manchester, 1900–1939* (Open University Press, Buckingham, 1992), p. 81.
4 J. Hargreaves, *Sporting Females: Critical Issues in the History and Sociology of Women's Sports* (Routledge, London, 1994), p. 113; emphasis added.
5 D. Fowler, *The First Teenagers: The Lifestyle of Young Wage-Earners in Interwar Britain* (Woburn, London, 1995), p. 1.
6 H. James and F. Moore, 'Adolescent leisure in a working-class district', *Occupational Psychology*, 14:3 (1940); 'Adolescent leisure in a working class district. Part II', *Occupational Psychology*, 18:1 (1944); J. L. Harley, 'Report of an enquiry into the occupations, further education and leisure interests of a number of girl wage-earners from elementary and central schools in the Manchester district, with special reference to the influence of school training on their use of leisure'. M.Ed. dissertation, University of Manchester, 1937; O. Morgan, 'A study of the training for leisure occupations offered in a senior girls' school in an industrial area, together with an enquiry into the use made of this training by the girls, after their entry into employment'. M.Ed. dissertation, University of Manchester, 1942.
7 B. Reed (ed.), *Eighty Thousand Adolescents* (George Allen & Unwin, London, 1950); P. Jephcott, *Some Young People* (George Allen & Unwin, London, 1954).
8 Harley, 'Report of an enquiry', p. 4.
9 James and Moore, 'Adolescent leisure in a working-class district. Part II', p. 33.
10 Morgan, 'A study of the training for leisure', pp. 193–4.
11 *Manchester Evening News* (hereafter *MEN*), 5 February 1920, p. 4.
12 *MEN*, 4 May 1925, p. 7.
13 *MEN*, 3 May 1920, p. 4.
14 *MEN*, 6 May 1920, p. 3.
15 *MEN*, 14 May 1930, p. 3.
16 J. White, *The Worst Street in North London: Campbell Bunk, Islington, Between the Wars* (Routledge & Kegan Paul, London, 1986), pp. 192–4; S. Alexander, 'Becoming a woman in London in the 1920s and 1930s', in D. Feldman and G. Stedman Jones (eds), *Metropolis, London: Histories and Representations Since 1800* (Routledge, London, 1989), pp. 256–8, 261–7.

17 *MEN*, 6 February 1920, p. 7.

18 *MEN*, 19 September 1925, p. 6.

19 *MEN*, 21 July 1930, p. 4.

20 *MEN*, 10 April 1950, p. 2.

21 *MEN*, 13 April 1950, p. 2.

22 B. Osgerby, *Youth in Britain since 1945* (Blackwell, London, 1998), p. 33.

23 *MEN*, 7 January 1955, p. 2.

24 *Ibid.*, p. 12. The 7-inch single and *New Musical Express* singles chart were introduced in 1952.

25 *Ibid.*, p. 12; *MEN*, 14 January 1955, p. 2.

26 M. Abrams, *Teenage Consumer Spending in 1959 (Part II) Middle Class and Working Class Boys and Girls* (London Press Exchange, London, 1961), p. 5.

27 Fowler, *The First Teenagers*, pp. 93–115.

28 Davies, *Leisure, Gender and Poverty*, pp. 102–8.

29 Osgerby, *Youth in Britain Since 1945* , p. 5.

30 E. Roberts, *Women and Families: An Oral History, 1940–1970* (Blackwell, Oxford,1995), pp. 33–4.

31 *MEN*, 28 October 1955, p. 8.

32 Morgan, 'A study of the training for leisure', p. 26.

33 Jephcott, *Girls Growing Up*, pp. 98–125; James and Moore, 'Adolescent leisure in a working-class district', p. 140.

34 Morgan, 'A study of the training for leisure', p. 213.

35 H. Llewellyn Smith (ed.), *The New Survey of London Life and Labour. Volume IX. Life and Leisure* (P. S. King and Son, London, 1935), p. 8.

36 A. H. Halsey (ed.), *Trends in British Society Since 1900* (Macmillan, London, 1972), p. 558.

37 James and Moore, 'Adolescent leisure in a working-class district', p. 140.

38 *Ibid.* It should be noted that the researchers included time dedicated to meals and travel, as well as the time spent performing household duties, in their definition of leisure time. As a consequence the share of *actual* leisure time taken up by visits to the cinema was even more spectacular. Moreover, the working boys surveyed for this study spent even more time at the cinema, with between 20 and 24 per cent of their non-working hours thus engaged (p. 139).

39 The percentage of non-working Saturday hours dedicated to the cinema declined from approximately 21 per cent at age sixteen to a low of 6 per cent at age eighteen, a time when opportunities to 'pick up' were perhaps most keenly sought. The hours engaged in picture-going then rose again to a maximum of 11 per cent at the ages of nineteen and twenty, before dropping off again at the age of twenty-one, perhaps reflecting the habit of cinema attendance among steady couples: James and Moore, 'Adolescent leisure in a working-class district. Part II', p. 29.

40 Harley, 'Report of an enquiry', p. 202; Morgan, 'A study of the training for leisure', p. 60.

41 Jephcott, *Girls Growing Up,* p. 116.

42 *MEN*, 15 November 1955, p. 6.

43 B. Seebohn Rowntree and G. R. Lavers, *English Life and Leisure: A Social Study* (Longmans, London, 1951), p. 230.

44 S. Jones, *The British Labour Movement and Film, 1918–1939* (Routledge & Kegan Paul, London, 1987), p. 7.

45 Mass-Observation Archive (hereafter M-O A): File Report (hereafter FR) 1871, 'The cinema audience', July 1943, p. 6.

46 *Ibid.,* p. 13.

47 M-O A: FR2429, 'The cinema and the public', October 1946, pp. 2, 11.

48 *The Times,* 24 June, 1932, p. 10.

49 *The Kinematograph Year Book 1955*, p. 305.

50 Richards notes that cinema audiences were not classless, and that classes rarely mixed at cinemas: J. Richards, *The Age of the Dream Palace: Cinema and Society in Britain, 1930–1939* (Routledge & Kegan Paul, London, 1984), p. 17.

51 Llewellyn Smith, *The New Survey of London Life and Labour,* p. 45.

52 Jephcott, *Girls Growing Up*, p. 118.

53 M. Gomes, *The Picture House* (North West Film Archive, Manchester Polytechnic, 1988), p. 40.

54 P. Jephcott, *Rising Twenty* (Faber & Faber, London, 1948), p. 155.

55 The *Rock Around the Clock* 'riots' received considerable newspaper coverage. See, for example, *The Times,* 15 September 1956, p. 4, col. c.

56 *MEN*, 10 February 1920, p. 4.

57 M. Hurstwitt, '"Caught in a whirlpool of aching sound": the production of dance music in Britain in the 1920s', in R. Middleton and D. Horn (eds), *Popular Music 3: Producers and Markets* (Cambridge University Press, Cambridge, 1983), p. 12.

58 *MEN*, 17 April 1925, p. 7.

59 For a fascinating account of attempts to 'stamp out freak steps', see R. McKibbin, *Classes and Cultures. England 1918–1951* (Oxford University Press, Oxford, 1998), pp. 404–6.

60 Morgan, 'A study of the training for leisure', p. 14.

61 Rowntree and Lavers, *English Life and Leisure*, pp. 279–80.

62 *MEN*, 24 October 1955, p. 2.

63 Harley, 'Report of an enquiry', p. 110.

64 M-O A: FR3150, 'Teen-age girls', August 1949, p. 2.

65 Elsie.

66 'Escapism' is used here in a literal sense, meaning a release from a particularly harsh material environment or set of domestic circumstances.

67 Harley, 'Report of an enquiry', p. 110; Morgan, 'A study of the training for leisure', p. 114.

68 Morgan, 'A study of the training for leisure', p. 114.

69 M-O A: Directive Respondent (hereafter DR) 1040, reply to January 1939 Directive.

70 Alexander, 'Becoming a woman in London in the 1920s and 1930s', p. 257.
71 Harley, 'Report of an enquiry', p. 111; Morgan, 'A study of the training for leisure', p. 114.
72 Celia.
73 Dorothy.
74 Davies, *Leisure, Gender and Poverty*, p. 91.
75 Rowntree and Lavers, *English Life and Leisure*, p. 281.
76 Morgan, 'A study of the training for leisure', p. 118.
77 M-O A: DR, replies to January 1939 Directive.
78 Morgan, 'A study of the training for leisure', p. 115.
79 Davies, *Leisure, Gender and Poverty*, p. 172.
80 Jephcott, *Rising Twenty*, p. 150.
81 For a discussion of gang violence in the Manchester and Salford dance halls of the interwar period, including the Devonshire Street ballroom, see Davies, *Leisure, Gender and Poverty*, pp. 92–4.
82 M-O A: DR1086, reply to July 1939 Directive.
83 M-O A: DR1289, reply to July 1939 Directive.
84 Harley, 'Report of an enquiry', p. 203.
85 Morgan, 'A study of the training for leisure', p. 119; James and Moore, 'Adolescent leisure in a working-class district. Part II', p. 31.
86 *MEN*, 7 January 1955, p. 2.
87 Jephcott, *Girls Growing Up*, p. 121.
88 A. Calder and D. Sheridan (eds), *Speak for Yourself: A Mass-Observation Anthology, 1937–49* (Jonathan Cape, London, 1984), p. 69.
89 M. Abendstern, 'Expression and control: a study of working-class leisure and gender, 1918–1939. A case study of Rochdale using oral history methods', Ph.D. thesis, University of Essex, 1986, p. 215.
90 M. Kerr, *The People of Ship Street* (Routledge & Kegan Paul, London, 1958), p. 32.
91 McKibbin, *Classes and Cultures*, pp. 395–6.
92 Jephcott, *Rising Twenty*, p. 150.
93 Kerr, *The People of Ship Street*, p. 32.
94 Llewellyn, *New Survey of London Life and Labour*, p. 268.
95 B. S. Rowntree, *Poverty and Progress: A Second Social Survey of York* (Longmans, Green, London, 1941), pp. 353–4.
96 *Ibid.*
97 M-O A: FR1873–7A, 'Juvenile drinking', June 1943, p. 88.
98 M-O A: FR1635, 'Report on women in public houses', March 1943, p. 7.
99 *Ibid.*, p. 4.
100 *Ibid.*, pp. 8–10.
101 M-O A: FR1873–7A, 'Juvenile drinking', June 1943, p. 93.
102 Jephcott, *Rising Twenty*.
103 *Ibid.*, p. 146.
104 Reed (ed.), *Eighty Thousand Adolescents*, p. 39.

105   Abrams, *Teenage Consumer Spending in 1959*, p. 7.

106   Osgerby, *Youth in Britain*, p. 58.

107   Morgan, 'A study of the training for leisure', p. 185.

108   Jephcott, *Rising Twenty*, p. 142.

109   P. Jephcott, *Some Young People* (George Allen & Unwin, London, 1954), p. 118.

110   Harley, 'Report of an enquiry', p. 81.

111   Jephcott, *Rising Twenty*, p. 103.

112   Rowntree and Lavers, *English Life and Leisure*, p. 180.

113   See, for example, *The Times*, 4 May 1934, p. 11, col. a; 14 September, 1935, pp. 7 and 11, cols d and a; 3, 4, 5, 9, 18 January 1952.

114   See P. Tinkler, 'An all-round education: the Board of Education's policy for the leisure-time training of girls, 1939–50', *History of Education*, 23:4 (1994); 'Sexuality and citizenship: the state and girls' leisure provision in England, 1939–45', *Women's History Review*, 4:2 (1995).

115   Jephcott *Some Young People*; Reed, *Eighty Thousand Adolescents*.

116   Rowntree, *Poverty and Progress,* p. 350.

117   Membership figures for these organisations in England and Wales for 1933–34 are as follows: Girl Guides, 474,408; Girls' Friendly Society, 158,000; Girls' Life Brigade, 40,242; S. Jones, *Workers at Play: A Social and Economic History of Leisure, 1918–1939* (Routledge & Kegan Paul, London, 1986), p. 69.

118   Llewellyn, *New Survey of London Life and Labour*, p. 63.

119   Morgan, 'A study of the training for leisure', p. 186; Harley, 'Report of an enquiry', p. 95.

120   Jephcott, *Some Young People*, pp. 20, 105.

121   *MEN*, 3 February 1950, p. 3.

122   Jephcott, *Some Young People*, p. 124.

123   *MEN*, 7 October 1960, p. 24.

124   *The Times*, 22 March 1958, p. 4, col. c.

125   *The Times*, 14 September 1935, p. 11, col. d.

126   Llewellyn, *New Survey of London Life and Labour*, p. 62; M-O A: FR2467, 'Saturday night', April 1947, p. 18.

127   Hargreaves, *Sporting Females*, p. 113.

128   *MEN*, 8 June 1925, p. 3; A. Warren, 'Sport, youth and gender in Britain, 1880–1940', in J. C. Binfield and J. Stevenson (eds), *Sport, Culture and Politics* (Sheffield Academic Press, Sheffield, 1993), p. 66.

129   Morgan, 'A study of the training for leisure', p. 112.

130   Irene, Joyce and Ivy.

131   Ada.

132   D. Caradog Jones (ed.), *The Social Survey of Merseyside*, vol. 3 (Hodder & Stoughton, London, 1934), p. 295.

133   Rowntree, *Poverty and Progress*, p. 397.

134   Warren, 'Sport, youth and gender in Britain', p. 66.

135   Llewellyn, *New Survey of London Life and Labour*, p. 61; M-O A: FR3150, 'Teenage girls', August 1949, p. 2.

136 Jephcott, *Some Young People*, p. 58.

137 Morgan, 'A study of the training for leisure', p. 108.

138 M-O A: FR3150, 'Teen-age girls', August 1949, p. 2

139 D. Bowker, 'Parks and baths: sport, recreation and municipal government in Ashton-under-Lyne between the wars', in R. Holt (ed.), *Sport and the Working Class in Modern Britain* (Manchester University Press, Manchester, 1990), p. 87.

140 T. Middleton, 'An enquiry into the use of leisure amongst the working classes in Liverpool', MA thesis, University of Liverpool, 1931, p. 106. This study was based upon questionnaire evidence solicited through workplaces, social clubs and churches.

141 *Ibid.*, p. 130.

142 *MEN*, 7 May 1925, p. 7.

143 *MEN*, 16 January 1930, p. 3.

144 Llewellyn, *New Survey of London Life and Labour*, pp. 65–6.

145 J. Williams and J. Woodhouse, 'Can play, will play? Women and football in Britain', in J. Williams and S. Wagg (eds), *British Football and Social Change: Getting into Europe* (Leicester University Press, Leicester, 1991), p. 91. For a report of the match at Manchester City's ground, see *MEN*, 5 May 1920, p. 5.

146 Williams and Woodhouse, 'Can play, will play?', p. 92.

147 Hargreaves, *Sporting Females*, p. 142.

148 A. Melling, '"Ray of the Rovers": The working-class heroine in popular football fiction, 1915–25', *The International Journal of the History of Sport*, 15:1 (1998), p. 98.

149 *Ibid.*

150 Williams and Woodhouse, 'Can play, will play?', p. 93.

151 L. Oliver, '"No hard-brimmed hats or hat-pins please": Bolton women cotton-workers and the game of rounders, 1911–39', *Oral History*, 25:1 (1997).

152 *Ibid.*, p. 43.

153 Middleton, 'An enquiry into the uses of leisure amongst the working classes in Liverpool', p. 106.

154 Manchester was the location of the first British speedway stadium, opened at Belle Vue in July 1926. Nationally, the peak year for attendance was 1945–46: McKibbin, *Classes and Cultures*, p. 363.

155 *MEN*, 2 May 1925, p. 5.

156 *MEN*, 12 September 1925, p. 5.

157 *MEN*, 27 April 1935, p. 1.

158 *MEN*, 25 July 1955, p. 2.

159 M-O A: Topic Collection Leisure, 80/1/C, Football/rugby counts, April/May 1947.

160 See, however, Davies, *Leisure, Gender and Poverty*, pp. 110–16, for a discussion of street relationships; and M. Tebbutt, *Women's Talk? A Social History of 'Gossip' in Working-Class Neighbourhoods, 1880–1960* (Scolar Press, Aldershot, 1995), for an assessment of the role of gossip within working-class communities.

161 Reed, *Eighty Thousand Adolescents*, p. 130.

162 Jephcott, *Rising Twenty*, p. 159.

163 There is also an echo here of the 'bedroom culture' identified by McRobbie and Garber in their study of girls and subcultures: A. McRobbie and J. Garber, 'Girls and subcultures: An exploration', in S. Hall and T. Jefferson (eds), *Resistance Through Rituals: Youth Subcultures in Post-war Britain* (Hutchinson, London, 1975), p. 213

164 McKibbin, *Classes and Cultures*, p. 187.

165 Osgerby, *Youth in Britain*, p. 41.

166 Jerry White has demonstrated that home-based leisure forms were pursued with difficulty in the crowded one-roomed dwellings of Campbell Bunk, London: White, *The Worst Street*, pp. 83–4.

167 Morgan, 'A study of the training for leisure', p. 29; M-O A: FR3150, 'Teenage girls', p. 2.

168 For a detailed study of girls' magazines, see P. Tinkler, *Constructing Girlhood: Popular Magazines for Girls Growing up in England, 1920–1950* (Taylor & Francis, London, 1995).

169 Fowler, *The First Teenagers*, pp. 101–3.

170 A. J. Jenkinson, *What do Boys and Girls Read?* (Methuen, London, 1940), p. 218.

171 Jephcott, *Rising Twenty*, pp. 111–13.

172 Jenkinson, *What do Boys and Girls Read?*, p. 213.

173 Abrams, *Teenage Consumer Spending in 1959*, p. 4.

174 Middleton, 'An enquiry into the use of leisure amongst the working classes in Liverpool', p. 147.

175 Morgan, 'A study of the training for leisure', p. 84.

176 *Ibid.*, p. 75.

177 *MEN*, 7 January 1930, p 3.

178 Jephcott, *Rising Twenty,* p. 142.

179 Harley, 'Report of an enquiry', p. 39.

180 M. Spring Rice, *Working-Class Wives: Their Health and Conditions* (Penguin, Harmondsworth, 1939), p. 49.

181 Nationally, the numbers of women employed in textiles across our period halved.

182 *Census of England and Wales 1931*, Occupation Tables, Table 3.

183 C. Parratt, '"Little means or time": working-class women and leisure in late Victorian and Edwardian England', in *The International Journal of the History of Sport*, 15:2 (1998), p. 28.

184 Tinkler, *Constructing Girlhood*, p. 32.

185 Doris.

186 Tinkler, *Constructing Girlhood*, p. 31.

187 Fowler, *The First Teenagers,* p. 109.

188 Morgan, 'A study of the training for leisure', p. 26.

189 Harley, 'Report of an enquiry', p. 200.

190 M-O A: FR1780, 'Youth questionnaire' May 1943, p. 4.

191 Jephcott, *Girls Growing Up*, p. 85.

192 M-O A: FR3150, 'Teen-age girls', p. 1.

193 Oliver, '"No hard-brimmed hats or hat-pins please"', pp. 42–3.

194 Middleton, 'An enquiry into the use of leisure amongst the working classes in Liverpool', pp. 133–4.

195 *MEN*, 7 August 1920, p. 2.

196 Roberts, *Women and Families*, pp. 33–4.

197 James and Moore, 'Adolescent leisure in a working-class district', p. 144.

198 James and Moore, 'Adolescent leisure in a working-class district. Part II', p. 30.

199 Morgan, 'A study of the training for leisure', p. 26.

200 Middleton, 'An enquiry into the use of leisure amongst the working classes in Liverpool', p. 155.

201 Dorothy.

202 Mary.

203 Jephcott, *Girls Growing Up*, pp. 126–7.

204 James and Moore, 'Adolescent leisure in a working-class district. Part II', pp. 29–30.

205 *Ibid.*, p. 29.

206 Davies, *Leisure, Gender and Poverty*, p. 58.

207 Jephcott, *Some Young People*, pp. 55–6.

208 M-O A: FR3150, 'Teen-age Girls', August 1949, p. 4.

209 Jean.

210 Joan.

211 E. Edwards, 'The culture of femininity in women's teacher training colleges 1914–1945', in S. Oldfield (ed.), *This Working-Day World: Women's Lives and Culture(s) in Britain 1914–1945* (Taylor & Francis, London, 1994), pp. 62–5.

212 *Ibid.*, p. 63.

213 Morgan, 'A study of the training for leisure', p. 193.

214 Harley, 'Report of an enquiry', p. 200; Morgan, 'A study of the training for leisure', p. 21.

215 For example, when Edith started at the foundry in 1925 she received fourteen shillings a week, with yearly rises thereafter. Joan left school at fourteen to work at the Co-operative biscuit-packing factory in 1935, and her first wage was twelve shillings and sixpence, a sum which had risen to one pound and sixpence by the time she left to marry in 1940.

216 Fowler, *The First Teenagers*, p. 93.

217 Jephcott, *Some Young People*, p. 166.

218 Osgerby, *Youth in Britain*, p. 25.

219 Jephcott, *Girls Growing Up*, p. 93.

220 Harley, 'Report of an enquiry', p. 101. Fowler uses this particular quotation as fuel for his thesis that gender did not impact upon levels of spends, and that young working-class workers 'retained around 50 per cent of their earnings, and some an even higher percentage'. Fowler rather disingenuously fails to cite Harley's evidence that out of an average wage of fourteen shillings, the

average amount returned to the girls in pocket money was just two shillings and sixpence: Fowler, *The First Teenagers*, p. 97.

221 Jephcott, *Some Young People*, p. 83.
222 Kerr, *The People of Ship Street*, p. 48.
223 Abendstern, 'Expression and control', p. 158.
224 Davies, *Gender, Leisure and Poverty*, p. 85.
225 E. Roberts, *A Woman's Place: An Oral History of Working-Class Women, 1890–1940* (Basil Blackwell, Oxford, 1984), p. 43.
226 Roberts, *Women and Families*, p. 46.
227 Jephcott, *Some Young People*, p. 83.
228 Fowler, *The First Teenagers*, p. 168.

4

'Do you come here often?' Courtship, sex and leisure

Constructions of youth which foreground heterosexual identity are omnipresent within much of the discussion of leisure experiences so far. This chapter addresses the relationship between leisure, sex and courtship in more detail. In effect, it introduces many of the themes concerning relationships between men and women which are integral to the final chapters, acting as an interlude between the exploration of leisure in youth and the examination of its nature in adulthood. Certainly, many of the activities engaged in by working girls were founded upon the opportunities they provided for meeting the opposite sex; social researchers during the late 1930s and 1940s believed that dancing was particularly popular because it fulfilled this function. 'Picking up' could itself be an enjoyable form of leisure, pursued, in the first part of this period, through rituals such as the 'monkey walk'. Furthermore, leisure venues such as the cinema often acted as arenas for courtship and sexual intimacy. Within a society where adolescent girlhood was constructed in terms of active heterosexuality, then, the realm of leisure was closely related to girl–boy relationships.

The onset of courting influenced a young woman's access to leisure. For example, an easing in parental control could accompany serious courtship. James and Moore discovered that as girls reached an age when relations with boys were socially approved of, they became less likely to have family demands, in the shape of chores, placed upon them.[1] There could also be a lightening of parental control as courtship became serious – although this was by no means automatic, as the personal testimony of Joan will demonstrate. Moreover, limited spends would go much further if leisure activity was paid for by a boyfriend, and a case study of debate over the question 'who pays' for courtship, drawn largely from the letters pages of newspapers and magazines, is included. The association between courtship and leisure could, however, act as a constraint as well as an opportunity. The way in which leisure arenas were designed to accommodate heterosexual couples could marginalise those who did not form part of such a unit, and the chapter will address the experiences of both those who remained single and those who sought sexual relationships with other women. Moreover, the interaction of courtship, sex and leisure was fraught with tension for young women, and the need to safeguard reputation and avoid pregnancy are also key areas of enquiry. Fundamentally, courtship could have a serious impact upon the pursuits of young women, disrupting established patterns of leisure and precipitating new forms of behaviour. It could also constitute important work for them; finding a 'good' husband remained a young woman's primary job throughout the period. Chapter 4, therefore, ends by returning to the theme of definitional fluidity and ambiguity in leisure which forms a subtext of the book as a whole.

Marriage as a 'career' for women

In her research on Manchester girls before the war, Harley observed: 'With some exceptions in the case of individual girls, their chief interest at this period is in boys.'[2] Pearl Jephcott recorded of the girls she encountered: 'The first spontaneous subject that the girls bring up, the thing that they want to talk about, and the one topic that is included in even the briefest of their letters has some bearing on a boyfriend.'[3] As girls progressed through youth, their own – and the wider community's – expectation was that they would actively seek a suitable partner for marriage. In a study of adolescents in Hulme, Manchester, James and Moore noted that from the age of sixteen, 'community tradition' accepted the 'open expression' of relationships between the sexes, and that courting activity was 'regarded by the adolescent as an indispensable mark of maturity'.[4] For the girls of Kerr's study, marriage was seen as 'an almost inevitable step'.[5] Indeed, as our period progressed, and the average age at marriage fell, girls were expected to take this step at an increasingly earlier point in the lives. In 1960, the *Manchester Evening News* reported the thoughts of a marriage guidance counsellor: 'Girls believe that if they are not married by the time they are 19 they are on the shelf.'[6] Jephcott concluded in 1948: 'The two things which stood out about these hundred war-time girls were first the extent to which their homes dominated their lives even up to the time they were twenty; and secondly how much their future marriage appeared to occupy their thoughts throughout adolescence.'[7]

Certainly, Ada remembered that in the 1920s, work for women of her background was viewed as an interval before the inevitable marriage:

> You see in those days girls got married young. You grew up with the idea you were going to get married. There was no, no thought of careers or anything. And, erm, you sort of went out to work for a few years ... er, before you got married. And, er, Mother had had two sisters, who'd had very happy lives in their various offices before they got married. Met very nice men to marry. They both married very happily and I suppose she thought it would give us more scope for finding future husbands.

Here the notion of husband-hunting as work for women, which should be planned for, and marriage as the ultimate career, is clearly evident. In 1960, the *Manchester Evening News* was prompted to publish a number of articles which posed the question 'Is this too soon for girls to wed?'[8] Pointing the finger of blame at mothers who encouraged their daughters into early matrimony, it asked: 'Why rush to marry off your daughter?'[9]

Class differences in attitudes to marriage are, however, evident. Jephcott noted: 'Marriage is more imminent for the shop and factory girl than it is for girls from the professional classes, which explains why the working-class girl of nineteen may be really perturbed and harp on the fact that she has not yet got a boy.'[10] It certainly seems likely that young women in possession of a good wage felt less urgency to marry than those in semi- or unskilled positions, where wages remained largely static after the age of twenty-one. The Manchester interviews point to class difference, in that the only women who did remain single were from lower-middle-class back-grounds. These women, however, were not uninterested in relationships with men. Ada, for example, admitted: 'I had romantic ideas. You know you go to a dance, you know. You meet someone and they whisk you off into romance. All that, I got really. I still have romantic ideas, you'd laugh if you ... I'm a very, very romantic ... (coughs).' She remembered clearly the point at which she recognised that she was unlikely to marry: 'And I remember I was in this American firm and when I got to thirty I walked down the office one day and I thought, I'm thirty and I'm not married. Why aren't I married? I didn't think it was anything I ought to do anything about.' Her sister, Freda, remembered the disdain with which she greeted those men she went out with: '*Did you ever have any proposals?* No. No. I always got either the sloppy sentimental young men, erm, I never got the right sort. *Yes.* Or, they probably never got the right sort. I was all right with them, you know, knocking about and playing tennis and badminton and all that but, er, I didn't. I've been out with several men, er, just on my own, but, nothing romantic about it.' Kate, too, admitted that she had high standards when vetting potential boyfriends: 'But I'm afraid I never used to look at boyfriends if they didn't go to the grammar school. *Why was that?* Well, they didn't seem intelligent enough for me.' She, too, remained single, although she did describe one relationship in particular and her reasons for ending it: 'It was no use, when he wanted sex I didn't like the idea at all. Not with anybody. I just didn't like it.'

Nationally, however, our period witnessed a substantial increase in the married proportion of the population and a corresponding decrease in the proportion of single people. In 1921, 53.5 per cent. of the female population of England and Wales were single and 38.3 per cent married; a decade later the figures stood at 50 per cent single and 41.3 per cent married. By 1951, only 40.5 per cent were single and 48.7 per cent were married; ten years later these figures had again shifted to 38.8 per cent single and 49.8 per cent married.[11] As Spring Rice observed of the working-class wives she surveyed in 1939: 'Throughout their lives they have been faced with the tradition that the crown of a woman's life is to be a wife and mother. Their primary ambition is therefore satisfied. Everyone is pleased when they get married, most of all the great public, who see therein the workings of natures divine and immutable laws.'[12] As the period progressed, then, more women married. These women did so at an increasingly early age. In both 1921 and 1931 only a quarter of women aged twenty to twenty-four were married; by 1951 the figure approached half and in 1961 exceeded that proportion.[13]

Yet despite the popularity of marriage and the centrality of heterosexuality to constructions of female adolescence across our period, there remained those, like the women discussed above, who stood outside it. In the first half of this period, a dramatic imbalance in the sex ratio, exacerbated by the high rate of male mortality during the First World War, ensured that the percentage of the female population which was single remained higher than that married. As Lewis notes, 50 per cent of those single and in their late twenties in 1921 remained unmarried ten years later.[14] However, what Oram has described as an increased focus on married heterosexuality as 'a social and psychological necessity for women' during the interwar period, founded upon the popularisation of sexology and psychology, led to a new perception of the single woman within society.[15] While the Victorian spinster had been marginalised both economically and socially, the new focus upon active heterosexuality as an essential element of woman's health and happiness sustained a notion of the spinster as 'an embittered, thwarted woman with overtones of sexual frustration or deviance'.[16] The romantic friendships between women which are evident in an earlier period were now more likely to be castigated as 'unnatural'; public interest in the prosecution of Radclyffe Hall's *The Well of Loneliness* precipitated the identification and castigation of the lesbian as a threat within society. By the 1950s an emphasis upon the heterosexual couple as the only acceptable form of relationship was reinforced in notions of the 'companionate marriage'; an emphasis which, in the realm of leisure, promoted the heterosexual couple and attendant nuclear family as the preeminent leisure unit for women. As the life histories presented in *Women Like Us* demonstrate, lesbian women across our period felt the full force of an exclusively heterosexual construction of girl/womanhood. For many, secrecy and discretion in personal relationships were a necessity; some even married to assuage family expectations. None the less, a sense of lesbian identity does emerge from their stories, and as we shall see such women constructed their own arenas for courtship both within and outside of heterosexual forums.[17]

Arenas for courtship

'Dancing is one of the recognised ways, particularly now that churchgoing has so declined, in which boys and girls expect to find their future partner.' asserted Jephcott in 1942.[18] Freda, whose youth spanned the 1920s, similarly pointed to the dance hall as an arena for courting: *'Did a lot of people find boyfriends and girlfriends at the dances?* Well, as I say, my sister met her future husband at the dance hall in Chorlton. Oh! it was the picking-up place. Oh! yes yes mmm.' Later in the period, Mass-Observation found that the usual way of meeting a boy was at a dance.[19] Clearly, commercial leisure venues did function as an arena for 'picking up'; in some circumstances the potential for meeting boys proved a key element in the attraction of particular leisure activities. 'It can be taken for granted', wrote Harley, 'that the 22 girls who go to dances are interested in boys. The girls who attend their local cinemas very frequently, no doubt, do so to meet the boys of their neighbourhood. Some may not do so deliberately, but the motive is present somewhere in the minds of nearly all of them.'[20] James and Moore observed that from the age of sixteen, 'activities that are readily adaptable to heterosexual purposes such as dancing and talk increase, whilst those less adaptable diminish or fail to increase'.[21]

Oral testimony points to the role of such activities in providing the opportunity to meet boys. Many of the women met boyfriends and even future husbands while dancing. Celia, for example, recalled that she met boyfriends either through work or at a dance hall: 'If I went to a dance you know they used to say can I take you home and do you come here often and that was the usual er, erm, that was it really. If you thought they were nice, you … it was all right.' However, dancing was not the only opportunity for this mixing of the sexes. Visits to the cinema, too, could be a source of potential boyfriends as well as a key arena for courtship activity, as we shall see shortly. Harley suggested that trips to the cinema provided girls with an opportunity to meet boys.[22] Indeed, in 1960, *The Times* reported a 'Cinema Ban on Girls' whereby:

> A Coventry cinema manager, Mr. John King, who claims that teenage girls use his cinema – the Standard – as a meeting place to look for boyfriends, has banned girls between 13 and 18 permanently from it. He said to-day that the ban did not apply to boys, who behaved themselves when the girls were not there to 'spur them on'.[23]

While this report shows that women were by no means passive actors within the rituals of courtship, it also demonstrates the oft-repeated belief that women were responsible for the leisure behaviour of men.

Lower-middle-class women were more likely to find alternative venues for the pursuit of boyfriends. Mary met her husband at a dramatics society, while Doris met her partner at Sunday school. Another woman met her husband through the Gaelic League, acknowledging the role which such groups could play in promoting relationships between members: 'Yes, a lot of, like all associations, there were lots of, er, romances built up, you see.'[24] Similarly, the workplace also provided opportunities for those who wished to meet men and those who sought relationships with women.[25]

For other women, particularly in the first part of the period, less formal activities such as the evening walk were used to gain introductions. Margaret remembered what she termed the 'walkabout': 'In those days Langford Park, which is in Stretford, used to be (laughs) the walkabout. There used to be a band there on a Sunday, and people used to go there and stroll and, pick up, like you do today at a jive. But we used to go in the park walking and eyeing up the boys and the boys eyeing up us.' Dorothy recalled her own Sunday-evening walks:

> What we did on a Sunday was erm, there was a parade of erm shops, that er, the boys walked on one side of the street and the girls walked on the other. You know. And you, you know, if you saw somebody you knew, you ... that's how we spent our Sunday evenings, you know in the summer. And I think they called it the monkey parade, the monkey walk and er, it was all very innocent you know.

Jane recalled that Cheetham Hill Road fulfilled a similar purpose during her youth in the 1940s, acting as what she termed the 'monkey run'. She also remembered that an ice-cream parlour and even a temperance bar on that road provided additional opportunities for girls to meet young men. Kathleen recalled the use made by courting couples of a park in Newton Heath during the war years and beyond:

> People all seemed to gather together and meet to talk and, you know, er, and they used to call it the Dell, which was part of Brookdale Park and it was thought rather naughty, if you went in the dell, never saw anything naughty actually, but it was, it was the dell where you went, if you wanted to do a bit of courting and it was only sitting on the seats and necking I suppose. But, er, that, we spent a lot of time doing things like that.

The Manchester monkey walk was, however, dying out by the late 1940s, precipitating an increased emphasis upon the dance hall as a venue for 'picking up'.[26] None the less, girls adapted alternative forms of leisure to the purpose of courting. The King George's Jubilee Trust survey, conducted between 1950 and 1952, observed that even cycling could be used as a way of picking up men: 'A cycle was regarded as essential for making encounters, since it is quite in order to pick up boys if one is on a bike – an altogether different matter from going after them on foot.'[27]

The dance hall and the monkey run catered for young heterosexuals in their search for potential boyfriends. Those who wished to meet partners of the same sex had to carve out their own opportunities. In 1925, the *Manchester Evening News* reported that female postal telephone staff had so enjoyed their female-dominated dances in wartime that they continued to hold annual women-only dances on an annual basis.[28] Yet in general, the period 1920 to 1960 witnessed a growing suspicion of the relationships women had with each other. As already suggested in this chapter, the lesbian became increasingly pathologised as an 'unnatural' threat to society; by the 1950s the heterosexual couple was widely viewed as the only acceptable sexual relationship. None of the women interviewed here spoke about lesbian lifestyles within Manchester; the subject merits a study of its own. None the less, Humphries records that pubs and clubs frequented primarily by homosexual men or lesbians did exist in many towns and cities, and has asserted that swimming or vapour baths were also popular as meeting-places.[29] In the 1950s Brighton was known as the 'gay Mecca', attracting lesbians and gay men from across the country.[30] Certainly, the life histories collected by Neild and Pearson demonstrate that lesbian women across our period and from different social backgrounds used established women-only organisations, as well lesbian-run clubs, as arenas to meet other women. For example, elementary-school-educated Eleanor, who was born in 1915, established contacts with other lesbian women through her membership of a Women's Evening Institute.[31] Other women recalled their membership of clubs such as the Gateways in Bramerton Street, London and the Coffee Ann, near Tottenham Court Road.[32] Never-theless, such venues operated with a discretion which could render them invisible to those who sought them out. Jackie Forster and Diana Chapman recalled the difficulties they experienced in the 1950s in even locating lesbian-friendly bars and clubs.[33]

Once young people were courting, the cinema provided them with an accessible place to meet. Mass-Observation found that the cinema was the most popular form of entertainment for the teenage couple of 1949.[34] Hannah remembered: 'It would be nine o'clock when he met me and we'd go in the news theatre and sit together and they used to have very com-fortable seats. Padded, you know, very nice and warm and we'd share this packet of pastilles. And watch the cartoons and news and whatever and then we'd come home together on the bus. That was our courting.' The cinema provided a cheap and comfortable venue for courting away from parental supervision. For working-class couples in particular, it served as an alternative to the public parks, which closed at dusk.[35]

While the cinema fulfilled a preferred requirement that early courting should be conducted away from parental supervision, the more established working-class couple might be given the freedom of the parlour where living space allowed, although they would rarely be left alone in the house.[36] Among poorer families, however, family circumstances were unlikely to

accommodate home-based courtship. Moreover, even where home conditions did not act as a barrier to social visiting, parental disapproval of a
girl's choice of mate might make secrecy in courtship a necessity. Among
the Manchester interviewees, Joan was compelled to conduct a secret
courtship for four years. A local boy, William, had first asked her to the
cinema when she was fifteen, an age both her parents believed to be too
young to start courting. While they permitted this one date, they made it
clear that it was not to be repeated. Joan, however, had felt differently,
noting: 'That started it off and we always felt after that, that we were sort
of semi, er, promised to one another. Compromised by the fact that he'd
taken me out and paid for my tickets, you know.' Subsequently, they met
in their lunch hours at a mutually convenient park, or Joan took the neighbour's dog for walks as a pretext for meeting him. Friends, too, were
instrumental in this courtship, calling for her to get her out of the house
in order to meet him. This secrecy continued until her father's death, when
the relationship finally came to light. The couple married shortly afterwards.

Sex

When women remembered the courting of their youth, they were often
most insistent about the 'innocence' of their particular age. Dorothy observed that during the war:

> They treated you with respect. You know they, they were lovely really. You
> know they, erm. *What do you mean by respect?* Well, you know, I mean you, you'd
> have to be taken out about three times to get a good night kiss, you know,
> whether they wanted it or not. You know. You know I mean, I mean when
> I say with respect I really mean that, you know … I mean our, our dating was
> company and being taken out and, erm, being paid for. Perhaps about six-
> pence to the cinema and erm, er, I think looking back you know, it was a
> lovely period.

Jane was similarly keen to stress the innocence of her youth, despite a recognition that her own activities often met the disapproval of her father: 'So
really, I, all our pastimes really were few, comparatively innocent, you know,
I mean I say innocent they're innocent now, but my father thought that they
were very very bad, especially when I started to go dancing, seriously.'

For these women, 'innocence' and 'respect' are used as a shorthand for
a limited knowledge about sex or a lack of pressure to become sexually
active. Oral testimony does point to an absence of sex education across

this period; as late as 1951, Rowntree and Lavers concluded: 'Sex is still surrounded for many adolescents by an atmosphere of mystery and stealth.'[37] In her study of central Liverpool in the 1950s, Kerr observed that children received barely any sex education from their mothers; some remained largely ignorant of the sexual act right up until their marriage.[38] As Celia remarked: 'Oh mind you we didn't learn about sex like they do now, at school and, I didn't, it's a miracle I never got led astray because I, I didn't know a thing, even when I got married, I was frightened to death I didn't know what was going to happen to me, you know.' She married in 1951. Many of the Manchester interviewees claimed that their mothers told them little or nothing about either menstruation or about sex. Jephcott observed that girls were more likely to learn such details from an older sister or 'the correspondence columns of the cheap magazines'.[39] Certainly, Manchester women often gleaned the necessary information from elder sisters, as Margaret explained: 'Being young in those days we were very ignorant of sex, and what it meant, I know I was, my sister told me about what was to happen with your monthly periods, not my mother.' Talk about sex was largely seen as something from which young unmarried women should be excluded. Ivy remembered being left out of street gossip about sex until her marriage in 1943: 'Yes even though they were rough people, you know you didn't, they wouldn't talk about anything like that. Sometimes you'd wonder why they'd all suddenly shut up, you know. And they'd all be looking at you – "go on!"'

For a number of women, sex education came directly from their future husband. A Mass-Observation Directive on age differences in 1939 received the following reply from a Kent housewife born in 1901: 'I didn't know until I was about 17 or 18 years old how babies were born. My mother told me nothing about sex matters, but I did not marry in ignorance as I found out and my husband and I discussed the subject before we were married – in this I don't suppose we differed from our parents, if they spoke the truth.'[40] Others found alternative sources of information. Kerr believed that the cinema provided an educational role here both in terms of film content and through the direct observation of other courting couples.[41] Jephcott listed the sources of information available to girls in the postwar period: female friends, sister, youth organisations, mother, women's magazines and booklets of the British Social Hygiene Council.[42] A respondent to the 1944 Mass-Observation directive on sexual morality offered the following thoughts on the subject:

I think we are still in a transitional period between the Victorian secrecy and the full realisation of sex as a clear normal part of life. So many people are still under the influence of the early secrecy and ignorance – my own mother, for example, believed that sex was a dirty subject for talk and would not have it mentioned … The women's magazines, with their free articles on all kinds of sex matters and their comments on correspondence are, I think, very sensible and are resulting in a level headed normal idea of sex and sex morality should benefit.[43]

In reply to an earlier directive on age differences, another panel member admitted : 'All of my information was obtained from talkative friends, books and stray conversations I may not have been supposed to hear; sex education seems to have been left to chance.'[44]

As the extract above makes clear, among the range of available sources of information, the role of friends or workmates was vital.[45] Joan was educated by the women at work: 'I remember what biscuits I was packing when I was told!' Jane recalled the jumbled information she gathered from school friends, and the advice she received from one particular work colleague:

When I first started going out with George I was working with a, an office boy in town, he was younger than me, but he had a girlfriend and he was very good, he used to tell me all the things he and his girlfriend used to do and he used to say why don't you try it, because George would like it, you know (laughs) and all this sort of thing. And, and it, this was it, this was how we got, we got our education.

Alice, who did not have sex until her marriage at the age of thirty-one, was advised by her workmates to take soap powder and a rubber sheet on her honeymoon.

Despite a certain lack of knowledge among the Manchester women interviewed, the fear of pregnancy did, however, loom large, and framed their attitude towards boys. Although Jephcott noted: 'Promiscuous and lengthy petting is quite likely to be encouraged and regarded as a perfectly satisfactory activity for girls and fellows of 17 to 25', many women were clearly petrified that a loss of control would lead to pregnancy.[46] Many of the interviewees talked about the 'shame' which a premarital pregnancy would bring at a time when the sexual double standard permitted men to gain sexual experience but prescribed chastity for women. Hannah, for example, pointed to the stigma attached to pregnancy outside marriage in the working-class community in which she lived during the 1930s: '*Were there very clear ideas about who was respectable and who wasn't respectable?* Well you weren't respectable if you got drunk and you weren't respectable if you had a baby before you were married. If you were in trouble, it was a great disgrace to the family.' Celia remembered the same attitude a decade later: 'I mean if anybody was having a baby it was quite a scandal really, it was, er, you know, they used to get married quick.' Edith, who fell pregnant after courting her first boyfriend for only a few months, married him shortly afterwards in 1931. Even in the 1950s, on the eve of the so-called 'sexual revolution', Amy recalled that pregnant girls were placed under enormous pressure to marry the father of their child as quickly as possible. As Humphries has asserted: 'The taboo on sex before marriage which was in part the legacy of the Victorian age remained intensely powerful right up to the 1950s – and arguably beyond.'[47]

The majority of women interviewed, however, maintained that they felt no pressure to become sexually active, and indeed had no desire to do so. For example, Amy claimed:

> I had loads and loads and loads of boyfriends, you know, but there was never any, they were just boyfriends. You went out, you know. You might have a bit of a snog at the front gate sort of thing, but that was it. There was no pressure to do anything else at all. I mean there were some people who went a bit farther than that, but if you didn't want to, it didn't matter or, or, you didn't feel you were expected to or, erm, it just didn't really rear its head. Not at all.

Joyce recalled that even after her engagement, she and her boyfriend opted for single rooms while holidaying together in Ireland: 'So, we went knocking on doors to try and get, er, single bed and breakfast, and of course these days you'd've got a double room and that would be it, but anyway, those days.' It should be noted here, however, that premarital sexual behaviour is one of the most difficult areas to gain accurate information about within an interview. As Rowntree and Lavers observed in 1951: 'In the whole field of human relationships there is probably no subject about which it is harder to get reliable information than about sexual promiscuity.'[48]

None the less, occasional glimpses of a different reality do emerge – for example, in the life story of Joan, whose wedding in 1940 was brought forward by her husband's behaviour: 'It was him, he was getting hot around the collar and I wasn't having that. Not when I was so near to being married. *So you had a rather rushed wedding?* Yes, Yes, Yes. Er, no I thought well right, just you wait a bit son (laughs). So, son was very good, he waited, er, he only waited cos he had the promise, you see.' The evidence of Mass-Observation is also helpful here, as the bond of confidentiality between the organisation and the Directive panel encouraged some women to write more freely about their sexual behaviour. For example, in response to a 1944 Directive on 'sexual morality', one woman wrote: 'I myself had sexual intercourse with my husband before we were married and I think that it is a good thing to do, especially when two people cannot get married for some years … Sexual intercourse with the man you are going to marry is accepted among some of my friends, but there are others who would strongly disapprove.'[49] In fact, 42 per cent of women aged under twenty when they married were already pregnant in 1938–39.[50] These figures suggest that sex before marriage was a more widespread social phenomenon than oral sources imply, although it was most likely to occur when a couple were already betrothed.

Moreover, despite a more commonly expressed shared mythology of the period 1920 to 1960 as an 'innocent' age, evidence does emerge from oral testimony which points to more problematic experiences. Jean recalled the threat which many felt to be posed by American servicemen during the war, and Margaret recalled a number of occasions where boys asked her 'to be sexy'. She explained her refusal in the following terms: 'In those days you see we didn't think anybody loved you if all they wanted was sex.' Indeed, throughout this period there is evidence of a contradiction between women's general recollections of their courting experiences, and the day-to-day reality about which they talked in interviews. One woman, who stressed the 'innocence' of her age, felt the need to take precautions to protect herself even on trips to the cinema: 'There's no way, I carried a hatpin in my … in my bag to go to the pictures. Cos it used to be regular at the pictures if, er, a hand'd come straying towards you.'[51] Another woman made the following – somewhat contradictory – assessment of her relationships with men in the 1930s:

> I'll say this for the men in those days, when you said no they took it as that. Some of them became great friends of mine, in fact, there was a gay fella that I knew, and he was the greatest friend I ever had when his friend or his lover or whatever you call them today went on holiday, he used to come out with me, people used to call me all sorts of names. But I didn't care because I knew he was, I could go out with him to the theatre or chip shop and know that I didn't have, have to fight for my virginity. He was a gentleman.[52]

Who pays?

For young girls in receipt of moderate spends, courtship could help to finance leisure activities, at least in the short term. As Jephcott observed:

> Weekly spending drops most gratifyingly when the girl has a boy. The fair return, when the matter is serious, is for her to put by, for their future home, the money that she personally has saved ... On the other side of the picture are those girls who really do prefer to pay for themselves when they go out with a boy, 'then they don't expect anything of you'; but this seems to apply more in the case of a fairly casual relationship than of a serious courting.[53]

Certainly, oral testimony points to both the frequency with which the boy would pay for courting activity, and the way in which this arrangement enabled limited spends to go further. Celia was clear in her acknowledgement that going out with a boy carried such benefits: 'Of course as I got a, you know er, if anybody asked you out, well that was all right then. You know it didn't cost any money then.' The surprise which Margaret felt at not being paid for by a boy she went to the cinema with only adds to a notion that this was the usual practice.

Other sources, however, point to some resistance to the idea that the financial responsibility for courting rested with the male. In 1930, a debate on the letters page of the *Manchester Evening News* concerned the issue 'who pays?' One writer argued that it was unfair for the boy to pay for both courting partners: 'Girls want as much as they can get for as little as they can give. They shout for sex equality, but if they got it, it would bring a rude awakening for many.'[54] In reply, one female reader suggested country rambles as a cheap courting activity: 'A. S. should join a rambling club, where girls are men, and pay their share without insistence.'[55] A male reader responded with the observation: 'I have found girls, with of course a few exceptions, always willing to bear a portion of the expense of courting'; while a 'Manchester typist' contended: 'Nine out of ten would be insulted if a lady offered to pay her own expenses.'[56] The notion that payment by a girl might destabilise the construction of gender roles within courting activity, even in the postwar period, was suggested in the response given to a letter to *Woman's World* in 1948. The girl who enquired: 'When a boy and girl go out together, and the girl wishes to pay her share of expenses, how should she do this?', was advised to give her boyfriend the money beforehand, 'and let the boy do the actual paying'.[57] This answer reflected a belief that boys should be seen to take financial responsibility for courting activity, even if the reality was somewhat different.

There was also some resistance to this arrangement from women within the period. When Mass-Observation asked its panel to comment on the question 'who pays?' in 1939, one thirty-eight-year-old housewife admitted: 'I've heard a lot about the modern idea of sharing expenses. I think in some ways it is a good idea. It gives the girl an independent feeling and does away with some young men's idea that they are entitled to some cuddling, kissing and other things in return for their "treat".'[58] A clerk from Northampton noted: 'Actually, I like paying my share of expenses and with certain friends this gives a much greater sense of freedom.'[59] The idea that in being paid for, a woman was actually compromising herself in some way is clear.

Even the predominantly middle-class Mass-Observation respondents, however, concluded that with few exceptions, the man generally paid for dates, and that once a couple were engaged, this would definitely be the correct practice. This arrangement did not simply reflect cultural expectations; the custom had a material basis in the higher wages which young men could expect from their work. As Jephcott noted of the girls she surveyed: 'They grow up in the knowledge that the boy does not have to do any of the housework, and that he has a better wage and more pocket money than they have.'[60] Moreover, once engaged, a girl would be expected to save her own money for the couple's married life together.

Leisure patterns and courtship

Throughout this period, particular forms of leisure were founded upon heterosexual activity. As a consequence of this, a boyfriend was a useful partner with whom to engage in such activity, regardless of any expectation of marriage, or whether or not he paid for the girl. In the *Manchester Evening News* of 1935, a 'modern girl' defended her right to go out with a man she had no intention of marrying: 'I want to go out. There are heaps of places dances, for instance – which are scarcely any fun at all without an escort.'[61] One of the Manchester interviewees used a relationship with a boy in a similar manner: 'I'm afraid I was a bit naughty really, I just used him to take me out, to dances and things and you know, I wasn't really that interested, but it was somebody to go out with.'[62] Clearly, leisure preferences which necessitated a male partner could be sustained through recourse to courting; thus providing evidence that the experience itself, rather than the opportunities it presented for meeting the opposite sex, sometimes provided the real appeal to young women.

The onset of courting could, however, disrupt already established leisure patterns and absorb a great deal of a young woman's spare time. 'Even the one who has a wide circle of friends', wrote Jephcott in 1948, 'may break with them if she becomes too engrossed in a boy.'[63] Commenting on her later study of London, Nottingham and Oxfordshire, she observed that courting superseded all other forms of leisure: 'all other activities must give way'.[64] Edith noted a movement away from close girl friends towards reliance upon the boyfriend: 'and then er, of course, the ... we all got boyfriends, I got him and Myra got her boyfriend, Lizzie and the girls in work all got boyfriends then. So we, we seemed to drift apart then. *Did you find that you didn't go out with your girl friends any more once you got your boyfriend?* Oh yes, that's right, yes. Oh yes, yes, funny isn't it? Yeah.' Others, however, reserved particular nights to spend with their friends. Moreover, the lower-middle-class single women interviewed found that female friendships remained, on the whole, constant, despite the courting activities of others. Freda continued to see her friend on a regular basis, even after her marriage:

> *Did you find that when your friends started going out with their husbands, was that a problem when you wanted to go out with them?* Oh no because I had so many friends you see. And in any case my friend's husband, Gwen's husband, he said I don't believe in, er, people dropping their single friends just because, you know, just because they get married. He saw his friends one night a week and she saw me, you know.

Yet courting could ultimately restrict the use which a girl might make of her leisure time. Jephcott found evidence of young women rejecting favoured ways of spending their time on account of a boyfriend; a notable example being the flight from the dance floor examined earlier in this chapter. She concluded: 'Even if the boy does not absorb all the girl's interests he tends to restrict her activities, particularly if she is conscientious.'[65] This restriction was grounded in the very nature of many activities as arenas for meeting girlfriends and boyfriends. Once courting, the girl often felt obliged to forgo such activities on the grounds that she had already found her mate. If the courting was serious, she might feel obliged to stay at home on those evenings she did not spend with her boyfriend, as a means of saving money for their future life together. The absence of boyfriends during the war could cause particular problems for the girl with spare time. Kathleen was warned by her mother of the consequences of an early engagement to the man she eventually married, who served in the air force during the war: 'She said if you get engaged, I want you here, you see there's no trotting about with Jane or anybody else.' Indeed, while he was away she did go out with other boys, although she acknowledged that there was 'nothing very serious'.

Other women found that their leisure patterns changed with the onset of courting as they began to pursue the favoured activities of their partner. Celia noted a change in her own leisure experience upon serious courting: '*And when you were courting, could you, erm, did your leisure pattern change at all or were you doing the same things?* Er, I didn't go dancing as much cos Jack, we, he didn't dance. We used to go to the pictures more then.' Similarly Kathleen remembered: 'Things didn't change very much, I mean, I still used to go to Newton Heath Palais occasionally, until David came along, and then David didn't like dancing of course so then it was, it was the cinema.' Jean recalled trips to see Oldham Athletic play football: 'I'm not saying that I was an enthusiast, you know, I suppose it was just one of those give-and-take things, well, you know.' Certainly, it seems likely that at least some of those women football spectators discussed in Chapter 3, were accompanying a boyfriend in his choice of leisure, rather than their own.

Some women did, however, refuse to alter their own leisure experiences to fit in with the demands of courting, providing examples of the ways in which women resisted prescribed gendered leisure patterns. Margaret parted with the man who was eventually to become her husband because he could not accept her right to separate leisure choices. As she explained: 'And the reason we fell out was because the RAF asked me to swim for them and I told him I couldn't go out with him one night and he said oh if you prefer that to this and the other. And we fell out. *So what was that about?* He didn't like the idea of me (pause) not ... having a date with him, rather than swimming for the RAF.' Mass-Observation interviewed one eighteen-year-old clerical worker in 1949 who was similarly not prepared to sacrifice her own varied interests for the sake of a boyfriend: 'I go to the jazz club, dancing, tennis, swimming, and listening to gramophone records. On Saturday, I went to the Bebop club in the evening and shopped in the afternoon, then a party at night ... I packed my boyfriend last week because he didn't like my going to bop clubs ... What do I want out of life? Just a nice husband, a baby, a home and "bop records".[66]

The women encompassed by this study often viewed youth as a golden age: a period in the life cycle when the pursuit of personal pleasure was felt to be both legitimate and possible. Freedom and independence in youthful leisure were founded upon a range of factors which combined to create a notion of 'earned' leisure. These included the assumptions of contemporaries, as well as participation in paid labour, within clearly defined hours, in exchange for financial reward. Chapter 3 examined the ways in which women pursued their pleasures over the period 1920 to 1960, it also illustrated the limitations which framed young women's experiences. This chapter has, however, shown that courting activity could precipitate a move away from much-loved activities, acting as an introduction to an adult world where the leisure preferences of others took precedence. Moreover, our period witnessed a falling age at marriage and a raising of the school-leaving age, ensuring that this period of relative independence in leisure became ever shorter. It seems probable that a reduction in the years between leaving school and marrying intensified the experience of youth, providing fuel for the youth culture of the 1950s. It is more difficult to prove a link between earlier marriage and the decline of those entertainments, such as the cinema, which depended upon the patronage of large numbers of young unmarried women over the years. However, such a link is indeed possible, as the lives of married women, despite their increasing participation in the labour force, became ever more home-focused. Certainly, as Chapter 5 will demonstrate, once they were married, the relationship between women and leisure changed markedly; duty and service replaced freedom and independence as its overriding characteristic.

Notes

1 H. James and F. Moore, 'Adolescent leisure in a working-class district', *Occupational Psychology*, 14:3 (1940), p. 144.

2 J. L. Harley, 'Report of an enquiry into the occupations, further education and leisure interests of a number of girl wage-earners from elementary and central schools in the Manchester district, with special reference to the influence of school training on their use of leisure'. M.Ed. dissertation, University of Manchester, 1937, p. 78.

3 P. Jephcott, *Rising Twenty* (Faber & Faber, London, 1948), p. 65.

4 H. James and F. Moore, 'Adolescent leisure in a working-class district. Part II', *Occupational Psychology*, 18:1 (1944), p. 31.

5 M. Kerr, *The People of Ship Street* (Routledge & Kegan Paul, London, 1958), p. 30.

6 *Manchester Evening News* (hereafter *MEN*), 2 January 1960, p 5.

7 Jephcott, *Rising Twenty*, p. 26.

8 *MEN*, 29 January 1960, p. 4.

9 *MEN*, 4 February 1960, p. 6.

10 P. Jephcott, *Girls Growing Up* (Faber & Faber, London, 1942), p. 135.

11 C. Rollett and J. Parker, 'Population and family', in A. H. Halsey (ed.), *Trends in British Society Since 1900* (Macmillan, London, 1972), p. 41.

12 M. Spring Rice, *Working-Class Wives: Their Health and Conditions* (Penguin, Harmondsworth, 1939), p. 95.

13 Rollett and Parker, 'Population and family', p. 43.

14 J. Lewis, *Women in England, 1870–1950: Sexual Divisions and Social Change* (Harvester Wheatsheaf, London, 1984), p. 4.

15 A. Oram, 'Repressed and thwarted, or bearer of the new world? The spinster in inter-war feminist discourses', *Women's History Review*, 1:3 (1992), p. 415.

16 A. Oram, 'Embittered, sexless or homosexual: attacks on spinster teachers, 1918–39', in A. Angerman *et al.* (eds), *Current Issues in Women's History* (Routledge, London, 1989), p. 183.

17 S. Neild and R. Pearson, *Women Like Us* (Women's Press, London, 1992).

18 Jephcott, *Girls Growing Up*, p. 123.

19 Mass-Observation Archive (hereafter M-O A): File Report (hereafter FR) 3150, 'Teen-age girls', August 1949, p. 10.

20 Harley, 'Report of an enquiry', p. 112.

21 James and Moore, 'Adolescent leisure in a working-class district. Part II', p. 31.

22 Harley, 'Report of an enquiry', p. 112.

23 *The Times*, 1 February 1960, p. 7, col. d.

24 Joyce.

25 Neild and Pearson, *Women Like Us*.

26 For a more detailed discussion of the monkey parade in interwar Salford and Manchester, see A. Davies, *Leisure, Gender and Poverty: Working-Class Culture in Salford and Manchester, 1900–1939* (Open University Press, Buckingham, 1992), pp. 102–8.

27 P. Jephcott, *Some Young People* (George Allen & Unwin, London, 1954), p. 58.

28 *MEN*, 10 November 1925, p. 3.

29 S. Humphries, *A Secret World of Sex. Forbidden Fruit: The British Experience, 1900–1950* (Sidgwick & Jackson, London, 1988), pp. 205–6.

30 Brighton Ourstory Project, *Daring Hearts: Lesbian and Gay Lives of 50s and 60s Brighton* (QueenSpark Books, Brighton, 1992), p. 59.

31 Neild and Pearson, *Women Like Us*, p. 33.

32 See Pat James's life history in Neild and Pearson, *Women Like Us*, pp. 57–62.

33 Neild and Pearson, *Women Like Us*, pp. 92, 99.

34 M-O A: FR3150, 'Teen-age girls', p. 12.

35 A debate in the pages of the *Manchester Evening News* in 1930 points to this function of the cinema. One correspondent claimed: 'Noisy talking which distracts attention is bad enough, but the conduct of some courting couples is worse.' In reply, another asserted: '[courting couples] are there because the parks close at dusk, and unfortunately, the back row accommodation is limited', *MEN*, 15 April 1930, p. 6; *MEN*, 16 April 1930, p. 6.

36 D. Caradog Jones (ed.), *The Social Survey of Merseyside*, vol. 3 (Hodder & Stoughton, London, 1934), p. 277.

37 B. Seebohn Rowntree and G. R. Lavers, *English Life and Leisure: A Social Study* (Longmans, London, 1951), p. 216.

38 Kerr, *The People of Ship Street*, pp. 72, 82.

39 Jephcott, *Girls Growing Up*, p. 139.

40 M-O A: Directive Respondent (hereafter DR) 2031, reply to July 1939 Directive.

41 Kerr, *The People of Ship Street*, p. 78.

42 Jephcott, *Rising Twenty*, pp. 88–9.

43 M-O A: DR1048, reply to April 1944 Directive.

44 M-O A: DR1329, reply to July 1939 Directive.

45 Humphries asserts that workmates were the most important educators of the young people he studied: Humphries, *A Secret World of Sex*, pp. 60–2.

46 Jephcott, *Rising Twenty*, p. 90.

47 Humphries, *A Secret World of Sex*, pp. 17–18.

48 Rowntree and Lavers, *English Life and Leisure*, p. 203.

49 M-O A: DR1346, reply to April 1944 Directive.

50 R. McKibbin, *Classes and Cultures: England 1918–1951* (Oxford University Press, Oxford, 1998), p. 297.

51 Alice.

52 Margaret.

53 Jephcott, *Rising Twenty*, pp. 74–5.

54 *MEN*, 8 May 1930, p. 6.

55 *MEN*, 10 May 1930, p. 4.

56 *MEN*, 12 May 1930, p. 6; *MEN*, 15 May 1930, p. 6.

57 *Woman's World*, 11 December 1948, p. 20.

58 M-O A: DR2031 reply to July 1939 Directive.

59 M-O A: DR1041 reply to July 1939 Directive.

60 Jephcott, *Girls Growing Up*, p. 39.

61 *MEN*, 3 January 1935, p. 3.

62 Amy.

63 Jephcott, *Rising Twenty*, pp. 75–6.

64 Jephcott, *Some Young People*, p. 66.

65 Jephcott, *Rising Twenty*, p. 76.

66 M-O A: FR3150, 'Teen-age girls', pp. 2–3.

5

'Pleasure loving mothers'?
Leisure in adult life

I f leisure in youth was often conceptualised in terms of freedom and independence, then women's leisure in adulthood was inextricably linked to notions of duty and service. While the paid work of youth legitimised leisure for young women, the unpaid domestic work of married women limited both the opportunities for and expectations of leisure. In effect, a notion of leisure as earned through full-time, paid labour framed women's own perceptions of their right to leisure. If the act of going out to work effected a separation between work and leisure for adolescent girls, women working in the home rarely experienced such a distinction. Moreover, while the relatively uncomplicated leisure status of young wage-earning adolescent girls was founded upon some measure of economic independence, the financial independence of married women was less certain. In the postwar period, the increased participation of married women in the workforce, as part-time or casual workers, did not promote a notion of earned leisure. Women were viewed as being able to combine two forms of work, but neither was perceived as a full-time job deserving of a leisure reward.

Oral testimony points to both changing experiences and differing perceptions of leisure as the life cycle progressed. Respondents often recalled that the years after marriage, and particularly after the birth of children, heralded fundamental changes in their relationship to leisure. Many of the women interviewed expressed the view that once married they no longer needed, deserved or even wanted leisure for themselves; most observed that in adult life the choices of other family members took precedence over their own use of time. Documentary sources, too, point to an indistinct notion of leisure for adult women; there was a widely promoted assertion that their pleasures were more dependent upon domestic circumstances than were those of any other family member. While occasional reference was made to the needs of women as individuals, women more generally, were addressed as part of – or, in the postwar period, representatives of – the family unit. In effect, the personal pleasures of youth were replaced by a leisure rooted largely within the family, with the family itself becoming the source of personal happiness. Certainly, the *Manchester Evening News* 'Home Page' made the link between a woman's happiness and her home explicit. In 1935 its editress proclaimed: 'It's not until you are married that you know what happiness is.'[1]

This chapter addresses the link between women's roles as mothers and wives and their experiences of leisure. It explores the ways in which adult women's leisure became rooted within the family, and examines the extent to which women actually serviced the leisure of other family members through their own work. The first section also considers additional arenas for service and duty in leisure, notably in work for church and youth organisations, and in caring for kin or neighbours. I will then move on to an examination of the day-to-day factors which acted as constraints upon women's leisure choices. Here the focus is upon issues of time and money; the extent to which the changing nature of the marital relationship impacted upon women's experiences is of specific concern. Chapter 5 concludes with an examination of those areas where women did carve out a space for their own pleasures, although these were only infrequently given the formal title 'leisure'. While change and continuity over the life cycle will be explored through an examination of dancing and picture-going, the emphasis in this section is upon informal, often home-based, experiences. In particular, attention is drawn to historical change in the arenas for socialising and the growing importance of the home as a leisure venue for family members. Throughout the chapter, there is a recognition that 'leisure' for adult women constituted a complex and ambiguous category. Definitions of the concept remained shifting and unclear across this period, and the boundaries between 'work' and 'leisure' were often difficult to draw.

Conceptualising 'leisure' in adult life

The problematic nature of 'leisure' as a category of historical analysis is acute when we are addressing the experiences of married women. In Chapter 1 it was suggested that the established definition of leisure as a reward for paid labour both ignores and distorts the experiences of those performing unpaid labour, notably housewives and those caring for children.

Here it is argued that this conception also actively framed women's own perceptions of their right to leisure, as well as determining social constructions of the relationship between adult women and the concept. In effect, while the paid work of youth engendered some notion of leisure as a right, the unpaid labours of adult life failed to produce a reciprocal notion of leisure entitlement.

Many of the Manchester interviewees did not consider that 'leisure' played a part in their lives after marriage – as Dorothy's evidence, cited below, will illustrate. Indeed, Elizabeth Roberts has argued that 'Women did not seek self-fulfilment at the expense of their family because they saw little distinction between their own good and that of their families.'[2] While Roberts's evidence for this assertion comes from working-class experience in the period 1890 to 1940, her assessment is supported by the working- and lower-middle-class experiences examined here. Moreover, social constructions of the 'good' wife and mother as someone who devoted her time to the needs of other family members could induce guilt in those women who sought to prioritise their own pleasures either within or outside the family. Certainly, the extent to which leisure often necessitated work by the wife and mother meant that so-called 'family leisure' rarely provided unmitigated personal leisure for the women involved.

Oral evidence suggests that marriage marked a disjuncture in experiences of leisure over the life cycle. Mary, for example, recalled her aspirations for married life: 'But you looked forward to a different sort of life, you see, looking after your own home. And we all looked forward to that.' As Judy Giles has demonstrated, the acquisition of 'a home of one's own' was particularly appealing to working-class women able to rent, or even buy, homes away from the slum conditions of the inner city in the first half of the twentieth century.[3] Other women observed that marriage effected a concentration upon the home and family which consumed their spare time. Hannah was questioned about the postwar period: '*When the war was over, and you'd already started your family, how did having children affect what you could do in your spare time?* Well you didn't really do anything very much apart from, er, home and children and garden.' The work of housewifery left such women with little time for leisure outside the family. As Celia noted: 'My life centred around, er, my husband … we didn't really bother going out. I was quite happy, you know, looking after the home.' Nor was the association between adult leisure and the family restricted to married women. The oldest interviewee, Ada, who lived with her father and stepmother, rarely left the house in pursuit of personal pleasure: 'No, I never wanted to go out. My interest is home and family.'

The decline of personal leisure after marriage was not just a by-product of family life; in some cases it was perceived as a necessary condition for it. Dorothy's analysis of her leisure over the life cycle demonstrates not only the extent to which family life superseded notions of personal pleasure, but also the way in which particular 'leisure' activities ceased to be perceived as such if they were conducted out of a sense of duty to others. Thus she demonstrates the need to ascertain the meanings which women gave to their experiences as well as the context within which they occurred, if we are to understand fully the work–leisure relationship in adult women's lives. Her words are quoted at length because they anticipate many of the central themes of this chapter, and demonstrate the complexity of interviewees' own understandings of their experiences over the life cycle.

Dorothy was born in 1925 and married in 1946. She spent her early years living in Ardwick, but later moved to Higher Openshaw, where she lived with her husband and three daughters. In Dorothy's youth, leisure had been a high priority. Dancing, in particular, had been a much-loved activity, and one which she had pursued several times a week throughout her wage-earning years. When she was interviewed, however, Dorothy asserted that her 'leisure' ended shortly after her marriage at the age of twenty-one. As she recalled:

> I'm awfully sorry that really my leisure ended when I started my family, which was 1948. But I thought you might just be interested in, you know, before that. Is there anything else you wonder about? *Well, I'm interested in the period afterwards as well. Did you feel that you would have liked more leisure after you had your children?* No, No. I was perfectly happy. No, I think, the fact that I had all this, I had quite a lot of, you, erm, I think probably I, I from about fifteen to meeting my husband at nineteen, erm, really that was enough for me, you know. I mean my husband and I did other things, erm, after we were married. I had the children, erm, we didn't have many baby-sitters but, erm, we managed to do things with the children. And we belonged to a church and you know, all their activities, with the children. And he then belonged to a dramatics society, and got two of the children interested in that. And erm. No I did honestly feel erm that I'd had enough of, you know, erm. We went to the cinema, but I, I, I did try going dancing when we couldn't get baby-sitters, or we couldn't afford them. And erm, we had one night out a week each, and erm, he went out about nine o'clock, for a drink, got back about eleven. And he had a game of cards. And I tried going back to the Ritz and, with my sister,

erm, but I didn't feel right, you know, I didn't feel right. *Why, why didn't you feel right?* Well I ended up dancing with other men when I had a husband at home, you know. I mean erm, er, erm, er, I went for a few weeks and er (pause) it just didn't seem right. So I didn't do it you know, I mean I stopped doing it, you know, and erm, er, then we more or less we ... except for the church dances. We waited until my eldest was about fifteen and then we danced a lot because we were able to do it, you know. ... So erm, no, I felt that I'd had a lovely teenage life and er, I wanted to settle down and erm, I really, not settle down that much but not do things without my husband. You know. You know, not, not too much anyway. I would perhaps have done something like gone to an evening class or something without him but not socially dancing, you know.

Although she spoke at length about family holidays, church activities, visiting and other areas which in other circumstances may be defined as leisure, Dorothy did not herself describe them thus. The fact that these were activities carried out in, and for, the family did not, in her experience, mark them out as leisure. For this woman, 'leisure' was equated with a particular notion of freedom and independence, specifically the freedom to dance, and this she really experienced only in her youth. After marriage, difficulties in acquiring baby-sitters, economic considerations, and the social meanings attached to her favoured activity constrained her movements. Of most importance in determining her experiences, however, was a funda-mental change in attitude towards the pursuit of personal pleasure: once she was married, the personal was replaced by the family. Dorothy's testimony thus demonstrates a clear shift in perceptions of 'leisure' over the life cycle. Her husband's weekly visits to the pub are suggestive of a contrasting continuity in male leisure patterns.

Historians of leisure utilising the unproblematic definition of the word outlined in the Introduction to this book have, largely, failed to address the changing ways in which women themselves understood the concept over the course of their lives. This is a criticism which can be levelled even at those who have explicitly addressed gender differences in access to leisure, including Andrew Davies' ground-breaking study of Salford and Manchester. While this study supports Davies' contention that 'Women's experience of leisure was subject to a series of financial, domestic and moral constraints', it argues that it is not enough to explore inequalities in access to leisure opportunity while taking definitions of leisure as given.[4] 'Leisure' is itself a fundamentally gendered concept; its very meaning and relationship to the category 'work' are rooted in gender difference. Oral testimony shows that the particular leisure experiences of adult women stemmed not merely from unequal access, but from a fundamental difference in the perceptions of – and notions of entitlement to – personal pleasure, between the sexes.

Women's leisure in the family

The forty years covered by this study witnessed considerable changes in the experience of leisure within the family. A reduction in family size, increased wages for many, and improvements in housing conditions heralded the rise of 'family leisure'.[5] This form of leisure was achieved by different classes at different times, but aspects of it were generally attainable by the end of this period. We will return to the forms which constituted 'family leisure' later in this chapter. Here, however, attention is drawn to notions of leisure entitlement within the family. Of specific interest is the extent to which women's work actually serviced the leisure of other family members, as wives and mothers became increasingly characterised as the custodians of family pleasure.

While the relationship between married women and personal leisure was often problematic, other adult family members experienced the concept in the defined terms of earned legitimacy. Chapter 3 has already outlined the extent to which young people of both sexes expected some measure of personal leisure. For men, this sense of legitimacy extended into married life, and was bolstered by an ideology of marriage which – although it shifted over the period, particularly in the demands it made on women – held at its core a husband's right to personal pleasure.[6]

In the 1930s, a number of *Manchester Evening News* writers urged women to accept their husbands' right to independent leisure and, in some cases, even suggested that they develop pursuits of their own in order to liberate their husbands from the demands of companionship. For example, Ursula Jeans suggested that a man should continue in his old sports, hobbies and acquaintances after marriage, while noting that '[for a wife] marriage is her be-all and end-all. It is everything to her although it is only a part of his life.'[7] In the same year, the composer Ivor Novello, writing as a guest for the *Evening News* series 'Husbands and Wives', was critical of a perceived tendency among women to see husband and self as one entity: 'Develop some hobbies of your own. Don't want to be always with him. There are times when the most affectionate man requires to be by himself.'[8] This advice appears to have been designed for a middle-class readership among whom notions of 'companionate marriage' were already gaining popularity in the interwar period.

Although the call for female hobbies was founded upon the needs of the husband, the idea that married women should have interests outside the home did coincide with a short-lived characterisation of housewifery for middle-class women as a modern, full-time job, deserving of a leisure reward. This characterisation had its roots in the decline of 'live-in' domestic service as an occupation and the downward expansion of the middle-class. Middle-class women became repositioned within society as housewives, aided by 'labour-saving devices' such as the vacuum cleaner, heated hot water, gas cooker, electric iron and electric radiators, but working to increasingly higher standards of cleanliness.[9]

As the period progressed, however, the project of 'companionate marriage' gained a cross-class, but never universal, ascendancy. Different demands were placed upon the wife within the sphere of leisure, as the inextricably linked concept of 'family leisure' also grew in currency. Rather than simply leaving her husband alone to enjoy his separate pursuits, the wife became responsible for the leisure choices of her partner. If leisure was to be enjoyed within the home, then that home must constitute an appropriate venue for male leisure. In an *Evening News* article in 1940, Ann Lewis castigated the archetypal 'lonely woman' whose husband spent every night in the pub or club: 'I'm willing to bet my new powder compact to a pair of clogs that you were to blame most of the time.'[10] By failing to maintain her appearance, or being too busy with her home to spend time with her husband, the woman was accused of driving him out of the family home. The solution, according to Lewis, lay in improved appearance, the acquisition of some games to play together, and the provision of the husband's 'favourite ale'. The onus was entirely upon the wife to create an environment in which her husband would want to spend his leisure time. Significantly, the wife carried this responsibility even in wartime. Later in the same year one writer warned the childless housewife contemplating taking a paid job in 1940 to ignore the need for leisure time at her peril: 'There must be a time for entertainment – free of domestic ties and work worries.' The consequences of omitting this consideration were perceived to be grave, chief among them being the impact which an absence of shared leisure might have upon the marital relationship. The piece ends with the admonishment: 'No sense of duty done will be adequate recompense for a lost husband.'[11] It appears that even the dictates of war could not outweigh a wife's responsibility for her husband's leisure.

At the end of the period, this expectation that women should take responsibility for servicing their husbands' leisure was again apparent within the pages of the *Manchester Evening News*. In 1955, Robert E. Gibbs advised married couples : 'Guard your marriage from that dreadful monotony. Go on. Enjoy yourselves together.'[12] 'Doing something together, enjoying a mutual pleasure, sharing an experience,' would, according to Gibbs, enhance a relationship. It was the woman alone, however, who was held responsible for organising the night out. The idea that a wife held a special responsibility for the maintenance of couple-based leisure was similarly evident in the response of the problem-solver Jane Dawson to a 'neglected wife' who complained of an absent husband. Dawson contended that this situation was likely to be of her own making, as a wife often, 'loses interest in him [her husband] as a man, gives all her time to children and home'.[13] Once again the wife was deemed culpable for her husband's leisure choices. This sense of responsibility was illustrated in an active way when a group of women succeeded in closing a gambling club frequented by their husbands by writing anonymous letters to the Oldham Police.[14] In this instance the action was necessary because the men 'gambled away their pay'.[15]

This brief survey of attitudes towards marital leisure evident within the pages of one local newspaper demonstrates both historical continuity and change. Husbands, throughout the period, were expected to enjoy some type of leisure activity in their non-working hours, although the forms this leisure took were not static over time. In contrast, wives were expected to service male leisure. In the earlier period this necessitated letting a husband alone to pursue his interests in peace. Later, with the advent of home- and couple-based leisure, it demanded the creation of a comfortable site for leisure, through the application of domestic skills within the home.

Women's role as facilitators of leisure within the family was not limited to the co-ordination of their husbands' leisure. While the advent of children could generally curtail the amount of time available to women for leisure, the leisure of children, like that of the husband, often necessitated work by the mother. Hannah, for example, remembered that in the 1940s and 1950s: 'School concerts, speech days, Scout and Brownie events occupied our spare time until the children grew older.' Those working-class women who remembered the Manchester Whit Walks recalled both the work and the self-sacrifice entailed in preparing children for these annual church-

and school organised processions into the city centre from the surrounding parishes.[16] *Manchester Evening News* reports claimed that the Church of England walk attracted approximately 20,000 children even in 1955, when the walks were beginning their decline.[17] The Catholic walk on Whit Friday attracted double that number of participants in the interwar period, although this figure had declined to 15,000 by 1955, probably as a result of city-centre clearance.[18] Each of these children was expected to walk in new clothes, and this created both additional work and worry for their mothers. As Joan recalled: 'You expected your mother to buy, er, an outfit for Whit Week and you wore it on the most important day, which was, for us, it was Whit Friday, and then Whit Sunday.'

Ivy recalled the struggles the women of prewar Ancoats went through in order to provide new clothes for their children at this time: 'They might go in the pawn shop the week after, but they had new clothes for Whit.' Irene said that her mother would probably do without to clothe them at Whit, and Dorothy remembered the walks as a time of worry for mothers: 'You know, I think they must have spent all their money on, erm, dressing the children up in all their finery, you know and erm, it was a big worry actually. A big worry. You know, erm, I think for lots of mums, even in my day you know, er, a big worry.' Certainly, those women who made their children's clothes themselves invested both time and money in the process, as both Ivy and Annie recalled. The extent to which the self-sacrifice of the mother released resources for other family members is evident in this extract from Kathleen's testimony:

> And my mother, I remember my mother telling me, and it was many years after, and she said I only missed one year. And I said, I didn't know cos I've got photographs of my mother in this big hat, you know. And er, and she said I, I only missed one year. And I said why did you miss, were you not so well? And she said, no to tell you the truth Kathleen I'd lent our Betty my shoes and I, I couldn't go. I said d'you mean you couldn't go because you'd lent one of my sisters your shoes and she said no I couldn't. And I said, did you only have one pair of shoes and she said yes. But, but we never went without anything.

While the Whit walks provide clear evidence of the work involved for Manchester women in servicing the structured leisure of children, the ambiguities inherent in defining 'work' and 'leisure' in adult women's lives are apparent elsewhere too. For example, what may appear to be out-of-house leisure activity could often involve the work of childcare. Walks, in particular, demonstrate the problems apparent in conceptualising leisure in terms of activity alone. As Davies has observed, trips to the park afforded a cheap form of leisure for many working-class adolescents and adults.[19] Chapter 4 demonstrated that the park provided young people with an arena for courting away from the supervision of parents or relatives. Mothers, however, rarely walked unaccompanied for pleasure; visits to the park were more usually related to the work of childcare.

Many of the women interviewed recalled walks with their mothers and visits to Manchester's many parks in their childhood. Others recalled their own experiences of motherhood in the postwar period. Irene described trips to the park with her sons in the 1950s: 'and as Paul got bigger we'd er, we'd go out and about and, er, we'd erm, go walking again with the pram, visiting my mother and Albert's parents and, er, we'd go to Belle Vue, of course that was, that was marvellous'. For some, the park provided an escape from overcrowded homes or, in the case of Hannah, from the watchful eye of her mother, with whom she lived during the war: '*So you had to look after him on your own. Did you find that hard?* Well it was really, with living with my mother. Cos it was only a little house you know and, er, with no bath or anything like that. I remember I used to trundle around for hours with him in the pram. To the park. *To keep out of the house?* Yes.' For others, visits to the park were undertaken largely for the benefit of their children. Spring Rice described one woman as: 'untiring in her devotion to and care of the children … taking them often to the park which is rather a long way off'.[20] Clearly, such activities did provide an element of leisure for mothers to the extent that they represented a legitimate means of escaping the confines of the home. Moreover, time spent with their children could be a source of joy and pleasure to mothers. As Alice suggested: 'My mother had pleasure with us as children taking us out to the parks and that, that's what I … I remember. The family was important to her.' None the less, it seems clear that child-centred forms of leisure, such as the walk or visit to the park, should be viewed as a complex synthesis of both duty and pleasure for adult women.

Spare time outside the family

So far, this chapter has concentrated upon experiences within the family, and has suggested that notions of service and duty framed adult women's relationship to leisure. However, the link between 'leisure', duty and self-sacrifice was evident not only within the realms of domestic life. Many of the women interviewed dedicated any spare time they did possess to the service of others outside the home. As Jessie noted when she talked about the guiding activities which constituted her abiding interest: 'I think that taught me to do, er, something for somebody else. And that's what I've been brought up to do.' Throughout her life, she involved herself in a variety of 'good causes' ranging from her work with young people to voluntary work at a hospital library. As she surmised: 'I don't suppose we did an awful lot, only do [things] for other people, I think that's what my life has been, doing for other people.'

For other women, their own work serviced the pleasures of others, while it often provided a sense of personal satisfaction. In the interwar period, in particular, churches provided an arena for women's voluntary work. Annie remembered the church socials of her youth in the 1930s, where it was always the women who prepared the food, and later dedicated the little spare time available to her to visiting the elderly members of her Methodist congregation. Jane believed that her own mother perceived her work for church fairs and gatherings as a duty rather than an enjoyable use of time; nevertheless, she dedicated precious time to the production of handicrafts and items of food to be sold at such occasions. Others performed work within alternative groups or organisations. Kathleen, for example, spoke about her involvement in the British Legion in the 1950s:

> *Would things like the British Legion, er, you know, preparing the food and things, would you see that as something you had to do or something that you enjoyed doing?* I er, well both. Both er, and, I mean … it was enjoyable, but it … and it was a … it was a good, it was a good thing to do. I mean the, the old men used to really look forward to it, you know. Er, and it was a good thing to do but we enjoyed doing it as well.

Here there is a clear recognition that a sense of duty and personal enjoyment could ultimately interact in a particular activity. Finally, some women spent what spare time they had caring for elderly or ailing relatives and neighbours. After her marriage, Elsie cared for both her mother-in-law and her father. As she put it: 'Erm, so I had my mother-in-law one side of the fire and my father at the other side. And they were both difficult people. But I coped.' Despite this, however, she freely devoted herself to the care of sick neighbours and friends, explaining her actions thus: 'I've always known that I could make them comfortable. And I put their comfort before my own feelings … it's hard to say why I did it because it was so natural for me to do it all my life. As though I couldn't do any other but step into the situation.' Some women, it would appear, did not feel easy in their spare time unless they were working for the benefit of others.

Adult 'leisure': duty and service?

Not all the women interviewed perceived leisure as constituting an arena for duty and service in married life: oral narratives demonstrate differing constructions of leisure as the life cycle progressed. For a minority, the transition from youth to adulthood was marked by a contrasting concept-ualisation of leisure. Those who had been subject to the greatest degrees of parental control over their youthful leisure behaviour sometimes espoused a different characterisation of leisure in adulthood. Jane, for example, was born in 1929 and lived in the Cheetham and Crumpsall areas of Manchester. She married in 1952; her two children were born three and thirteen years respectively after her marriage. Like Dorothy, this woman's chief interest was dancing, an activity she had pursued in her youth despite her father's active opposition. After marriage she continued to dance, ac-companying her husband to dance halls at which he played as a member of a jazz band. Even after the birth of her first child she continued this lifestyle, as her mother was available to baby-sit for them. As the following extract shows, the constraint upon her use of time experienced by Jane in her youth caused her to associate her married life, not her youth, with notions of freedom in leisure:

> And when we got married, the day we got married, we went home after the wedding, er, to where we were going to live and he [her husband] said to me, Well you're a married woman now and you can do as you like and you can smoke if you want to and you can listen to Radio Luxembourg. That's free-dom (laughs). That's freedom for you (laughs). Cos my father wouldn't let me do any of those things.

Overall, however, oral testimony supports a notion of 'leisure' in adult-hood as rooted in the home and interwoven with caring for the family. Most of the women interviewed did conceptualise leisure as a youth-based experience, and related this to their role as full-time, paid workers. After marriage, and particularly after childbirth, personal pleasure was no longer the most pressing priority. Most commonly, women's own individual leisure preferences were subsumed into those of the family, with 'leisure' becom-ing a vehicle for service to husband and children. This is not to say that the women resented this. In many cases, the women themselves perceived their lives to be necessarily discontinuous and talked about embracing their new role, with the family itself becoming a source of pleasure. As one twenty-five-year-old from Pinner told Mass-Observation in 1939: 'Mother seems to live a completely reflective life (I don't mean pensive – perhaps I should say "enjoys others pleasures and not too often her own").'[21] Elizabeth Roberts contends: 'There can be no doubt that many women found great happiness and contentment in bringing up their children.'[22]

However, oral evidence suggests that, retrospectively, women did feel that they had given up something of themselves in their progression through the life cycle. Dorothy, for example, said: 'I only do what I want to do now, because for years I've done what everybody else wanted to do (laughs).' Similarly Elsie, whose mother-in law lived with her for twenty years, acknowledged a sense of personal freedom which she associated with the deaths of both mother-in-law and husband: 'And er, she died in the May, and, erm, then my husband died one month after. But I, I felt a terrific sense of freedom, I thought suddenly, you know, less to do, it was wonderful.'

Time and money: the constraints upon leisure in married life

Notions of leisure in adulthood as rooted in service and duty clearly framed many women's experiences over this period. Limitations of time and money constituted a day-to-day constraint upon the pursuit of leisure by adult women. As Chapter 2 has shown, the nature of domestic labour led to a fragmentation of time; the demands of family and home limited its availability. Even when time was available, unequal access to perhaps very limited family resources dictated the nature of women's experiences. In the second section of this chapter, therefore, the constraints upon leisure choices are addressed. The focus here is less upon the very nature of work in the home and more upon those factors outside of the work itself which shaped women's access to spare time. In particular, I examine the influence of the marital relationship upon women's leisure experiences.

Gendered work within the home

The ideology of 'family leisure' assumed that the home constituted a venue for the enjoyment of leisure. This chapter has already demonstrated how women were increasingly encouraged to create a pleasing leisure environment for their husbands over the course of this period. Yet for both the full-time housewife and the woman who combined family with outside labour, the home could never be an uncomplicated leisure site. Work within the home was allocated according to gender; housework and childcare remained a largely female province. This is not to say that men performed no work within the household. The evidence which follows will present a picture of an increasingly active masculine role. However, household labour remained fundamentally gendered, a situation which both promoted and sustained gender-specific notions of spare time among married couples.

The contributions which a husband might make to household chores and childcare could increase a woman's potential leisure time; the extent to which a woman did not receive such help often had an adverse effect upon her resources of time. As one of the working-class wives surveyed by Spring Rice observed:

> I believe myself that one of the biggest difficulties our mothers have is that our husbands do not realise that we ever need any leisure time … So many of our men think we should not go out until the children are grown up. We do not want to be neglecting the home but we do feel we would like to have a little look around the shops, or if we go to the clinic we can just have a few minutes … It isn't that the men are unkind. It is the old idea that we should always be at home.[23]

When Mass-Observation asked its panel of volunteers for their thoughts on housework in 1948, a major reason given by women for male help in the house was that it would free time up for leisure. As one thirty-one-year-old secretary put it: 'Men benefit from shorter hours and five-day week etc. and unless they use some of that time to alleviate woman's domestic work the woman gets absolutely no break at all which is manifestly unfair. Why should she toil from morning till night seven days of the week while the husband's responsibilities are ended when he gets back from his office at 6 p.m.?'[24] A twenty-three-year-old housewife added: 'The main reason is that if my husband helps me we then have more time to do other things together. If I have to do everything myself I get tired and irritable and we have no time to garden together or go for walks or cycle rides and I have no time to read or write.'[25]

Analysis of the *Manchester Evening News* reveals a lively debate across our period about the extent to which men should help in the running of the home. Like many of the debates within the newspaper's pages, the picture presented was one of ambiguity and complexity – the same year, and even the same edition, often yielding contradictory and contrasting evidence. Yet there was a clear acknowledgement in much of the newspaper discussion that the distribution of household chores had a fundamental impact upon the time available for leisure. It was where the husband appeared to be sacrificing his own right to 'earned' leisure that the most vociferous debate occurred.

In 1940, Ann Lewis delivered what she termed 'a few scornful words to the wives of Mary Ann husbands … Those poor chaps who have regular household duties to perform, sometimes when they come home from work in the evenings – and almost certainly on Saturday afternoons and Sunday mornings.'[26] Here, the encroachment of housework into a husband's non-working hours was regarded as particularly regrettable. A decade later, a similar debate was provoked by the letter of a 'lucky wife' who wrote of a husband who helped her with all the household duties, giving her a full day off each Saturday 'to be able to go out and enjoy myself'.[27] Other readers responded with horror. One woman wrote of her own husband as 'a man doing a man-sized job', boasting that he never raised a finger to help her in the home: 'I wouldn't exchange him for all the dish washing Mary Anns in Manchester.'[28] A male bus driver enquired about 'lucky wife's' use of the spare time her husband's labour afforded her, labelling her a 'good time girl'.[29] Another male reader thought it likely that her husband was 'glad to be rid of her for a day'; while yet another asked: 'I wonder what "lucky wife's" unlucky husband does in his spare time?'[30] Clearly, the division of labour within this woman's household transgressed a gender norm in the division of time into work and leisure, which readers – including some women – found distasteful. Roberts has identified four reasons why some women in the postwar period refused to let their husbands perform more than a limited range of chores: social conditioning; a sense of 'fairness' if they did not go out to work full-time; their own sense of housework as a skilled occupation and their desire to maintain control within the household.[31]

While their contributions were less numerous, a number of the newspaper's readers did, however, reject these arguments, providing evidence of a demand for help in the home. For example, one letter of 1930 on the subject 'My ideal … ' suggested that an ideal husband would help in the home and spend his leisure time with the family.[32] Ten years later, another reader responded to Ann Lewis's comments concerning 'Mary Ann husbands' in scathing terms: 'No Ann Lewis, the trouble is that there are far too few husbands like mine – and far too many wives who do every single thing for their husbands.'[33] Towards the end of our period, a retired male reader commented upon the respective work of men and women over the life cycle, noting: 'men who make their 44-hour-a-week "man sized job" their excuse for wanting their wives to wait on them hand and foot will no doubt dig up some other excuse for "dodging the column", domestically, when they retire from work. But when will their wives retire?'[34] The benefits for women of a husband's help in the home were more often articulated in women's magazines over the period. For example, *Woman's Own* encouraged women to train their husbands to help with domestic labour: 'At first he will be only too eager to help you with the dishes. Don't make the mistake of refusing! In a year or two he won't even offer.'[35]

The extent to which men did, or did not, help their wives within the home can be traced through oral evidence and the snapshot perspective offered by replies to the Mass-Observation Directive on housework in 1948.[36] The picture presented here is one of measured historical change over the period, within a wider framework of continuity in female responsibility for the running of the home. None of the women interviewed remembered her father performing domestic tasks with any degree of regularity. Ivy, for example, was asked about her father's activities in inter-war Ancoats: *'And would your father help your mother in the house?* No, not really. He always polished our shoes, polished our shoes and things like that. And dried our hair, you know, when we'd had our hair washed. We liked Dad drying it, he was much gentler than my mother (laughs).' Dorothy, too, recalled her father's lack of assistance within their home in Ardwick:

> I mean my mother worked herself to death, she literally did and never went out to work. *Did your father help in the house?* Oh no, no, no I don't think my mother expected it. I mean he, erm, he worked on the railway, he didn't have a very, er, taxing job … But he did work rather long hours, and my mother, er, you know my mother, erm, liked housework really I suppose. And er, erm, she, you know, she was always on the go. Always cooking. I never saw her sit down ever. And when she was tired she went to bed. You never saw my mother sitting down like this.

The work which Dorothy's mother performed in the home left her little opportunity for even the most basic form of leisure: leisure as rest.

Other women recalled that their own husbands, in the interwar and postwar periods, similarly made no contribution to the running of the home. Edith married in 1931, and subsequently brought up four children, in the Collyhurst and later New Moston districts of Manchester. Although she continued to work full-time at a local foundry throughout her married life, her largely unemployed husband made no contribution to the work of bringing up their family. As a consequence, her double shift of paid and unpaid work left her with little time to herself. As she stated: 'By the time I came home here, I'd have all me housework and bath the kids and put them to bed, you know, really, and do me washing. And cook before I went to work of a, you know of a morning.' Doris, who enjoyed a comfortable lower-middle-class existence until the death of her husband at the end of this period, recalled:

> No, no he didn't do anything in the house, no. *Would you have liked him to?* Well, men weren't expected to in those days. You didn't expect them to and my father never did. So no you didn't, not like they do these days, they take their turn don't they, usually. But they didn't then. That was why I was so put out when he expected me to help with the garden. *Did you see that as his role, then?* Yes. Cos it had always been my father's role, the garden, you see.

A married thirty-eight-year-old Mass-Observation panel member admitted that:

> If and when I am in the house my husband doesn't lift a dish. For instance on Sundays immediately after breakfast he rises from the table and goes out. He comes back about 1.30 p.m. and has his meal. After this he rises from the table and sits down by the fire to read and have a sleep. Every Sunday when I am washing up I envy women who are helped and think what a difference it would make to me if he would help. Also in the evening about supper time I get very tired and would appreciate an offer to make the supper. My friends often discuss the subject and most of them do get help of some kind, some more than others. My husband's point of view is, that he doesn't ask me to go to the office to help him.[37]

As this extract suggests, the postwar period witnessed a growing resentment among women, particularly those engaged in part-time employment outside the home, at the lack of help offered by their husbands. Certainly, the vast majority of those who replied to the Mass-Observation directive of 1948 felt that the man should definitely help out. As one housewife exclaimed: 'Yes, I think they should help in the evenings and at weekends because we need time off at these times just as much as they do and we are tired too.'[38] Oral testimony provides evidence of this demand for assistance. Dorothy, for example, acknowledged: 'I haven't my mother's enthusiasm for, er, housework. My husband didn't help in the house actually. We had a few rows about that, but he said he had three daughters and, er, he did his own jobs, his decorating his gardening and er, and that.' (The rise of 'masculine housework' will be addressed shortly.[39]) Others employed strategies to enlist their husbands' help. Ivy, for example, described the way in which she persuaded her husband to perform work which she particularly disliked: 'My bugbear the stairs (laughs) cleaning them. Oh I used to hate vaccing the stairs, used to do everything and then I'd say to Dennis, now I've done it all, I've only the stairs to do when I get back. So I'd know that when I came back he'd've done the stairs (laughs). He never cottoned on (laughs).'

Some women insisted upon a more consistent and wide-ranging contribution from their husbands. Jean married in 1955 and spent several years in full-time paid work before the birth of her first daughter. The demands she made of her husband within the home were explicitly founded upon her own parents' experiences. Her words are quoted at length because they demonstrate generational change particularly clearly:

> *And did your husband help you in the home?* Oh yes, yes, yes. That was one of the things that I say, I think I realise now that I was just, I was a bit forward-thinking, without, without feeling that I was forward-thinking, cos it was something I did stipulate when we, when we were engaged, erm, that you know when we got, after we'd both been working, you know, that we both had to do jobs. Because that was something my father didn't do, when he came in, he liked to have the meal and I can remember there was, erm, a … a difficulty, that would be sort of all around the early fifties that Mother and him were getting in at the same time, you know, and if the fire wasn't lit and you know, there were all these things that seemed to have to be done. Erm, it wasn't that he wouldn't do jobs at all, er, I mean he quite happily years ago, on the bank holiday I mean it was like what, 'Oh I'll whitewash the ceiling' or you know. It was all right when he had the whole day, but there wasn't this sort of doing, doing jobs when you got in, you know. He'd, he, he because he'd, he'd been used to this having, having the meal ready more or less, you know, even though he was all over the place during the war. So I could see that I wouldn't be able to cope with that, so er, so we did, we did used to do things together.

It should be noted, however, that Jean was the only respondent who demanded and experienced an equitable division of labour within the home over this period.

As Jean's words suggest, the work which men more generally performed within the household was of a particular type. The sexual division of labour often allocated specific, time-limited chores to the husband, and the less defined, more time-consuming ones to the wife, with attendant consequences for the distribution of spare time within the marital relationship. Masculine housework constituted a series of 'jobs' rather than an omnipresent 'duty'. As Lady Muriel Kirkpatrick asserted in a *Manchester Evening News* article in 1930:

> There is room for only one boss in the kitchen. An Englishman's home may be his castle, but in the domestic sphere there is room for only one overlord, and its natural ruler is the wife. Certain little jobs like getting coal, chopping wood, and locking up seem to be natural for a man to perform. But there are definite limits in this matter of housework, past which, I am sure, the average housewife would not care for her husband to go.[40]

In the same year a reader described her ideal husband as a man who would adhere to strict gender roles: 'My ideal is a real man – not half a maid. Helpless at the kitchen sink when full of dirty dishes, but all right at the kitchen tap when a new washer is required.'[41]

The oral evidence already presented points to particular arenas for masculine work within the home: gardening and decorating have been described as the jobs most usually performed by men. The Mass-Observation panel added mending and fixing, carrying the coal, chopping firewood, lighting the fire, washing up, table-setting and window-cleaning.[42] Joanna Bourke has argued that the advent of new housing, particularly in the postwar era, combined with a reduction in working hours and increases in real incomes to effect an expansion of 'manly housework' within this period.[43] In some instances, the distinction between what was 'manly' and what was not appeared slight, yet was of great significance in work allocation within the home. Margaret, for instance, felt it only 'fair' that she should perform the bulk of household chores while her husband earned money for the family. However, there were limits to the work she was prepared to undertake, as the following story concerning the cleaning of shoes illustrates:

> I said what you put these here for? He says will you clean them and have them ready, I said, me clean your shoes! He said well my mam always used to, Margaret, he wasn't, wasn't nasty, it was how he'd been brought up. I said from now on, dear, you clean your own shoes or you'll go out mucky. I said,

in the air force who cleaned your shoes for you, he said I cleaned them myself. I said well carry on. I wasn't going to start where his mother left off. I did the baking, the cooking, looking after him, he always had a clean shirt and clothes, he always had food on the table but clean his shoes? Not on your nelly.

Lower-middle-class women had recollections of their fathers' pursuit of gardening, a work activity which was also capable of providing a sense of satisfaction and personal pleasure. As Freda recalled: 'What spare time he had, he would … very good gardener, very keen on gardening.' As better housing became more affordable, working-class husbands and fathers also embarked upon home improvements in their spare time. Edith recalled that the only work her husband did perform in the home was the deco-rating, after they had moved into Corporation housing in 1938: 'Some-times he used to – listen to this – he used to do paper over paper, decorate paper over paper. It was horrible.' Kathleen recalled that her husband did his own particular jobs within the home: '*So did you split the work in the house then between you?* No, not really. No. David was … David was always a handyman, he was always a … he and all the – that kind of work. But he never did housework. I never expected him to really.' In the 1950s, a do-it-yourself revolution encouraged even more men into the field of home improvement.[44] However, housing conditions did not improve for all sections of society. Into the 1960s there remained those whose homes lacked gardens and were not of a condition to encourage home improve-ment of any type. The 1961 census revealed that over a quarter of Man-chester families remained without the use of a fixed bath, and that nearly a fifth were without the use of a hot-water tap.[45]

Shared or separate leisure?

While a husband's attitude towards work in the home would influence the amount of spare time available to women, the nature of the individual marital relationship itself could influence women's experiences of leisure. The notion that men earned leisure while women facilitated it framed gendered experiences of leisure within a marriage. The view offered above – 'our husbands do not realise that we ever need any leisure' – often found expression in the separate pleasures of men and their unwillingness to accompany their wives at leisure.[46] The *Manchester Evening News* letters page provides plentiful evidence of men pursuing their own leisure preferences at the expense of their wives. For example, 'an unlucky one' wrote of a husband who frequented public houses daily: 'I know a wife to-day who has given her husband fatherhood and all the rest but he does not hurry home from business. Oh no, he goes for a drink first and comes home after closing time; although he knows that his meal is waiting for him and two lovely children are waiting to kiss him good-night.'[47] A Withington woman condemned a husband who went out every night, 'just treating me like a servant, going out himself and leaving me every evening'.[48] In the postwar period, too, similar complaints were evident, although less prevalent. One woman reader recorded: 'He [her husband] does not take me out, although I have pleaded with him. He goes on holiday alone. He says he wants to be alone.'[49] Certainly, one study of leisure patterns in a Yorkshire mining community at the end of our period found that men and women continued to move in 'different spheres' even in the last decade of our study, a lifestyle accentuated by a still strongly defined sexual division of labour within the home.[50]

Historians of the interwar period have emphasised the continuation of separate patterns of leisure among many working-class couples[51] – although, as Roberts has observed, 'the extent to which women and men wanted to share their leisure time varied very much from marriage to marriage'.[52] Interviewees often contrasted the separate nature of leisure in their parents' marriages with their own, more shared, experience in the postwar world. For example, Irene and her husband Albert spoke at length about the division of leisure within the working-class communities of Ardwick in which they grew up:

> *Were there different ideas about what men and women could do in their leisure time?* (A) Well, in those days most of the women, married women never went out, their husbands went down to the pub or whatever. (I) There was a lot they would go to a football match. (A) But the women hardly ever went out, did they? (I) Well my mother didn't. Except to the cinema of course. (A) I can't remember my mother going anywhere on her own, except church on Sunday, you know. And I don't think the men used to expect them to want to go with them, my dad never said well, what, are you going to come with me, you know, I mean they just used to say I'm off now, and that would be it, you know. (I.) Well the only time my mum and dad went out was, er, perhaps at weekend when they went to Shudehill market.[53]

Celia similarly remembered her father as a man who would go out drinking, while her mother's time was taken up with household labour:

Can you remember your mother ever taking time for herself to do things that she enjoyed?
Not, not really. Time was taken up making meals and yes, quite sad really.
They didn't, er, they had no leisure time did they, or their time was taken up
looking after us I think, really. *Would your father go out at all?* He liked going to
the pub, Claire, he used to go in, and have a drink. And that was his life really,
it was, er, my mother didn't like going in the, er, she was well too busy looking
after us I think, and the house, you know. She was, er, now the husbands
seem to help the wives or with the children, er, but, er, I think my mother,
which a lot of her generation, they, they went off and left them and they did
all the ... brought the children up didn't they really. They had quite hard lives
didn't they you know, really.

However, separate leisure was not the only marital pattern, even in the
interwar period; other women noted that their parents might occasionally
visit the cinema or local pub together. As Ivy recalled: 'They didn't really
go out much together. They might go for a drink, you know, Saturday
night, cos there was a pub on every corner.' While pubs segregated their
customers according to gender, the snug, parlour or 'best' room was presented as a room in which women could drink with or without their
husbands. In contrast, the vault or taproom was closed to women.[54] Andrew
Davies found that the pub constituted a venue for shared leisure in the
working-class districts he examined.[55] A Mass-Observation directive of 1939
received the following reply from a woman born in 1901: 'I have never
been in a "pub" by myself. I don't suppose I ever shall. When I am out
with my husband we sometimes go into the private bar or saloon bar or
lounge – he drinks a glass of ale or something similar and I will have a
"gin and t" or just lime.'[56] Other respondents to the same directive recorded that they generally 'didn't go into pubs' but would frequent establishments in the countryside with their husbands. In the postwar period,
Mass-Observation's study of a typical postwar 'Saturday Night' found that
this night was the 'family night' for pub-going.[57] Adult women clearly did
frequent pubs across our period, sometimes in the company of their husbands. However, the pub remained a predominantly masculine arena. As
Rowntree and Lavers asserted in 1951: 'A large proportion, probably a
majority, of women of all classes of society never enter public houses.
Indeed, in some parts of Britain, particularly in the north, there is strong
feeling against women entering them at all, unless there is a special room
set apart for them.'[58]

Interviewees' own experiences of marital leisure were diverse. For some,
separate patterns of leisure spanned their married life. Edith recalled:

[I] never went out with my husband, love. *Never? Why was that?* My never, my husband never took me out. I don't know why. When I used to come home from work, in fact, er, he ... he did drink, my husband, when he got the chance, you know what I mean, but no. No, because he could be nowty ... irritable, you know what I mean, and they have the gift of the gab ... Yeah. No I, no I never went out with my husband. *Did he go to the pub on his own, then?* Yes, this is it, yes. Yeah. No I never went out with my husband. I went out with him plenty when I was courting but that was it after I was married, I was a slave. I was a slave. You know what I mean, I was the mother, the father and everything.

The extent to which his leisure patterns reduced her own spare time is clear. Lower-middle-class women, too, found that their husbands pursued separate leisure, although none of the women interviewed spoke of the extreme separation experienced by Edith. While the pub provided an often segregated venue for working men's leisure, clubs and organisations such as the Masons fulfilled a similar function for middle-class men. As Mary recalled, her husband regularly attended Masonic meetings alone. While Ladies' Evenings did provide an opportunity for shared leisure, it was her husband's interests which were pursued. The extent to which 'shared' leisure was often founded upon the interests of the male partner is apparent in the testimony of interviewees who found themselves attending football matches or accompanying their husbands on fishing trips. As Alice observed: 'I went, but not to do the fishing, er yes and it was a case of being, because of your husband, whereas, er, it wasn't my own pleasure, you know what I mean.'

Many of the women interviewed, however, recalled a more equitable distribution of time within the marital relationship, regardless of whether leisure was shared or separate. Margaret's nieces baby-sat while she went to a whist drive and her husband visited the cinema, and Kathleen and her husband both had time for themselves: 'I got out a couple of times a week and I should say perhaps the same for David, perhaps three times.' Some women in the postwar period pursued separate leisure with enthusiasm, as Joyce explained: 'I've always said this that I don't think any couple should just spend all their time going out together, I think you've got to have other interests, because if one of them goes you're, you're absolutely more devastated ... than ever.' Many more women recalled forms of leisure which were shared, thus reflecting the postwar ascendancy of 'companionate marriage'. Dorothy claimed that neither partner wished to go out without the other: 'But erm, no I, I certainly, erm, didn't want to do much without my husband. And I, don't think he did with me, although he, you know, he had sports, you know, he played sports. But, not to go out at night, erm, doing, you know, something. I mean he wouldn't have dreamt of going to a dance without me.' Of course her husband did pursue his own interest, sport, alone. Jane recalled that marital companionship stemmed from an enjoyment of leisure in the home in the 1950s: 'Once we got married we didn't need to go outside for activities the same, you know looking for company, because we had it in the house so we used to, as I say, do things, in the house.' For some, the pursuit of shared leisure could have isolating consequences. *And did you tend to spend most of your leisure time together once you got married?'* Barbara was asked. 'Oh yes. yes. *You didn't go out separately?* I … I've got no friends now, because, er, you know I sort of let them all drift to be with him.'

For particular women, the project of shared leisure was pursued with vigour. Joan acknowledged that her husband had little inclination to pursue separate leisure activities: 'I don't think my husband had any idea of, he didn't drink so there was no, separate life like him going in the pub and me staying at home, baking the pies, he should worry (laughs) I'd have him baking the pies and I'd be out.' However, her desire to maintain a mutuality in leisure led her to limit her own activities:

> I was crafty, I never learned to drive, I'm sorry now, very very sorry. But I wouldn't then because I thought it'd separate us. Because he'd say oh you go. Oh you take the car, you. Because he was very generous about, he wasn't like my father, jealous, you could go anywhere you wanted, if you wanted to, but of course I didn't want to go anywhere.

The advent of children

Oral evidence suggests a movement towards shared leisure within the marital relationship over this period. The advent of children, however, could have a significant impact upon the distribution of time within the home. Certainly, children could break down any established pattern of shared leisure between partners, with consequences that were more severe for the mother than for the father. As a letter to the *Manchester Evening News* in 1920 explained: 'The expense of the family lowers one's standards of living, saps one's strength in the endeavour to do justice to them, and leaves a woman no freedom morning, noon or night.'[59] Two decades later, Spring Rice observed: 'Where there are a lot of young children it is miraculous that any real leisure is procurable. Many women say they cannot leave the children in the evening; a woman in Blackburn says "Never go to market or cinema. Sister used to come and look after children and let me go out, but has now removed from the town."[60] *Working-Class Wives* contains frequent references to women unable to take time for themselves because of the duties of childcare.[61] And yet this period witnessed a trend towards smaller families across all classes, thus ensuring that the majority of women were freed from a lifetime of childbearing and rearing.[62] Such a trend might have been expected to increase the amount of time available to adult women. Indeed, middle-aged women in this period probably did enjoy more spare time than had those of previous generations. However, as Lewis has noted, while a decline in the birth rate, allied to gradual improvements in healthcare and housing conditions, theoretically gave women more time and energy for activities outside the home, a reformulation of domestic ideology led to a renewed emphasis upon the home as the woman's sphere.[63] More time was to be taken up with more intensive housewifery, and in the postwar period a powerful ideology of motherhood ensured that women remained the chief carers for those children they did have. As Finch and Summerfield note: 'No longer were women being told that they ought to have opportunities to pursue "outside interests" even if only in order to do their social duty and preserve their marriages. Children were expected to be their consuming passion.'[64]

Women continued to be responsible for the work of childcare throughout our period; indeed, as Finch and Summerfield have demonstrated, motherhood became laden with additional expectations, a development which reinforced the conflation of women's personal time and family life.[65] Within the *Manchester Evening News,* there is clear evidence that women felt that their work as mothers limited their own access to pleasure, or even rest. In a letter to Jane Dawson, for example, one mother asked why she should not be able to go to a cinema matinée or do a bit of shopping on her own, and Dawson herself wrote of the real need that mothers had 'for a little rest and relaxation'.[66] In his survey of working-class life in York, undertaken between 1938 and 1939, Rowntree noted: 'There is no doubt that working-class women with young families have far fewer hours of leisure on which they can definitely count than the men.'[67] In 1960, the *Manchester Evening News* problem page received the following plea for leisure outside the home and away from children:

> Don't you think husbands might stay in more, not less, when their wives are tied by small children? In my experience most of them jump at the chance of

going out with 'the boys', and never seem to think that having been shut up with the children's pretty but nerve-racking prattle all day, it's the wives who need the change! What can we do about it?[68]

Women who did seek an escape from their children's 'nerve-racking prattle' generally relied upon informal types of childcare. As the experience of the Blackburn woman cited by Spring Rice and recorded above shows, access to a baby-sitter, usually a mother or other relative, could free up time for individual women; the absence of such a service could greatly limit a woman's spare time and effectively imprison her within the home. Several of the women interviewed noted that their mothers provided this valuable service for them. Irene's mother baby-sat occasionally, and Jane continued to go to the pictures regularly, 'because my mother used to come and baby-sit and, er, we did go out, but of course we didn't go out as often'. Similarly, Kathleen's mother-in-law enabled her and her husband to go to the first showing at their local cinema:

> Cos you see they had two houses then at the cinema you know an early one and a later one. And David's mother very kindly, she said that we could go to the early one. And what used to happen is, that I used to get the children, or Linda, or later both of them. I used to bath them, get them undressed, and David's mother and father used to come to our house. David and I went to the first-house pictures … And, erm, then his mother would dress them, over their nightclothes, in their bonnets and their coats and cover them up in the prams and they'd walk down to the cinema or where, whichever one we'd gone, cos we only went to Mossley. And she used to wheel the children down to the cinema, and then they'd go into the cinema, and we'd wheel them back home again.

Other women shared the burden of childcare among themselves, as Hannah did when she moved to a postwar Corporation prefab: 'And the kids played in the garden with one another cos they had plenty of friends, cos everybody was the same, kind of thing. And we had the school run. Bring them home at lunch time and take them back again and bring them home at home time. But we did it turns each so we didn't have the same thing to do every day.' Indeed, Melanie Tebbutt has argued that within the new housing estates of this period, a shared interest in children was a way of re-creating the female sociability which was sometimes lost in the move out of the close-knit communities of the inner city: 'A collective identity with other women was still maintained through the children, who played an important part in redefining concepts of neighbourliness.'[69] For the women of Spring Rice's study in the interwar period, state interest in the health of their children provided them with an opportunity for some form of leisure: 'The success of the Infant Welfare Centre is in some degree attributable to the pleasures the mother finds in spending an afternoon away from home and in meeting kindly doctors and nurses as well as other women with whom she can talk.'[70]

For women who relied upon friends and family to give them a break from the work of childcare, spare time was a precarious commodity. The death of a relative, a fall-out with a friend, or geographical relocation away from family and friends could curtail personal time.[71] Certainly those who could not afford to pay for baby-sitters, and whose family could not perform this service, found that their spare time was extremely limited, or had to be enjoyed on a rota basis. As Doris recalled: 'Of course my husband and I couldn't go out together, when Ruth was little we used to take it in turns going to the pictures, say, you know, on a Saturday.' For others, such as Ivy, childcare consumed time: 'I had Daniel I, er, well you just, life was the babies then. You know. Then I had Michael two years after and Peter two years after him. So I didn't really go anywhere then.'

The household economy

Even those women whose domestic arrangements left them time for leisure may not have had the money to continue the commercially based activities of their youth. Certainly, many of the women interviewed noted that after marriage they had less disposable income for leisure. As Davies has demonstrated, the leisure patterns of men as well as women were regulated by economic circumstance: his study of interwar Manchester and Salford has shown that poverty could keep men out of the pub and away from football matches and excluded them from street betting.[72] None the less, the financial arrangements of the home were often founded upon the husbands' right to spend money on their own pleasures; like the adolescent, they expected an amount of pocket money, because they felt that this had been earned. Women in command of a limited budget often had economic priorities other than the pursuit of personal pleasure. As with the notion that women did not deserve leisure time for themselves because they had not engaged in full-time paid labour, there was a belief, often internalised, that they had not earned the right to take money for themselves. As the *Manchester Evening News* noted in 1920:

> In the poorer classes a husband always spends more on himself than a woman.
> He must have his tobacco, his football matches and his drinks. The well-to-
> do man must also have his tobacco, his club, and his drinks. But what does
> the woman get? If she goes twice a week to the pictures or once to a theatre
> in one week she is thought extravagant, yet this is her only diversion ... A
> man takes it for granted that he must have certain relaxations. Very many
> men spend a pound per week on amusements alone. I include tobacco and
> drinks in amusements of course. Well, a man could save on this. But a woman
> has nothing she can cut down, for her money goes to pay for necessary, not
> for luxury, things.[73]

Even towards the end of our period, Kerr observed that the Liverpudlian
mothers she surveyed over a five-year period would often go without
necessities, never mind luxuries, in order to feed and clothe their children.[74]
She recorded the words of a sixteen-year-old girl, who admitted: 'My mother
never buys herself any clothes. If Dad gives her money and tells her to buy
something for herself, she buys clothes for the children.'[75] In one Yorkshire
mining community, women rarely spent money on their own amusements
without the prior 'permission' of their husbands.[76]

Studies of working-class communities in the interwar period have demonstrated that it was generally women who organised the weekly budget.[77]
Interview evidence supports this analysis; women recalled that it was their
mothers who held responsibility for the financial running of the home.
While such women often went without, in order to provide for their
families, control of the household economy could be an important source
of power for working-class women within this period.[78] Kerr explored 'the
economic power of Mum', describing the lengths to which women would
go to defend this power against children and husbands who threatened to
renege on their end of the financial bargain.[79] None the less, despite this
evidence, she believed that the traditional control exercised over the wage
packet by the mother was in decline.[80] Certainly, control over the family
economy became more complex in the postwar period. Some women did
continue to administer money within the family. Dennis, Henriques and
Slaughter found that Yorkshire miners' wives in the early 1950s received a
housekeeping 'wage' from their husbands which was sufficient only to
cover regular weekly expenses.[81] Margaret – who married in 1946, and
whose husband was an electrical engineer – recalled:

> Once or twice we had a row about money, and it, and he said to me I am not
> having anything to do with it, he said, I earn it you spend it. *So you were very
> much in charge of things?* I, I had to do the finances. As long as he had his

spends and his tobacco, he was a happy man. Except for the fortnight we went on holiday. Then he used to bring his three weeks' wages home, and I used to bring my three weeks' wages home, we'd pay out what we had to do for the three weeks, not leave any debts, and then he'd have the whole lot in his pocket and then he'd give me some, and say spend that on yourself. But I didn't have to pay for groceries, hotels, travel, anything. Nothing. The money was mine.

The importance to Margaret of having money of her own to spend during the family holiday only underlines the extent to which housekeeping was more generally viewed as a family, not personal, resource.

Other women within this period maintained control of the housekeeping, while employing a shared ownership of the family income through the use of a joint bank account. For example, Doris, a lower-middle-class woman, strictly controlled the money that was spent, but did not allocate specific spends to her husband:

> I think Jack's wage was about four pounds, when we got married, about four pounds ten. That was supposed to be a good wage. And erm, er, you'd got to pay the rent, we rented a house, the first house we had, when we were first married, it was eighteen shillings a week. And then I used to, erm, do the shopping you know, and I used to reckon up how much I'd spent at the greengrocer's, how much for the grocer's, how much for the butcher's. I used to have it all written down. And if my money didn't balance, in my purse, I was up all night wondering where it had gone (laughs). *So what did you do with the spare money, did you split that between you?* No we had, er, a joint, we've always had a joint account, a joint bank account, everything's been joint. *So you didn't give Jack spending money?* No it's never been a case of erm, that's you know, yours and that's mine, er, we've always had it erm you know what money was over well, it, it was in erm, in the desk, you know, you'd just go and get what you wanted. We didn't kind of say oh well, you know, that's for you and that's for you, we, we just had it joint, and whatever we wanted we got, you know.

Within other marriages, control of the finances rested entirely with the husband. As Barbara remembered: 'James used to manage the money when he was here, cos he loved money.'

In her oral history study of working-class families up to 1970, Elizabeth Roberts asserted that the postwar period witnessed a decline in women's power within the household which was rooted in a weakening of control over the family finances.[82] Identifying changing ideas concerning the ownership of money within the family, she argued that notions of shared responsibility actually weakened a woman's position. Certainly, the increasing tendency of married women to perform paid labour outside the home does not seem to have engendered a notion of personal income for such women.[83] While more women worked than in the interwar period, 'indigenous' women at least, were seen as earning money to pay for family 'extras', yet carried a burden of guilt regarding the impact of their out-of-house activities upon their families. As Dorothy recalled of her own part-time labours: 'I had to do really to afford any kind of small luxury.' Margaret emphasised: 'Our daughter came first, before the money. But she benefited by it.' The money she earned helped in the purchase of a car, family holidays and, ultimately, the family home. In contrast, those married working-class women who had performed paid labour in the earlier period, had done so only if it was absolutely necessary to sustain the family economy. Roberts argues that this shift in the value of married women's paid labour was an important aspect of the changing power relationships within families over the period.[84] It also informed notions of who 'earned' leisure and who did not. The notion that women could combine part-time work with domestic work sustained a conception of women workers as inferior workers, certainly not breadwinners. Women's wages were conceptualised as a supplement to the family income rather than a vital contribution, despite evidence that women continued to work out of necessity when circumstances dictated.[85] Moreover, working-class women's traditional skills of managing, making and budgeting became less valued in an age of consumer goods and rising incomes.[86] Domestic work, being unpaid, was undermined within this mass consumer society; the interwar profession of housewifery became a role which could be combined with paid work for the benefit of the family. In contrast, migrant women in the postwar period were excluded from this discourse, being positioned as workers first and foremost, and frequently performing full-time rather than part-time work.[87] Constructions of leisure within such women's lives probably differed substantially from the 'white' experience addressed within this study.

Allocating family resources

While poverty would clearly limit the leisure activities of all family members, it was often the wife who suffered most. The work of housekeeping was compounded by an absence of money, and could fill all a woman's time. As Spring Rice observed:

> It is little short of a miracle that some women, even some of the most hard-worked, find time and mental energy to belong to such organisations as the

Women's Co-operative Guild, the Salvation Army or a branch of their political party where they can hear and talk about the wider aspects of their own or other people's problems. It is, however, very rare to find amongst the active members of these organisations, the women whose poverty and consequent hard work demand the greatest measure of consideration and carefully planned reform. The poorest women *have no time* to spare for such immediately irrelevant considerations as the establishment of a different system, a better education, a more comprehensive medical service, or some sort of organised co-operation.[88]

Even where time was available, poverty could deny women the most favoured pleasures of youth, notably trips to the local cinema. Spring Rice frequently recorded comments such as 'Have never been to the "talkies"', 'I have no money for pictures', and 'There is no money to spare anyhow for the pictures, or very seldom.'[89] In their 1943 study of picture-going preference, Mass-Observation received the following reply from a sixty-two-year-old housewife from Orpington: 'I haven't been able to afford to go to the pictures *and* smoke, so I gave up the pictures – I fancy smoking may have to follow suit.'[90]

Certainly, there was a clear acknowledgement within the pages of the *Manchester Evening News* that women were often left short of money by husbands who reneged upon the expected notion of handing their wages over to the wife. In 1935, a woman who signed herself 'worried Margaret' wrote to the postbag about her own husband:

> My husband's views are that out of a wage of £4 10s. (earnings at the moment of which I would not be aware only that I have had to pay income-tax) he should have £1 10s. for his weekly expenditure out of which he pays 5s. in a clothing club for his clothes. He has no other expenses. I buy cigarettes. He spends the balance entirely on his own pleasures, never takes me anywhere or buys me anything … I am supposed to be an attractive woman and would dearly love to go out with my husband and meet other people, but he says a wife's place is at home, or I can go to the pictures with a relative. Yet he says he loves me.[91]

A woman in 1950 complained that her husband 'goes out every night spending money on his own pleasures'.[92]

Other sources, too, provide evidence of inequality in the allocation of family resources. A national Mass-Observation survey of 1949 found that women had much less money for personal expenditure than men.[93] Eight times as many women as men claimed that they had no dedicated money for themselves at all, and average weekly allocations were markedly unequal.[94]

The survey of 2,040 people found that the average male spend was one pound three shillings and sixpence while the average figure for women was seven shillings and sixpence.[95] In fact, 52 per cent of women spent less than five shillings on themselves compared to only 14 per cent of men.[96] Moreover, it emerged that some of the women questioned had no exact knowledge of their husbands' income at all, and one in three of those men whose pay increased did not pass the increase on to his wife.[97] Oral evidence also provides cases of inequality in the allocation of family resources. Irene's husband, Albert, recalled that his father 'kept too much money for himself to spend on drink', giving his wife just sixpence a day for housekeeping. In the later period, Elsie stated that her husband would not share the use of the family car with her. The majority of women interviewed did not, however, articulate such grievances. Most seem to have assumed that their husbands had earned their right to spend money on personal pleasures. As long as a husband's spending did not have a detrimental impact upon the well-being of the family as a whole, women of both working- and lower-middle-class status acquiesced in their husband's perceived right to enjoy the leisure which his wage-earning activities apparently justified.

Opportunities for leisure in adult life

Despite the emphasis placed upon leisure as an arena for service and duty to the family, the constraints of time and money which married women experienced, and – fundamentally – the problems inherent in defining 'leisure' within adult women's lives, both documentary and oral sources do point to a demand for leisure and demonstrate some of the ways in which women attempted to pursue their own pleasures over the period 1920 to 1960. The final section of this chapter, therefore, shifts attention to those areas where adult women did carve out a leisure space, although it recognises that these experiences were only rarely called 'leisure'.[98] In effect, the chapter examines a range of experiences from the commercial and organised to the less tangible, but no less important, realm of 'rest' and 'social life'. The aim is to illustrate the various components of a conception of leisure which has real meaning to women within the context of their everyday lives.

Commercial leisure in adulthood

On the whole, those activities in which women did engage during their adult lives tended to be less formalised and less commercially based than those of their youth. The primary reason for this was that they lacked the clearly defined time, and often the financial resources, to pursue such activities, although – as this chapter has already shown – notions that married women did not 'deserve' leisure in the same way as wage-earning adolescents and men had a clear impact upon the types of activity pursued. Moreover, those activities most frequently enjoyed in youth – dancing and picture-going – also carried certain meanings outside their pursuit as leisure activities. As Chapter 4 has shown, both these activities were closely related to the act of courting: the dance hall provided an arena for meeting boys, and the cinema acted as a venue for courtship away from the gaze of parental supervision. While it has been shown that many young women enjoyed these leisure forms for their own sake, it is clear that the meanings which they carried across the life cycle encouraged the participation of women at some points and actively discouraged their participation at others.

Visits to the cinema were the most probable of these two commercial forms of leisure to be continued into adult life. In 1951, Mass-Observation found that where housewives did enjoy outside activities, these were focused on the cinema.[99] Kathleen Box's survey of 1946 revealed that only 25 per cent of adult women never went to the cinema; adult women accounted for 62 per cent of the adult civilian cinema audience in that year, despite accounting for only 54 per cent of the adult civilian population.[100] However, the gender balance of cinema audiences did shift in the final decade of our study, so that by 1960, 47 per cent of the cinema audience were women compared to a figure of 53 per cent for men.[101] In the 1935 *New Survey of London Life and Labour*, it was suggested that 'Women mainly attend the afternoon performances. It is no uncommon sight to see women slipping into the cinema for an hour, after they have finished their shopping and before the children come home from school.'[102] Like so many of the pursuits of adult life, cinema-going was, it would seem, fitted in around the timetables of other family members.

The cinema itself was used by women for a variety of purposes – something which has sometimes been overlooked by historians who have focused upon the medium itself, rather than the meanings attached to the activity by picture-goers.[103] Often, the act of 'going to the pictures' seems to have been of more importance to women than the content of the films they actually saw. Certainly, Box described cinema-going as a 'real habit', and claimed that 23 per cent of the regular cinema-goers she surveyed would frequent the same cinema whatever film was being shown.[104] For some, particularly working-class women of the interwar period, visits to the cinema constituted a valuable break from household labour. Spring Rice described how 'a woman in a country town in Essex, with seven children all under thirteen, and in a good Council house, makes a point of going once a week to the pictures with her husband, "for a rest and a little pleasure".'[105] Oral history also provides evidence of weekly trips to the cinema as a rare form of rest experienced by married women. Dorothy recalled her mother's visits to Manchester cinemas: 'Now that was the only time she did sit down. You know she enjoyed it and, erm, she took me in occasionally at night. But you know, in the house, you know if she was in the house, she was working.'

However, the cinema also provided an arena for childcare, with women taking their children to the cinema throughout this period. As Rowntree and Lavers observed just after the war: 'Babies in arms, who are not infrequently both seen and heard in cinemas, particularly in the after-noons, are admitted free.'[106] One Manchester city-centre picture-house manager observed in 1925: 'We get a very mixed crowd nowadays – mothers and fathers, sisters and brothers. In fact we get family parties.'[107] Weekly visits to the cinema could also constitute a shared form of leisure between husbands and wives. Both Jessie and Dorothy, for example, attended the pictures with their husbands. As Jane recalled: 'We went to the pictures, we went to the pictures quite regularly until they got so expensive and then they got really so dear, going to the pictures.' The Mass-Observation leisure survey of November 1948 found that over half of those women who went to the cinema did so with their husbands, paying prices ranging from one shilling to two shillings and ninepence, but an average of one shilling and ninepence.[108] The others went with children, friends or alone. Certainly, Doris visited the cinema alone while others looked after the children. For such women, the cinema was a valuable personal interest: in the case of Irene it consumed her spare time throughout her life – as she observed, 'It was always the cinema.'

Dancing, however, proved less amenable to pursuit over the life cycle. The association of the public dance hall with the act of courting – or, more directly, the act of 'picking up' – actively discouraged married women from attending. For example, Dorothy, whose words were quoted at the beginning of this chapter, had danced frequently during the war at public dance halls, and yet ceased to dance upon her marriage. The reasons she gave point clearly to the association of dancing with the rituals of courtship; fundamentally, she felt awkward dancing with other men when she 'had a husband at home'. As she explained: 'It just didn't seem right. So I didn't do it you know, I mean I stopped doing it, you know.' Dorothy did, however, return to the dance floor later in the life cycle, when her eldest daughter was old enough to baby-sit and her husband could accompany her. The fact that her husband's presence was so important points clearly to particular notions of how women could appear in 'public', and with whom.

Certainly, marriage seems to have curtailed many women's dancing activity. Replies to a Mass-Observation directive in 1939 contain evidence of this phenomenon, as well as reaffirming the real pleasure which women of this period had found in youthful dancing.[109] For example, a middle-class housewife aged thirty-six said: 'Since I married twelve years ago I have practically given it up and dance about once in three years'; while a twenty-nine-year-old woman who gave her occupation as 'musician and farm worker' noted: 'I very seldom go to dances. I like dancing but my husband does not.' As a Gateshead housewife born in 1887 stated: 'Dancing was a joy when I went before marriage. It is a joy to my daughter.' In the last decade of this study, Kerr noted repeatedly that women who loved dancing in their youth gave it up immediately upon marriage.[110]

For some, the propriety of attendance at a dance was maintained through the accompaniment of daughters, or even sons. In 1925, a debate occurred in the letters page of the *Manchester Evening News* concerning the dancing activities of 'pleasure loving mothers'. Here it was argued that mothers were pursuing leisure opportunities as keenly as their daughters, accompanying them to dances and actually participating in the dancing themselves.[111] While there was some concern about this behaviour – one writer commenting, 'What can we hope for the women of the future when the women of today spend half their time dancing and the rest of it gadding about?'[112] – most contributors defended a mother's right to dance, albeit on the assumption that she accompany her daughter. As one reader asserted: 'There is no need to condemn modern mothers for indulging in dancing and similar delights. These things keep us young and more fit to be companions to our children than any of the old-fashioned parents were.'[113] Another explained:

> Although on the wrong side of fifty I still like to dance. I accompany my daughter aged 21, and another friend's daughter of the same age, every Saturday evening to a dance and generally have about six dances myself. Of course I

do not dance the new dances, the fox trots and one-steps, but the lancers and waltz, I seldom miss … I shall dance as long as I can, as I feel sure it keeps me feeling fit and young. Why should a woman be compelled to spend more than half her life in the home? So long as she brings up her children, why should she not have a little recreation?[114]

Oral history, too, points to the phenomenon of mothers accompanying their daughters to the dance. Margaret remembered attending dances with her own daughter: 'I used to go there [church dances] with our Lynne and most of the time I sat on my bum, but she danced every dance.' Rowntree and Lavers recorded the words of one fifty-year-old housewife in 1951: 'When the children were small, I never had the chance to go out much. Now I go to a dance every week with my eldest son. It's the only pleasure I ever get, and I love it.'[115]

Other women, however, found their enjoyment of dancing broken by the advent of children. Ivy had been a committed ceilidh dancer at the Gaelic League during the war, but noted: 'Then I got married, of course, and then I had three children. And, er, well the ceilidhing stopped then (laughs) for a while anyway.' However, she did return to dancing with her husband in her late forties, after her children had grown up. In contrast, some women continued to dance throughout their married life, although the nature of the dances attended altered. Mary, for example, frequented dinner dances with her husband: 'You see, er, we met, we went out with other friends to a dinner dance. Now we, we'd go to, say the Royal at Hayfield, they had … the cricket clubs always had dinner dances. Now we'd go there.' Joan paired up with an old friend from the biscuit factory: 'Er so erm, I, my social life began after the war, with her. We used to go to dinner dances and things like that.' Those – mainly middle-class – women who responded to the Mass-Observation Directive of January 1939 also attended different types of dance in their married life, including dinner dances, hotel dances and church socials.[116] Only one of the interviewees, Jane, continued to frequent the public dance halls, and this she did in the company of her husband, who played in a jazz band. As she recalled, she perceived no fundamental difficulties in dancing with other men while he played, although his presence on the stage probably did act as a safeguard for her: 'and lads'd sometimes come up and say can I take you home. I'd say oh no, no er I'm going home with my boyfriend like he's in the band, or my husband as he was then. And they'd say, is your husband in the band and doesn't he mind you dancing with people and I'd say oh no no no, not at all.' Their assumption that he *would* object to her dancing with other men demonstrates the strict etiquette which more generally accompanied married women's experience of dancing.

Sport and physical activity

While we have already seen that in their youth many women found enjoyment in sporting activities, in adulthood they were unlikely to continue these pursuits. The cost and physical demands of sporting activity ensured that only a minority of adult women chose to dedicate any spare time they did have to more active leisure forms. In September 1948, Mass-Observation conducted a major leisure survey which asked the following questions: 'Do you yourself go in for any sport?' and 'Do you yourself watch any sort of sport?' Of those housewives asked, only 7 per cent stated that they did indeed 'go in for sport', usually bowls, tennis and swimming.[117] While Oliver's work on Bolton shows that participant sport was not the exclusive province of the young, wealthy or male,[118] and the ascendancy in the 1930s of a movement for physical culture encouraged membership of organisations such as the Women's League of Health and Beauty, the vast majority of married women did not participate in active sports, either being too tired or lacking the necessary financial outlay.[119] None the less, Mass-Observation found that a far greater proportion of the housewives surveyed were spectators (37 per cent), with football, cricket and tennis the most popular choices. Other sports cited included speedway, golf, rugby, hockey, netball, bowls, wrestling, boxing, dog racing, swimming and athletics. Once again, however, the majority of women did not watch sport, and this tendency was most pronounced among working-class women.

Oral testimony suggests that while sport spectatorship could often be a way of sharing leisure between married couples but often, in fact, actually constituted the husband's personal interest, for other women watching sport was a real pleasure. One of the oral history interviewees had been a fanatical Manchester United supporter throughout her life, noting that she nearly refused to start courting her future husband when she discovered that he supported Manchester City. As we have already seen in Chapter 3, newspaper coverage of interwar football and cricket matches often drew attention to the presence of women in the crowd. The *New Survey of London Life and Labour* observed the presence of 'considerable numbers' of women at London greyhound tracks.[120] Sport was clearly not an entirely male preserve across this period, yet men still constituted its chief clientele.

Other forms of organised leisure

The extent to which women were more generally engaged in formal, organised leisure, was, however, limited. Some of the women interviewed recalled the involvement of both their mothers and themselves in the Mothers' Union and other church-based organisations.[121] Spring Rice, too, found evidence of more formalised leisure among the women she surveyed – Mrs N. of Bolton, for example, attended lectures and women's meetings, and a woman in Leeds attended Mothers' meetings at the Chapel.[122] In his study of York, Rowntree noted that women's weekly meetings provided an opportunity for women church members to socialise; for those who were too busy on a Sunday to attend a service they provided 'the principal link with their church'.[123] Some women, it would appear, could not find time even for their religious devotions. In rural areas, the Women's Institutes (1915) provided an array of amenities, classes, talks and outings for women of different social classes; in towns the Women's Co-operative Guild (1883) and Townswomen's Guilds (1928) similarly provided cultural space for women, as well as opportunities for campaigning activity. However, as Spring Rice noted: 'Such cases however are the exception. It is much more usual to read that in effect such leisure time as there is is spent in some sedentary occupation as a rest from the long hours of standing – and that it is spent entirely in mending.'[124] Kerr observed that in the 1950s, few of the women she surveyed had time for church or its associations.[125]

While clubs were a focus for debate concerning the leisure behaviour of young women, clubs for adult women were less widely proposed. Certainly, many women were unable to carve out the time needed for regular attendance at a club or society, and as we shall see later, their leisure, such as it was, often revolved around less structured forms of pleasure. The major Mass-Observation leisure survey of spring 1947 included the question: 'Do you belong to any clubs or organisations or a union or anything like that?'[126] The results clearly demonstrate the inability of clubs to attract a mass female membership. While well over half of those middle-class women surveyed enjoyed membership of the Women's Institute or Women's Conservative Association, the women with which this study is concerned proved less 'clubbable'. Only a tiny proportion of Class D, working-class women, were members; while amongst Class C, lower-middle-class women, a greater, but still small, proportion were club members. Moreover, even those who were club members sometimes claimed that this membership was due to the interests of other family members. One housewife with two children whose husband was a railway official said that she was a member of a cricket club, adding: 'My husband and boys play in the cricket here so of course I take a big interest in that.' Once again we see adult women's personal leisure intimately linked to the leisure choices of other family members.

Social life

By far the largest proportion of women's leisure in adult life was taken up with less structured kinds of spare-time activity. Informal leisure such as doorstep gossip, socialising with friends and family, or visits to other houses demanded less in terms of time and money from those involved. It also fitted the largely fragmented time structures of married women working in the home and, if conducted within the home, enabled children to be cared for simultaneously without recourse to a baby-sitter. As Melanie Tebbutt has observed in her study of the role of gossip within working-class communities: 'In some respects, gossip reflected the seamless quality of many working-class women's lives, since there was often no clear demarcation between the multitude of monotonous tasks which had to be completed every day.'[127] Moreover, the importance of social intercourse as a form of leisure for women should not be underestimated. As Dame Janet Campbell noted in the introduction to Spring Rice's *Working-Class Wives*:

> People who lightly censure the woman gossiping on her doorstep, untidy and even slatternly as she may seem, often fail to realise how completely she is tied to her own small home, and how few opportunities she has of escaping from the wear and tear of family life at close quarters. The cinema has done something to bring mental peace and refreshment, but it costs more money than she can afford; the wireless is beyond the means of many homes.[128]

Certainly, socialising seemed to account for a great deal of any spare time available to Spring Rice's working-class wives; her study often recorded comments such as 'visit friends', or 'visit a neighbour'.[129] Kerr found that 'women after marriage seem to do little else in the way of recreational activities except visit members of the family or be visited by them'.[130] In fact, within the area she surveyed, visiting was almost exclusively a family affair within which the mother–daughter relationship reigned supreme. Towards the end of our period, Dennis, Henriques and Slaughter found that in Ashton, Yorkshire, 'callin'' was the main leisure activity for women.[131]

Oral testimony reveals that a premium was often placed upon informal socialising; Tebbutt has illustrated the recreational function of gossip, as well as its role in the exchange of information and its function as a community policing system.[132] However, there were clear distinctions among women in the forms that such activity took – distinctions rooted in material circumstance and historical moment. For working-class women in the inter-war period, socialising and gossip provided an informal break from work which did not necessitate travelling out of the immediate vicinity of the neighbourhood. Spring Rice recorded the words of one woman: 'I haven't any outdoor clothes, so I chat to neighbours two or three times daily and sit on back step mending and darning.'[133] In this way work activity could be enhanced by the introduction of an element of social life. Certainly Ivy recalled that her Ancoats-based mother 'used to sit on the step, you know, the front step and chat'; while Jean recalled her own mother's street gossip on wash day.

Historians such as Tebbutt and Elizabeth Roberts have pointed to the importance of neighbourhood networks in providing mutual aid and support to working-class women who often inhabited overcrowded housing and juggled inadequate material resources. As Lewis notes: 'In large part it was neighbourliness that distinguished the behaviour of working-, from lower middle-class women.'[134] Within this context, 'neighbourliness' was defined differently to friendship, and lacked the intensity of kinship. None the less, working-class women had a strong sense of locality: a sense of place which often differed markedly from that of women of other social backgrounds. For example, interview evidence shows that those women who lived within inner-city Manchester tended to view the city in significantly different terms from those located in the suburbs. Many of the former discussed the city in terms of their immediate locality, and related this locality to poverty, either their own or that of other families in the district. Edith, who lived in Collyhurst during the 1920s and 1930s before moving to a council house in New Moston in 1938, recalled: 'I mean it was all very poor, down there, you know. I mean it was what you call Collyhurst.' She proceeded to talk about the details of the family home in Collyhurst Buildings and the help which neighbours gave each other. In comparison, women of lower-middle-class backgrounds recalled a wider notion of 'Manchester', dwelling less upon their immediate vicinity and more upon the city as a whole. As Freda recalled of the 1920s:

> You see Manchester was a thriving flourishing city when we came. In 1920, a wonderful city. *How do you remember it?* Oh. There were beautiful big shipping offices in Whitworth, oh gorgeous things and lovely calico printing associa-

tions, down Oxford Street, there'd be whole long, er, windows with beautiful materials … it was a beautiful city when we first came.

Or, as Mary stated: 'I mean I don't like Manchester now. I think it's a filthy city. But at one time I was proud of it. I loved Manchester.' Clearly material circumstance dictated perceptions of the city itself, and notions of identity within it.

The interwar period, however, witnessed the beginnings of a movement away from the 'traditional' working-class communities as what has been termed a 'housing revolution' heralded slum clearance, new council-owned suburban housing estates and a growing trend towards owner-occupation.[135] Hughes and Hunt have outlined the implications which a move out of the inner city had for the new inhabitants of the Wythenshawe 'satellite town' council estate in Manchester, noting in particular the commitment to privacy which the estates encouraged and the intense family-based lifestyle which emerged. As they observe: 'In most of the oral evidence from Wythenshawe residents a favourable contrast is drawn between the new estate, where people kept themselves to themselves, and the intrusive older communities.'[136] Certainly socialising on the new estates was restricted. McKibbin offers a number of explanations for this phenomenon including the predominance of young, busy families on the estates and the absence of forums for easy neighbourliness such as the corner shop or pub.[137] Shopping in the new precincts was a more solitary affair, and lacked the casual sociability already explored in Chapter 2.

Women within these estates tended to relax inside their home, rather than in the street; certainly the new housing did not *necessitate* the street-based existence which stemmed from inner-city squalor.[138] Such women began to experience forms of social life similar to those of middle-class women, whose increased access to both time and money enabled socialising to be conducted away from the home, or at least apart from the work of running that home. As Mary recalled of her own lower-middle-class existence:

I quite enjoyed it. Yes because I'd always got friends to go out with, it was afternoon teas, morning coffee and, er, all that sort of thing. Did a lot of that. *Socialising and entertaining?* Yes. Yes. Yes. Very much so. Erm, yes eveybody had coffee mornings and afternoon teas and you filled in your time very nicely. And you'd meet in town, and do the shops and have tea together.

As the period progressed, then, interviewees recalled a more home-, rather than street-based experience of socialising – one which involved reciprocated, and sometimes organised, visits to each other's houses. Tebbutt, however, rejects a view of the new estates of the 1930s and 1950s as bereft of the informal socialising of an earlier period.[139] As this chapter has already demonstrated, women often used their position as mothers to make contacts with others. Elsewhere, the increasing participation of married women in the workforce provided a social outlet for women which was often highly prized. If contacts with other women were less easy, women continued to rely upon them for their personal leisure in the form of social life. For example, Edith recalled Friday-night trips to the pub with her friend, who lived across the road: 'Sometimes we'd go for a little drink in the Gardener's Arms. Go about half-past nine and have a little drink and a talk and then come home, you know. Could never go by myself.' Kerr observed married women, who would not feel comfortable visiting each other's houses, meeting regularly in the pub for a little social time together.[140] In contrast, Dennis, Henriques and Slaughter found that only older women would attend Ashton pubs unaccompanied during the week.[141]

None the less, oral evidence is suggestive of a postwar movement towards a more family- and couple-based experience of leisure. Home-based forms will be addressed shortly, it should be noted here, however, that social life also took on a more couple-based appearance over the period *across* social classes. Celia recalled her married life in Miles Platting: 'We used to have friends to come, and, you know for a meal and, er, entertain them, or have an evening with them but er, er, we used to go to their house as well.' Joyce, a lower-middle-class teacher, similarly remembered: 'We'd have friends round for supper, yes and, er, either have a discussion or if they liked to play cards er we'd play, we'd play cards. And then we'd go to them, for, er, for a supper. Wasn't so much … it's more dinner parties now, isn't it?' Jean constructed her own rota in order to keep her visits in order, and recalled the work which such visits necessitated: 'I was, I was developing this net, social life in, in Trafford Park, so it was all visi … you know, it was sort of, er, keeping up with your housework, because then these people would be coming at, at the weekend.'

Leisure in the home

While social life itself became more home-based over the course of the period, leisure activities more generally became focused upon the home as so-called 'family leisure' became the dominant motif. The development of home-based forms of leisure such as the wireless, and later the television, both contributed to and reflected this social shift. The interwar period, for example witnessed a rapid growth in ownership of the wireless, so that while 24.7 per cent of United Kingdom households held a broadcast licence in 1926, 79.2 per cent held one in 1937.[142] This type of rapid diffusion of a leisure commodity was repeated with the advent of television after the Second World War. While just 4.3 per cent of the population owned a television set in 1950, 81.8 per cent possessed one a decade later.[143] The trend was clearly towards home-based, family leisure, with the car becoming an extension of that privatised home for those with the means to purchase it.[144] The relative decline of the cinema in the 1950s and its more dramatic decline in the 1960s was symptomatic of this shift.

This chapter has already assessed the work for wives and mothers necessitated by the project of 'family' leisure. Here the focus is upon women's own use of the home as a site for leisure experiences. As we shall see, however, the personal spaces which adult women did carve out for their own pleasures within the home were often fragmentary and fraught with definitional ambiguity.

In the interwar period, Margery Spring Rice identified games as one way in which working-class wives might find a little relaxation. As she observed:

> Very occasionally games are mentioned, played with the children or husband. A woman in Sheffield who is very poor, lives in a slum house, and has four children, is in extremely bad health. She says she must rest sometime during the day - and she sometimes plays cards or ludo 'as that is cheaper than the pictures – I have no money for pictures'. Another woman mentions jig-saw puzzles – and another crossword puzzles.[145]

Card games in particular appear to have been popular among women of working-class and middle-class backgrounds throughout our period. Joyce remembered her mother's whist evenings in interwar Hulme as well as her own evenings spent playing cards with friends, and Margaret recalled that she attended weekly whist drives as well as enjoying card games within the home in the years after the Second World War. In 1933, *Good Housekeeping* actually admonished women bridge players for 'killing the art of conversation' by approaching the game too seriously;[146] later in the same decade, *Woman's Friend* advised its readers on the provision of food 'at your next card party'.[147] Certainly, despite *Good Housekeeping*'s reservations, card games did provide a form of entertainment to be shared with those who paid social visits, and as the period progressed they constituted an important arena for couple-based leisure. Dorothy, for example, recalled inviting friends to her house in order to play cards in the 1940s and 1950s:

> We played cards a lot, yes. And erm, had friends in, you know and erm, you know, people that didn't have children that could come round and, er, play cards, and we played till late, I mean we played till two and three you know, I mean we just and, erm, they [the husbands] might slip out for a drink, and then when they came back we'd start playing cards you know.

Jane similarly enjoyed evenings spent in the home playing cards in the postwar period, particularly the game Canasta (she held regular Canasta parties): 'So we used to have people come in and stay for the night and that and talk and play cards or whatever … it was mostly er, again, activities created around the home … It all sounds very boring now, when I repeat it to you, but it never seemed boring at the time.'

Other home-based activities were less overtly social in character. When Mass-Observation surveyed leisure activities in 1947, two in particular were most popular among the female interviewees.[148] Needlecrafts and reading were the favoured spare-time activities of a third of those surveyed. The first activity was favoured by a majority of those whose family incomes were below ten pounds a week; the second was the preferred choice of a higher proportion of those whose incomes lay above this figure.

Reading constituted an activity which fitted easily into the fragmented nature of women's time, while it was also a means of stating a claim to time for oneself, even when remaining within the home.[149] As Kathleen recalled: 'I've always read. I've always read. *Would you read in snatches or for longer periods?* Oh no. Oh no. Snatches. Yes. Because I, you know with, with the two young ones, er, you don't get a lot of time and you know when they're asleep you've got to do, wash nappies or do something else and, but I, I always went to the library, you know.' As well as public libraries, the '2*d*. libraries', which charged for the loan of what Rowntree termed 'thrillers and sentimental love stories', also catered for the female reader.[150]

Magazines such as *Good Housekeeping* (1922), *Woman's Friend* (1924) and *Woman's Own* (1932) provided a particularly accessible home-based form of leisure reading, and their consumption constituted a valuable but class-stratified leisure experience for adult women. Generally, magazines approached women's lives holistically; leisure and work were not clearly differentiated. Magazine content reflected a notion of women's time which frowned upon the enjoyment of pure leisure. Consequently, the pleasurable aspect of magazine-reading was mitigated by a belief that useful information on housework/childcare/being a wife was also provided. Magazines also reflected the fragmented nature of women's time, being easy to pick up and then put down in the course of a day's work. So, although they were not unproblematic as a 'leisure' product, magazines did provide a real opportunity for relaxation of a type which fitted the realities of women's everyday lives.

As women's magazines flourished, so local and – in the postwar period – even national newspapers began to identify a specifically female audience, making ever-increasing efforts to attract women readers through the provision of regular 'women's pages'. The *Social Survey of Merseyside* claimed in 1934 that the local evening paper was 'the mainstay of many homes';[151] in 1959, it was asserted that women constituted 60 per cent of all readers of national daily newspapers.[152] Certainly the *Manchester Evening News* targeted women as readers of the newspaper in their leisure time, and produced a recognisable 'women's page' throughout the period. In 1920, 'For the Ladies' comprised three or four paragraphs on high-society fashion and a recipe which, paradoxically, stressed thrift. Later in the decade, what the paper called 'topics interesting to women readers' appeared throughout the week under the different titles 'Through a woman's eyes', 'From a woman's notebook', 'The world of women' and 'From a woman's point of view'. Such titles gave an 'otherworldly' flavour to the pages, and indicated that the offerings were for – and written by – a sex whose viewpoint was particular, and different from men's. The articles themselves focused upon the latest fashions, recipes, new fads, dress patterns, topical news, women's sport and the household, and included profiles of famous women.[153] Even in wartime regular items targeted at a female audience appeared, as Jane Dawson provided answers to personal and practical problems, the weekly home page cook supplied recipes for rationed goods, and other articles concerned household chores, clothes and beauty. In the postwar period, women continued to be addressed as a defined section of the readership, but what was written for them was positioned almost entirely within the domestic realm, with women appealed to directly as consumers of domestic products. Fashion advice, household tips, recipes, sewing suggestions and notes on childcare constituted the staples of provision for women. By the end of 1955 the women's section, renamed 'The Women's Club', appealed to its audience in the following manner: 'Please! Slip this section out while father and the children concentrate on their favourites elsewhere in the paper.'[154]

Handicrafts, as we have already seen, are more difficult to define as 'work' or 'leisure' within women's lives, and their greater popularity among women from lower economic groups again reinforces the suspicion that these were often tasks performed out of necessity rather than personal choice. Nevertheless, it is clear that while some women pursued these activities as work which had to be done, others extracted real pleasure from the process of 'making things'. A wide variety of handicrafts presented an opportunity to pick something up and put it down as time allowed; thus, like magazine-reading, these activities fitted well into the working days of many adult women. Half of the women interviewed by Mass-Observation in 1948 claimed that needlecrafts of various types constituted their most significant leisure activity, and oral testimony attests to the continued popularity of these forms up to the end of our period. [155]

Certainly, sewing, embroidery, knitting and other handicraft advice formed a staple of women's magazines and 'women's pages', so that two of the most widely enjoyed leisure experiences of adult women were fundamentally linked. *Woman's Own* provided its own 'craft expert', Priscilla Knox, advising its readers thus: 'If you are interested in sewing, knitting, or crochet write to her for any special advice you may require'; *Woman's Friend* included 'Kathleen Pym's needlecraft corner', while *Good Housekeeping* provided a regular 'pattern service' for its readers.[156] Magazines like these provided sewing and knitting patterns, often using them to sell the magazine by advertising patterns worn by models on their covers. In 1938, for example, *Woman* used its front cover to advertise its 'ready to sew glamorous satin nightie'.[157] In the same edition this particular magazine offered its readers a total of seven patterns to knit or sew, including those for a dress which could, apparently, be transformed into five different outfits; a negligée to complement the glamorous nightie, a pair of slippers and a 'bluebell jersey'. In the postwar period magazines relied less upon sheer weight of patterns for their sales, but continued to advertise knitting patterns, dress patterns to buy and needlecraft accessories on their covers. For example, in 1955 *Woman's Own* offered '2 new knitting designs by James Norbury' and a pattern for a suit which could be purchased from the magazine's 'pattern shop'.[158]

Both hand knitting and sewing retained their popularity among women across the period, with particular fashions evident at key moments – the 1920s, for example, heralded a 'jumper craze'; while in the 1930s and 1940s hand-knitted swimwear proved popular.[159] Moreover, while magazines provided needlecraft advice for the generalist, specialist publications catered for the more serious needleworker; these included journals such as *Fancy Needlework Illustrated*, numerous texts which included *The Complete Knitting Book* (1934), and booklets like *Woolcraft* (seventeen editions between 1914 and 1962). By the 1950s, the BBC even employed a television knitter in the shape of James Norbury to advise its viewers on correct knitting habits.

The popularity of needlecrafts should not, however, lead us to ignore the wide range of alternative handicrafts enjoyed by women, many of which were intimately related to the work of home-making. From exhortations to 'go gay with your glass' – that is, to paint tumblers and wineglasses – to suggestions on better rug-making, women's magazines reflected and encouraged the pleasure which many women derived from the act of 'making things', particularly items for their own homes.[160] While it is clear that home-focused handicrafts were definitionally ambivalent in nature, so that personal creativity could melt seamlessly into necessary work, handicraft activities did undeniably constitute a much-valued form of personal pleasure for many adult women across the period 1920 to 1960.

As our period ended there was a clear perception that the creative pleasures outlined above were threatened by the advent of television as it became *the* focus for home-based leisure. As Jane recalled, television quickly began to dominate home life in the 1950s:

> And I had a knitting machine and I used to do knitting and that, my husband used it as well and a sewing machine, and I used to sew. But the television stopped all that, cos when we, er got the television we couldn't use the knitting machine cos you couldn't hear the television for the noise of the knitting machine. And sewing and things like that all went by the board because we all became obsessed with the television.

Certainly, the fear that television would threaten long-standing leisure forms is apparent in responses to a Mass-Observation directive of 1949. A number of women expressed their concern that television, unlike the radio, would overwhelm their creative leisure pursuits and, crucially, prevent them from combining work and leisure within the home. One twenty-eight-year-old housewife observed: 'The worst of television from a housewife's point of view is that it requires a darkened room so that knitting or mending is out of the question, whereas to "mend" while listening to the wireless makes a tedious job less irksome.'[161] Tellingly, however, others noted that in fact this might not be a bad thing, allowing the housewife to enjoy a purer form of leisure rather than the complex mixture of leisure and work which was their more usual experience. As one woman observed: 'Yes I suppose it would affect my other pursuits if we had a television set, after all one cannot sit and knit, sew or read whilst watching the television, but on the other hand during that time one can completely relax which is a very good point in favour of television.'[162]

Women's 'leisure' in adulthood, over the period 1920 to 1960, constituted a complex and ambiguous category. Difficult to separate out from the fabric of women's everyday lives, it often appears to be redundant amid the competing demands made of women as wives and mothers. While some women did continue to enjoy the commercial activities of their youth, the meanings attached to these types of leisure, as well as the forms they took, changed. Women more usually filled any spare time available to them with 'casual' leisure experiences. Socialising and home-based activities were particularly popular across the period and across social classes: the former because it could be fitted into the working day; the later because it was easily combined with the roles of wife and mother.

As in their youth, adult women experienced a number of constraints upon their leisure choices. Time and money were often limited, and the activities of other family members could have a decisive impact upon the resources available to them. However, the transition from youth to adult-hood was accompanied by a different conception of leisure entitlement, one which was of fundamental importance in framing adult women's ex-periences and contributed significantly to the development of the wife/mother identity. Once they were married, many women did not believe that they had a legitimate right to personal leisure, primarily because they had not *earned* it through full-time paid labour. Social constructions of the adult woman's role emphasised service and duty as overriding characteris-tics. The 'personal' was superseded by the 'family', and 'leisure' itself be-came an arena for service and duty to others.

Notes

1 *Manchester Evening News* (hereafter *MEN*), 28 January 1935, p. 6.

2 E. Roberts, *A Woman's Place: An Oral History of Working-Class Women, 1890– 1940* (Basil Blackwell, Oxford, 1984), p. 203.

3 J. Giles, 'A home of one's own: women and domesticity in England 1918– 1950', *Women's Studies International Forum*, 16:3 (1993).

4 A. Davies, *Leisure, Gender and Poverty: Working-Class Culture in Salford and Manchester, 1900–1939* (Open University Press, Buckingham, 1992), p. 171.

5 D. Gittins, *Fair Sex: Family Size and Structure 1900–1939* (Tavistock, London, 1982).

6 See J. Finch and P. Summerfield, 'Social reconstruction and the emergence of companionate marriage, 1945–1959' in D. Clark (ed.), *Marriage, Domestic Life and Social Change* (Routledge, London, 1991), pp. 7–32, for an examination of the development of 'companionate marriage' in the second part of this period.

7 *MEN*, 21 April 1930, p. 3.

8 *MEN*, 3 April 1930, p. 3.

9 S. Bowden, 'The new consumerism', in P. Johnson (ed.), *Twentieth Century Britain: Economic, Social and Cultural Change* (Longman, London, 1994), pp. 253–4.

10 *MEN*, 2 January 1940, p. 2.

11 *MEN*, 28 February 1940, p. 2.

12 *MEN*, 27 June 1955, p. 2.

13 *MEN*, 11 November 1955, p. 4.

14 *MEN*, 19 September 1955, p. 5.

15 The family economy is examined in the next section of this chapter.

16 None of the lower-middle-class women interviewed recalled walking in the Whit processions.

17 *MEN*, 1 June 1925, p. 4; *MEN*, 30 May 1955, p. 2.

18 *MEN*, 5 June 1925, p. 4; *MEN*, 3 June 1955, p. 2.

19 Davies, *Leisure, Gender and Poverty*, pp. 138–41.

20 M. Spring Rice, *Working-Class Wives: Their Health and Conditions* (Penguin, Harmondsworth, 1939), p. 73.

21 Mass-Observation Archive (hereafter M-O A): Directive Respondent (hereafter DR) 2147, reply to July 1939 Directive.

22 E. Roberts, *Women and Families: An Oral History, 1940–1970* (Blackwell, Oxford, 1995), p. 151.

23 Spring Rice, *Working-Class Wives*, p. 94.

24 M-O A: DR2012, reply to March/April 1948 Directive.

25 M-O A: DR0884, reply to March/April 1948 Directive.

26 *MEN*, 2 February 1940, p. 4.

27 *MEN*, 28 June 1950, p. 2.

28 *MEN*, 30 June 1950, p. 2.

29 *Ibid.*

30 *Ibid.*

31 Roberts, *Women and Families*, pp. 39–40.

32 *MEN*, 14 January 1930, p. 3.

33 *MEN*, 7 February 1940, p. 2.

34 *MEN*, 6 July 1950, p. 2.

35 *Woman's Own*, 22 October 1932, p. 65.

36 As Roberts has observed, male work in the home was always characterised in terms of 'help' rather than 'responsibility': Roberts, *Women and Families*, p. 37.

37 M-O A: DR1605, reply to March/April 1948 Directive.

38 M-O A: DR0174, reply to March/April 1948 Directive.

39 Joanna Bourke employs this term in her study of working-class culture: J. Bourke, *Working-Class Cultures In Britain, 1890–1960: Gender, Class and Ethnicity* (Routledge, London, 1994), p. 81.

40 *MEN*, 7 October 1930, p. 3.

41 *MEN*, 17 January 1930, p. 3.

42 M-O A: replies to March/April 1948 Directive.

43 Bourke, *Working-Class Cultures*, pp. 81–94.

44 *Ibid.*, p. 90.

45 *Census of England and Wales 1961*, County Report. Lancashire, p. 393.

46 Spring Rice, *Working-Class Wives*, p. 94.

47 *MEN*, 26 March 1935, p. 6.

48 *MEN*, 1 January 1935, p. 4.

49 *MEN*, 17 June 1960, p. 10.

50 N. Dennis, F. Henriques and C. Slaughter, *Coal is Our Life: An Analysis of a Yorkshire Mining Community* (1956; Tavistock, London, 1969) pp. 170, 182.

51 Davies, *Leisure, Gender and Poverty*; M. Abendstern, 'Expression and control: A study of working class leisure and gender, 1918–1939. A case study of Rochdale using oral history methods', Ph.D. thesis, University of Essex, 1986.

52 Roberts, *A Woman's Place*, p. 115.

53 As Davies has observed: 'Touring the markets brought men and women together, in contrast to activities like drinking which tended to keep couples apart.' Davies, *Leisure, Gender and Poverty*, p. 131.

54 V. Hey, *Patriarchy and Pub Culture* (Tavistock, London, 1986), pp. 45–7.

55 Davies, *Leisure, Gender and Poverty*, p. 56.

56 M-O A: DR2031.1, reply to June 1939 Directive.

57 M-O A: FR2467, 'Saturday night', April 1947, p. 13.

58 B. Seebohn Rowntree and G. R. Lavers, *English Life and Leisure: A Social Study* (Longmans, London, 1951), p. 175.

59 *MEN*, 11 February 1920, p. 4.

60 Spring Rice, *Working-Class Wives*, p. 109.

61 See, for example, *ibid.*, pp. 33, 121.

62 Between 1901 and 1931, working-class birth rates were halved, so that even the families of manual workers, who generally tended to have more children than non-manual workers, had an average 2.5 children: Bourke, *Working-Class*

Cultures, p. 58.

63 J. Lewis, *Women in England 1870–1950: Sexual Divisions and Social Change* (Harvester Wheatsheaf, London, 1984), p. xi.

64 Finch and Summerfield, 'Social reconstruction and the emergence of companionate marriage', pp. 11–12.

65 *Ibid.*, p. 30.

66 *MEN*, 28 July 1950, p. 7; *MEN*, 11 August 1950, p. 6.

67 B. Seebohn Rowntree, *Poverty and Progress: A Second Social Survey of York* (Longmans, Green, London, 1941), p. 332.

68 *MEN*, 23 September 1960, p. 8.

69 M. Tebbutt, *Women's Talk? A Social History of 'Gossip' in Working-Class Neighbourhoods, 1880–1960* (Scolar Press, Aldershot, 1995), p. 157.

70 Spring Rice, *Working-Class Wives*, p. ix.

71 Wendy Webster points out that childcare was a particular problem in the postwar period for migrant women who were often separated from their mothers and other support networks: W. Webster, *Imagining Home: Gender, 'Race', and National Identity, 1945–64* (UCL Press, London, 1998), p. 143.

72 Davies, *Gender, Leisure and Poverty*, pp. 30–54.

73 *MEN*, 16 February 1920, p. 7.

74 M. Kerr, *The People of Ship Street* (Routledge & Kegan Paul, London, 1958), p. 52.

75 *Ibid.*, p. 52.

76 Dennis, Henriques and Slaughter, *Coal is Our Life*, p. 201.

77 Roberts, *A Woman's Place*, p. 110; C. Chinn, *They Worked all Their Lives: Women of the Urban Poor in England, 1880–1939* (Manchester University Press, Manchester, 1988), p. 51.

78 Roberts, *A Woman's Place*, p. 124.

79 Kerr, *The People of Ship Street*, pp. 46–8

80 *Ibid.*, p. 48.

81 Dennis, Henriques and Slaughter, *Coal is Our Life*, pp. 187–9.

82 Roberts, *Women and Families*, pp. 89–93.

83 While in 1931 only 10 per cent of married women were recorded in the official employment figures, by 1951 the figure has risen to 22 per cent: P. Summerfield, *Women Workers in the Second World War* (Croom Helm, London, 1984), p. 188.

84 Roberts, *Women and Families*, p. 139.

85 Kerr, *The People of Ship Street*, p. 30.

86 Roberts, *Women and Families*, pp. 92–3.

87 Webster, *Imagining Home*, p. 141.

88 Spring Rice, *Working-Class Wives*, pp. 95–6.

89 *Ibid.*, pp. 99–100, 110, 112.

90 J. Richards and D. Sheridan (eds), *Mass-Observation at the Movies* (Routledge & Kegan Paul, London, 1987), p. 270.

91 *MEN*, 26 October 1935, p. 4.

92 *MEN*, 2 June 1950, p. 6.

93 M-O A: FR3075, 'Present-day cost of living', January 1949, p. 3.

94 *Ibid.*, p. 13.

95 *Ibid.*, p. 5.

96 *Ibid.*, p. 13.

97 *Ibid.*, p. 5.

98 M. Devault, 'Talking and listening from women's standpoint: feminist strategies for interviewing and analysis', *Social Problems*, 37:1 (1990), p. 111.

99 M-O A: *Report Bulletin, New Series 42*, 'The Housewife's Day' (May/June 1951), p. 13.

100 M-O A: FR2429, 'The cinema and the public', 1946, pp. 3, 6.

101 S. Harper and V. Porter, 'Cinema audience tastes in 1950s Britain', *Journal of Popular British Cinema*, 2 (1999), p. 67.

102 H. Llewellyn Smith (ed.),*The New Survey of London Life and Labour. Volume IX. Life and Leisure.* (P. S. King & Son, London, 1935), p. 46.

103 See, however, J. Stacey, *Star Gazing: Hollywood Cinema and Female Spectatorship* (Routledge, London, 1994), pp. 94–105.

104 M-O A: FR2429, 'The cinema and the public', pp. 8–10.

105 Spring Rice, *Working-Class Wives*, p. 110.

106 Rowntree and Lavers, *English Life and Leisure*, p. 232.

107 *MEN*, 24 November 1925. p. 6.

108 M-O A: Topic Collection Leisure, 80/5/B, Questionnaire responses, November 1948.

109 M-O A: replies to January 1939 Directive.

110 Kerr, *The People of Ship Street*, p. 32.

111 *MEN*, 13 May 1925, p. 7.

112 *MEN*, 14 May 1925, p. 11.

113 *Ibid.*, p. 11.

114 *MEN*, 16 May 1925, p. 4.

115 Rowntree and Lavers, *English Life and Leisure*, p. 283.

116 M-O A: replies to January 1939 Directive.

117 M-O A: Topic Collection Leisure, 80/4/B-C, Questionnaire responses, Spring 1948.

118 L. Oliver, '"No hard-brimmed hats or hat-pins please": Bolton women cotton-workers and the game of rounders, 1911–39', *Oral History*, 25:1 (1997).

119 See J. Matthews, '"They had such a lot of fun": the Women's League of Health and Beauty between the wars', *History Workshop Journal*, 30 (1990). p. 23, for an exploration of the meanings attached to the League by its members.

120 Llewellyn Smith,*The New Survey of London Life and Labour*, p. 55.

121 This chapter has already demonstrated, however, the extent to which such activity could be performed out of a sense of 'duty' as well as because of personal preference.

122 Spring Rice, *Working-Class Wives*, pp. 109–10.

123 Rowntree, *Poverty and Progress*, p. 426.

124 Spring Rice, *Working-Class Wives*, p. 114.

125 Kerr, *The People of Ship Street*, p. 101.

126 M-O A: Topic Collection Leisure, 80/2/B-E, 80/3/A-C, Questionnaire responses, Spring 1947.

127 Tebbutt, *Women's Talk?*, p. 57.

128 Spring Rice, *Working-Class Wives*, p. ix.

129 *Ibid.*, pp. 109, 112.

130 Kerr, *The People of Ship Street*, pp. 32–3.

131 Dennis, Henriques and Slaughter, *Coal is Our Life*, p. 170.

132 Tebbutt, *Women's Talk?*

133 Spring Rice, *Working-Class Wives*, p. 115.

134 Lewis, *Women in England*, p. 9.

135 A Kidd, *Manchester* (Keele University Press, Keele, 1993), p. 212.

136 A. Hughes and K. Hunt, 'A culture transformed? Women's lives in Wythenshawe in the 1930s', in A. Davies and S. Fielding (eds), *Workers' Worlds: Culture and Communities in Manchester and Salford, 1880–1939* (Manchester University Press, Manchester, 1992), p. 90.

137 R. McKibbin, *Classes and Cultures: England 1918–1951* (Oxford University Press, Oxford, 1998), p. 194.

138 See R. Unwin, 'The influence of housing conditions on the use of leisure', *International Labour Review*, 9:6 (1924) for a contemporary assessment of the impact of housing conditions upon home-based leisure forms.

139 Tebbutt, *Women's Talk?*, p. 154.

140 Kerr, *The People of Ship Street*, p. 105.

141 Dennis, Henriques and Slaughter, *Coal is Our Life*, p. 155.

142 J. I. Gershuny and K. Fisher, 'Leisure in the UK across the 20th century'. *Working Papers of the ESRC Research Centre on Micro-social Change*. Paper 99–3 (University of Essex, Colchester, 1999), p. 25.

143 A. H. Halsey (ed.), *Trends in British Society Since 1900* (Macmillan, London, 1972), p. 552.

144 In 1949, 7.2 per cent of the population owned a car; by 1966, this figure stood at 53.1 per cent: Halsey, *Trends in British Society* p. 551.

145 Spring Rice, *Working-Class Wives*, p. 112.

146 *Good Housekeeping*, July 1933, p. 46.

147 *Woman's Friend*, 19 June, 1937, p. 1.

148 M-O A: Topic Collection Leisure, 80/2/B-E, 80/3/A-C, Questionnaire responses, Spring 1947.

149 J. Radway, *Reading the Romance: Women, Patriarchy and Popular Literature* (1984; Verso, London, 1987), p. 93.

150 Rowntree, *Poverty and Progress*, p. 472.

151 D. Caradog Jones, (ed.), *The Social Survey of Merseyside*, vol. 3 (Hodder & Stoughton, London, 1934), p. 274.

152 M. Abrams, 'The home-centred society', *The Listener*, 26 November 1959, p. 915.

153 For a representative example, see *MEN*, 8 January 1925, p. 8.

154 *MEN*, 7 January 1955, p. 9.

155 M-O A: FR3067, 'A report on work and leisure', November 1948, p. 10.

156 *Woman's Own*, 22 October 1932, p. 54; *Woman's Friend*, 19 June, 1937, p. 5; *Good Housekeeping*, February 1934, p. 65.

157 *Woman*, 3 December 1938, front cover.

158 *Woman's Own*, 10 February 1955.

159 R. Rutt, *A History of Hand Knitting* (B. T. Batsford, London, 1987), pp. 139–43.

160 *Woman's Life*, 28 October 1933 p. 9; *Woman's Friend*, 8 October 1948.

161 M-O A: DR1488, reply to February 1949 Directive.

162 M-O A: DR4004, reply to February 1949 Directive.

Conclusion

> The condition of woman is a seamless web; it is difficult even to unpick the different threads so that they may be examined separately.[1]

Of all the subjects of historical research, women's leisure is perhaps the most amorphous. The study of this particular topic necessitates an understanding of a wide range of other histories including those of work, the family, housing, and standards of living. Leisure cannot be understood in isolation; it touches – and is touched by – almost every sphere of human experience. Hard-and-fast definitions of the concept are often impossible to draw; the historian may even despair in the face of the complex definitional fluidity which attends her chosen field of research. Yet an understanding of the relationship between women and leisure is vital if we are to achieve a rounded picture of women's lives in the twentieth century.

The approach to leisure employed within this book is a holistic one. A central aim has been to develop an understanding of leisure which gets nearer to encompassing the totality of the particular experiences of women. Instead of accepting definitions of 'leisure' as given, the very nature of the category, as it operated within women's lives and across a particular historical period, has been problematised. Throughout, attention has been paid to the meanings allocated to particular experiences and the different contextual backgrounds within which they occurred. Specific consideration has been given to the complex – and often ambiguous – relationship between work and leisure: a relationship which can really be understood only if it is studied in the context of everyday life. In addition, the impact which a characterisation of leisure as 'reward' had upon women's experiences over the life cycle has been addressed. In this way, the book suggests a feminist, leisure studies-inspired theoretical underpinning to the field of leisure history – a field which is, at present, seriously undertheorised.

The methodologies adopted have grown out of feminist theoretical concerns; in the absence of appropriate methodologies from within the field of leisure history, the approach has been interdisciplinary in nature, but firmly rooted in a range of historical evidence. The use of oral history, in particular, has proved to be an important means of accessing both perceptions and experiences of leisure at the local level, allowing for the examination of interpretation and motivation as well as patterns of behaviour.

Within this theoretical framework, *Women's leisure in England* has not been unduly concerned with the intricate development of institutional forms, nor with the specificity of experiences defined by the researcher as of historical importance. Rather, the aim has been to draw attention to the complex nature of leisure experiences within the context of everyday lives. It is hoped that the book has gone some way towards providing a historical understanding of the 'informal, day to day, private content' which Bailey identified as an absence within leisure history in 1989.[2] It is suggested that this particular approach has also facilitated the examination of the 'fragments of leisure' which Davies acknowledged to be missing from his own study of leisure in Manchester and Salford.[3]

While I have not given equal attention to all social groups, a focus upon lower-middle-class and working-class experiences has allowed me to examine difference and similarity in leisure experiences over the period. Interestingly, similarities seem to have been more evident than differences. Although women of the lower middle class generally held an important economic advantage, their patterns of behaviour often diverged very little from those of working-class women. It was generally the quality of the experience rather than its nature which was different. For example, in youth, they were more likely to attend the more luxurious cinemas, to enjoy rambles further afield and to play tennis more regularly. The constraints upon their use of leisure time were, however, of a similar nature to those experienced by working-class girls. The regular performance of housework and other household duties; parental control and discipline, and the procedures which surrounded tipping up and the allocation of spends – all these had an impact upon young women of contrasting social backgrounds. In adulthood, women of both classes held the primary responsibility for household labour and childcare, and this, as we have seen, was the most significant factor in structuring experiences of – and notions of entitlement to – leisure. None the less, both housing conditions and the availability of domestic appliances exercised a crucial influence upon the performance of work in the home. Moreover, class-based patterns of residence, and the nature of the home itself, played an important part in framing the character of social life and had an impact upon the pursuit of leisure within the nuclear family. In the later part of this period, however, women of both working-class and lower-middle-class backgrounds seem to have experienced their social life in a more home-centred fashion. For example, a woman who had grown up in the slum districts of Miles Platting and a teacher whose parents had owned a profitable grocer's shop both attested to a more family-, home- and couple-based experience of leisure in the postwar period.

In examining the central years of the twentieth century, it has been possible to assess change and continuity in leisure experiences over a period of forty years. Perhaps the most significant change was the movement away from street-based forms of social life towards those located within the home and family. This movement, as we have seen, was rooted in the changing nature of housing provision, allied to rising standards of living and a low birth rate, which made a home-centred existence possible. Change has also been identified in the attitudes towards women's leisure exhibited within local and national sources. Certainly, attitudes towards – and experiences of – leisure were not static over this period. This study has demonstrated considerable change in the forms which leisure took over time. Ultimately, however, the evidence presented here has emphasised continuity over change. In particular, definitional ambiguity concerning the nature of leisure, and the inextricably linked category work, within women's lives has been evident throughout the period and across social classes. We have seen, for example, that conceptual confusion surrounding the nature of housework and childcare, often defined in terms of 'duty' rather than 'work', had a profound, and constant, effect upon opportunities for and expectations of leisure over this period.

The need to examine the fluidity within which specific experiences gained definitional validity as 'leisure' or 'work' has formed a central tenet of the theoretical framework employed here. The blurring of work into leisure, and the difficulties inherent in defining each concept within women's lives, are apparent throughout. Analysis of activities such as the family holiday, shopping, homecrafts and personal grooming, as well as a consideration of the courtship rituals of youth, have illustrated the futility of an approach in which work and leisure are considered as definitional opposites. Leisure often included aspects of work; the two could coexist within the same activity. Time and again this book has illustrated the importance of centring meaning and context if we are fully to understand women's historically specific leisure experiences.

Within this study, I have considered a number of key contextual backgrounds against which the experiences of women must be understood. The one factor which has emerged as a critical determinant of the leisure experiences addressed within this study, however, has been life-cycle stage: women's experiences of leisure were fundamentally structured along life-cycle lines. Both oral and documentary sources depicted youth as a period of legitimate leisure, characterised by freedom and independence. The experience of earning a wage and engaging in clearly defined hours of work lent the work–leisure relationship in youth a clear sense of definition; women felt that they deserved personal leisure in these years, and enjoyed the independent resources with which to pursue favoured activities. Once they were married, the relationship between work and leisure in women's lives changed. While the paid work of youth legitimised leisure for young women, the unpaid work of married life limited both the opportunities for and expectations of leisure. In effect, a notion of leisure as earned through paid labour framed women's own perceptions of their right to it. Moreover, social constructions of the 'good' wife and mother as a person devoted to other family members militated against the exercise of personal leisure time, and could induce guilt in those who sought to maintain more individual interests. More generally, the sources describe a notion of leisure in adulthood which was rooted in the home and dovetailed with caring for the family. Most commonly, the personal leisure preferences of youth were subsumed into those of the family, with 'leisure' becoming a vehicle for service and duty to husband and children. The transition from youth to adulthood thus heralded a crucial shift in the experience of leisure: the personal was superseded by the family. Despite a number of changes in leisure behaviour over the forty years encompassed by this study, these gendered notions of leisure entitlement exhibited an overriding continuity.

There is, of course, a great deal of research to be conducted on women's leisure within the twentieth century. It is to be hoped that this book will stimulate further work which might, for example, foreground 'difference' more explicitly than I have been able to. While this study has hinted at the role played by ethnicity in leisure choices, the relationship between ethnicity, 'race' and leisure merits specific and detailed attention. The focus here has been largely upon the urban experience, yet we urgently need to address the leisure patterns of rural women, about whom we know very little. In addition, an examination of the leisure experiences of middle-class women would add to our understanding of the way the work–leisure relationship works within different women's lives and might, usefully, challenge some of the findings within this book. Certainly, attention to leisure in later life would enhance our understanding of the life cycle as a key framework for leisure experience.

According to Philip Larkin, sexual intercourse 'began' three years after our period ends.[4] The 1960s brought what has been defined by some as a 'sexual revolution'; later in the decade and into the 1970s, radical politics, including a revitalised feminism, challenged discourses of gender and 'race'. This study closes as these apparently transformative cultural and political forces gathered momentum. Future studies might, then, ask how women's experiences of leisure changed during a period often characterised as one of profound social upheaval and, crucially, explore the extent to which life-cycle stage continued to frame those experiences.

Notes

1　E. Wilson, *Only Halfway to Paradise: Women in Postwar Britain, 1945–1968* (Tavistock, London, 1980), p. 61.

2　P. Bailey, 'Leisure, culture and the historian: reviewing the first generation of leisure historiography in Britain', *Leisure Studies*, 8:2 (1989), p 118.

3　A. Davies, *Leisure, Gender and Poverty: Working-Class Culture in Salford and Manchester, 1900–1939* (Open University Press, Buckingham, 1992), p. 56.

4　P. Larkin, 'Annus Mirabilis', in *High Windows* (Faber & Faber, London, 1974).

Appendix 1

The Manchester interviews

Interviews were conducted with twenty-three women, contacted through local newspapers and an appeal on local radio, whose dates of birth ranged from 1907 to 1936. More than half of the women spent at least part of their lives living in, or near, central Manchester; those who did not lived in the northern and southern suburbs of the city. Only three of the women did not marry, and only one of those who married did not have children. Seven of these women described their family background as middle-class, while the remainder defined themselves as working-class.

The majority of the interviews were conducted within the respondents' homes on a one-to-one basis. In three cases, however, the women were interviewed in the presence of male partners.[1] In keeping with a commitment to examine leisure in the context of everyday life, the interviews rejected the fixed, topic-based, questionnaire approach in favour of one founded upon the life cycle.[2] Consequently, where specific, agenda-setting questions were necessary, these centred around different life stages rather than particular leisure activities. Working with the life cycle in this way helped to contextualise leisure experiences. It also limited the introduction of researcher-defined, activity-based notions of the concept 'leisure' into the interview situation. More generally, however, interviewees were encouraged to lead the conversation, and my responses were conditioned by the points they made. As Anderson and Jack put it: 'in order to listen, we need to attend more to the narrator than to our own agendas'.[3]

The Manchester interviews were also informed by a suspicion that asking women about their 'leisure' might exclude experiences which did not fit the 'out-of-house', activity-based, commonly held conception of the term. I therefore used a variety of words in order to transmit the idea that women should talk about the broad range of their experiences, not only about sporting activities or trips to the cinema and dance hall. In initial contacts with women, the term 'spare time' was adopted as one which, while not unproblematic in itself, might be more likely to tap into their experiences than the term 'leisure'. Within the interviews, the field of enquiry was set out as widely as possible; in order to encourage women to talk more fully about their experiences of 'leisure', a variety of terms were used. Each interview began along the following lines: 'I want to talk with you about all the things you did in your spare time. Your hobbies, what gave you pleasure, fun, leisure if you use that term.'[4] Here the term leisure was used, but given no particular precedence over other terms. Over the course of the interviews, particular attention was paid to the words which women themselves chose to articulate their experiences.[5]

Notes

1 The impact of the presence of a partner during the interview varied. Elsie's partner adopted an intrusive stance, continually interjecting with episodes from his own life story, while Annie's husband made only infrequent contributions to the conversation. Irene had already been interviewed alone before a second interview in the presence of her husband. Within this interview, the couple encouraged and prompted each other's memory in a fruitful manner.

2 A questionnaire was used to elicit basic biographical details about the respondents before the interview. This information was used to create the skeleton of a life structure for each interviewee, which was referred to within the interview as a source of prompts.

3 K. Anderson and D. Jack, 'Learning to listen: interview techniques and analyses', in S. Gluck and D. Patai (eds), *Women's Words: The Feminist Practice of Oral History* (Routledge, London, 1991), p. 12.

4 Within the sociology of leisure, different researchers have employed different terms in their attempts to access women's experiences. Green, Hebron and Woodward, for example, used notions of pleasure and enjoyment; Wimbush questioned women using the concept of well-being; and Deem asked her interviewees to talk about enjoyable and pleasurable aspects of daily routines, or to hypothesise about how they would spend a free period of time: E. Green, S. Hebron and D. Woodward, *Women's Leisure. What Leisure?* (Macmillan, London, 1990); E. Wimbush, *Women, Leisure and Well-Being: An Edinburgh Based Study of the Role and Meaning of Leisure in the Lives of Mothers with Pre-School Age Children* (Centre For Leisure Research, Dunfermline College of Physical Education, Edinburgh, 1986); R. Deem, *All Work and No Play: The Sociology of Women and Leisure* (Open University Press, Milton Keynes, 1986).

5 For further discussion of the use of oral history for the study of women's leisure, see C. Langhamer, 'Women and leisure in Manchester, 1920–c.1960', Ph.D. thesis, University of Central Lancashire, 1996.

Appendix 2

Brief biographical details of the Manchester interviewees

Note: Pseudonyms were used in all cases.

Ada

Born	1907
Parents	Father, railway signalman; Mother, housewife (died 1922)
Siblings	Two sisters
Occupations	Clerical/secretarial
Marriage	None
Children	None
Husband's occupation	None
Location	Withington

Freda

Born	1909
Parents	Father, railway signalman; Mother, housewife (died 1922)
Siblings	Two sisters
Occupations	Clerical/secretarial
Marriage	None
Children	None
Husband's occupation	None
Location	Withington

Edith

Born	1911
Parents	Father, worked at a brewery; Mother, in service prior to marriage, afterwards casual cleaning work and took in washing
Siblings	Three sisters and three brothers

Occupations	Foundry worker
Marriage	1931
Children	Two girls and two boys
Husband's occupation	Unemployed (ill-health); Part-time warehouseman
Location	Collyhurst, New Moston

Mary

Born	1911
Parents	Father, commercial artist; Mother, housewife
Siblings	None
Occupations	Insurance clerk, housewife
Marriage	1939
Children	One boy
Husband's occupation	Public health officer
Location	Fallowfield, Didsbury, Withington

Jessie

Born	1914
Parents	Father, wages clerk; Mother, tailor prior to marriage, afterwards took in sewing (died 1928)
Siblings	None
Occupations	Book-keeping machine operator, housewife, returned to previous job when children at grammar school
Marriage	1941
Children	One girl and one boy
Husband's occupation	Textile designer, worked with textile rollers
Location	Crumpsall

Elsie

Born	1916
Parents	Father, journeyman saddler; mother, mill girl, after marriage owned corner shop, worked as a waitress (parents separated)
Siblings	One brother
Occupations	Clerical/secretarial, housewife, part-time corsetière
Marriage	1945
Children	One girl and one boy
Husband's occupation	Centre-lathe turner, charge hand, shop foreman
Location	Hulme, Stretford, Sale

Hannah

Born	1916
Parents	Father, baths attendant (Corporation worker); Mother, cotton-weaver
Siblings	Two sisters and one brother
Occupations	Clerical/secretarial, housewife
Marriage	1942
Children	One girl and two boys
Husband's occupation	Moved from clerk to departmental manager within same firm. After redundancy retrained as a teacher
Location	Crumpsall, Blackley

Doris

Born	1917
Parents	Father and mother owned first a drapery and then a tobacconist's shop (mother died 1938)
Siblings	None
Occupations	Clerical/secretarial, housewife, social worker.
Marriage	1940
Children	One girl
Husband's occupation	Technical officer for telephone company
Location	Higher Broughton, Whitefield

Margaret

Born	1917
Parents	Father, worked at Metropolitan Vickers; Mother, lady's maid, housewife
Siblings	Two sisters and one brother
Occupations	Tea-checker, WAAF, part-time shop assistant, garage assistant
Marriage	1946
Children	One girl
Husband's occupation	Electrical engineer
Location	Urmston, Stretford

Joan

Born	1920
Parents	Father, sanitary inspector; Mother, printer's assistant, housewife
Siblings	Two sisters and one brother
Occupations	Biscuit-packer, shop assistant, clerk, housewife, shop assistant

Marriage	1940
Children	One girl
Husband's occupation	Charge hand at chemical factory
Location	Harpurhey, Blackley

Ivy

Born	1920
Parents	Father, collier, printer; Mother, mill worker, housewife
Siblings	Three sisters (two brothers died in infancy)
Occupations	Machinist, bus conductor, housewife, part-time work
Marriage	1943
Children	One girl and two boys
Husband's occupation	Pit worker, Gas Board worker
Location	Ancoats, Bradford, Beswick

Annie

Born	1920
Parents	Father, kiln worker; Mother, mill worker
Siblings	One sister and two brothers
Occupations	Clerical, nurse
Marriage	1955
Children	One girl and one boy
Husband's occupation	Technical representative
Location	Hulme, Old Trafford, Davyhulme

Barbara

Born	1921
Parents	Father, brass finisher; Mother, weaver. Parents then owned a confectionery shop
Siblings	One sister
Occupations	Comptometer operator, NAAFI
Marriage	1957
Children	None
Husband's occupation	Bus conductor, salesman
Location	Hulme, Chorlton Cum Hardy

Irene

Born	1922
Parents	Father, miner, labourer, night-watchman; Mother, in service before marriage, afterwards cleaner and barmaid.

Siblings	One sister
Occupations	Clerical, munitions, cleaner
Marriage	1952
Children	Two boys
Husband's occupation	Jewellery apprentice, army, warehouseman, caretaker
Location	Ardwick, Chorlton Upon Medlock

Dorothy

Born	1925
Parents	Father, railway wheel taper; Mother, mill worker, housewife
Siblings	Two sisters and one brother
Occupations	Clerical, munitions, part-time shop assistant
Marriage	1946
Children	Three girls
Husband's occupation	Engineer's draughtsman
Location	Ardwick, Higher Openshaw

Alice

Born	1926
Parents	Father, glazier (died 1927); Mother, service, mill work, housewife (died 1944)
Siblings	Six sisters and two brothers
Occupations	Service, nursing
Marriage	1957
Children	Three boys
Husband's occupation	Master tailor, textile foreman
Location	Harpurhey, Blackley

Kathleen

Born	1927
Parents	Father, company secretary; Mother, seamstress, housewife
Siblings	Three sisters and three brothers
Occupations	Tracer, housewife, clerk
Marriage	1949
Children	Two girls
Husband's occupation	Electrician, RAF
Location	Miles Platting, Newton Heath, Mossley

Celia

Born	1929
Parents	Father, cable joiner; Mother, housewife
Siblings	One sister and one brother
Occupations	Clerical/secretarial
Marriage	1951
Children	One boy
Husband's occupation	Engineer
Location	Miles Platting

Jane

Born	1929
Parents	Father, tram and bus driver; Mother, tailoress, milkmaid, machinist, waitress
Siblings	One brother
Occupations	Secretarial
Marriage	1952
Children	One girl and one boy
Husband's occupation	Joiner
Location	Cheetham Hill, Crumpsall

Joyce

Born	1930
Parents	Parents owned a grocer's shop
Siblings	One brother
Occupations	Schoolteacher
Marriage	1954
Children	One girl and two boys
Husband's occupation	Motor engineer
Location	Hulme, Davyhulme

Kate

Born	1930
Parents	Father, senior clerk; Mother, housewife
Siblings	One sister and one brother
Occupations	Clerical
Marriage	None
Children	None
Husband's occupation	None
Location	Burnage

Jean

Born	1930
Parents	Father, engineer; Mother, clerical, housewife
Siblings	None
Occupations	Clerical, part-time shop assistant
Marriage	1955
Children	Two girls
Husband's occupation	Cotton-worker, merchant navy, electrical engineer, salesman
Location	North Reddish, Urmston

Amy

Born	1936
Parents	Father, master baker; Mother, housewife
Siblings	None
Occupations	Domestic science student, secretary
Marriage	1959
Children	One girl and two boys
Husband's occupation	Farmer
Location	Chorlton Cum Hardy

Appendix 3

Map showing the geographical spread of the Manchester interviewees

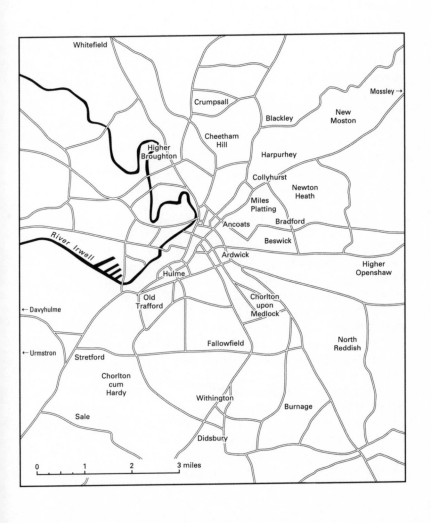

Select bibliography

Primary sources

Newspapers and magazines

Good Housekeeping
Home Chat
Kinematograph Year Book
Manchester Evening News
The Times
The Vote
Woman
Woman's Friend
Woman's Life
Woman's Own
Woman's World

Mass-Observation Archive, University of Sussex

File reports

FR24, 'The cinema in the first three months of war' (January 1940)
FR337, 'Leisure' (August 1940)
FR445, 'Film questionnaire' (October 1940)
FR689, 'Diary comparisons' (May 1941)
FR1611, 'Women in pubs' (March 1943)
FR1632, 'Some notes on the use of leisure' (March 1943)
FR1635, 'Women in public houses' (March 1943)
FR1780, 'Youth questionnaire' (May 1943)
FR1837–7A, 'Juvenile drinking' (June 1943)
FR1871, 'The cinema audience' (July 1943)
FR1882, 'Juvenile drinking' (August 1943)
FR1911, 'Juvenile drinking' (September 1943)
FR1970, 'Women in pubs' (December 1943)
FR2429, 'The cinema and the public' (October 1946)

FR2467, 'Saturday night' (April 1947)
FR3016, 'Drinking habits' (July 1948)
FR3067, 'A report on work and leisure' (November 1948)
FR3075, 'Present-day cost of living' (January 1949)
FR3078, 'The importance of leisure' (January 1948)
FR3150, 'Teen-age girls' (August 1949)
New Series Bulletin, 42, 'The housewife's day' (May/June 1951)

Directive replies

January 1939, 'Jazz'
June 1939, 'Class'
July 1939, 'Jazz and age differences'
April 1944, 'Sexual morality'
March/April 1948, 'Housework'
February 1949, 'Television'

Topic Collection, Leisure, TC80

Box 1: Leisure 1940–47
80/1/C: Football/rugby counts, April and May 1947.
Box 2: Leisure survey, Spring 1947
80/2/A: Questionnaires, codings and instructions
80/2/B-E: Questionnaire responses
Box 3: Leisure survey, Spring 1947 (continued)
80/3/A-C: Questionnaire responses
Box 4: Leisure survey 9/2 (1948)
80/4/A: Questionnaires, coding and instructions
80/4/B-C: Questionnaire responses, September 1948
80/4/D: Leisure survey 9/2. Analysis sheets, October 1948
Box 5: Leisure survey 9/3
80/5/A: Questionnaires and coding
80/5/B: Questionnaire responses, November 1948

Printed primary sources

Abrams, M., 'The home-centred society', *The Listener* (26 November, 1959).
Abrams, M., *Teenage Consumer Spending in 1959 (Part II) Middle Class and Working Class Boys and Girls* (London Press Exchange, London, 1961).
Burns, C. D., *Leisure in the Modern World* (McGrath, Washington D.C., 1932).
Caradog Jones, D. (ed.), *The Social Survey of Merseyside*, vol. 3 (Hodder & Stoughton, London, 1934).
Conservative Political Centre, *The Challenge of Leisure* (C.P.C. series no. 203, 1959).
Dennis, N., F. Henriques and C. Slaughter, *Coal is Our Life: An Analysis of a Yorkshire Mining Community* (1956, Tavistock, London, 1969).
Evans, R. and A. Boyd, *The Use of Leisure in Hull: A Survey Prepared for the 'Use of Leisure' Sub-Committee* (Hull, 1933).

Harrison, T. and C. Madge, *Britain by Mass-Observation* (Penguin, London, 1939).

Hoggart, R., *The Uses of Literacy* (1957; Penguin, London, 1992).

James, H. and F. Moore, 'Adolescent leisure in a working-class district', *Occupational Psychology*, 14:3 (1940).

James, H. and F. Moore, 'Adolescent leisure in a working-class district. Part II', *Occupational Psychology*, 18:1 (1944).

Jenkinson, A. J., *What do Boys and Girls Read?* (Methuen, London, 1940).

Jephcott, P., *Girls Growing Up* (Faber & Faber, London, 1942).

Jephcott, P., *Rising Twenty* (Faber & Faber, London, 1948).

Jephcott, P., *Some Young People* (George Allen & Unwin, London, 1954).

Kerr, M., *The People of Ship Street* (Routledge & Kegan Paul, London, 1958).

Labour Party, *Leisure for Living* (London, Labour Party, 1959).

Llewellyn Smith, H. (ed.), *The New Survey of London Life and Labour. Volume IX. Life and Leisure* (P. S. King and Son, London, 1935).

Mass-Observation, *The Pub and the People: A Worktown Study* (1943; Seven Dials Press, London, 1970).

Reed, B., *Eighty Thousand Adolescents: A Study of Young People in the City of Birmingham by the Staff and Students of Westhill Training College for the Edward Cadbury Charitable Trust* (George Allen & Unwin, London, 1950).

Richmond, A. C., 'The action of voluntary organisations to provide occupation for unemployed workers in Great Britain', *International Labour Review*, 37 (May 1938).

Rowntree, B. S., *Poverty and Progress: A Second Social Survey of York* (Longmans, Green, London, 1941).

Rowntree, B. S. and G. R. Lavers, *English Life and Leisure: A Social Study* (Longmans, London, 1951).

Spring Rice, M., *Working-Class Wives: Their Health and Conditions* (Penguin, Harmondsworth, 1939).

Unwin, R., 'The influence of housing conditions on the use of leisure', *International Labour Review*, 9:6 (1924).

'The leisure of women and children', *The Listener* (2 March 1932), p. 328.

'Spare time in the country', *International Labour Review*, 9:6 (1924).

Secondary sources

Books

Bailey, P., *Leisure and Class in Victorian England: Rational Recreation and the Contest for Control, 1830–1885* (Routledge, London, 1978).

Bourke, J., *Working-Class Cultures in Britain, 1890–1960: Gender, Class and Ethnicity* (Routledge, London, 1994).

Bowlby, J., *Maternal Care and Mental Health* (World Health Organisation, Geneva, 1952).

Brighton Ourstory Project, *Daring Hearts: Lesbian and Gay Lives of 50s and 60s Brighton* (QueenSpark Books, Brighton, 1992).

Burnett, J., *A Social History of Housing 1815–1970* (David & Charles, London, 1978).

Calder, A. and D. Sheridan (eds), *Speak for Yourself: A Mass-Observation Anthology, 1937–49* (Jonathan Cape, London, 1984).

Chinn, C., *They Worked all Their Lives: Women of the Urban Poor in England, 1880–1939* (Manchester University Press, Manchester, 1988).

Clarke. J. and C. Critcher, *The Devil Makes Work: Leisure in Capitalist Britain* (Macmillan, London, 1985).

Cross, G., *Worktowners in Blackpool: Mass-Observation and Popular Leisure in the 1930s* (Routledge, London, 1990).

Cunningham, H., *Leisure in the Industrial Revolution, 1780–c.1880* (Croom Helm, London, 1980).

Davies, A., *Leisure, Gender and Poverty: Working-Class Culture in Salford and Manchester, 1900–1939* (Open University Press, Buckingham, 1992).

Davies A. and S. Fielding (eds), *Workers' Worlds: Cultures and Communities in Manchester and Salford, 1880–1939* (Manchester University Press, Manchester, 1992).

Deem, R., *All Work and No Play: The Sociology of Women and Leisure* (Open University Press, Milton Keynes, 1986).

Dixey R. and M. Talbot, *Women, Leisure and Bingo* (Trinity and All Saints College, Leeds, 1982).

Ferris, P., *Sex and the British: A Twentieth-Century History* (Michael Joseph, London, 1993).

Fielding, S., P. Thompson and N. Tiratsoo, *'England Arise!' The Labour Party and Popular Politics in 1940s Britain* (Manchester University Press, Manchester, 1995).

Fletcher, S., *Women First: The Female Tradition in English Physical Education, 1880–1980* (Athone Press, London, 1984).

Fowler, D., *The First Teenagers: The Lifestyles of Young Wage-Earners in Interwar Britain* (Woburn, London, 1995).

Gavron, H., *The Captive Wife: Conflicts of Housebound Mothers* (1966; Routledge & Kegan Paul, London, 1983).

Giles, J., *Women, Identity and Private Life in Britain, 1900–50* (Macmillan, London, 1995).

Gittins, D., *Fair Sex: Family Size and Structure 1900–1939* (Tavistock, London, 1982).

Gluck, S. and D. Patai (eds), *Women's Words: The Feminist Practice of Oral History* (Routledge, London, 1991).

Gomes, M., *The Picture House* (North West Film Archive, Manchester Polytechnic, 1988).

Green, E., S. Hebron and D. Woodward, *Women's Leisure: What Leisure?* (Macmillan, London, 1990).

Griffin, C., *Typical Girls? Young Women from School to the Job Market* (Routledge & Kegan Paul, London, 1985).

Griffiths, D. (ed.), *The Encyclopedia of the British Press 1422–1992* (Macmillan, London, 1992).

Halsey, A. H. (ed.), *Trends in British Society Since 1900* (Macmillan, London, 1972).

Hamer, E., *Britannia's Glory: A History of Twentieth-Century Lesbians* (Cassell, London, 1996).

Hargreaves, J., *Sporting Females: Critical Issues in the History and Sociology of Women's Sports* (Routledge, London, 1994).

Heron, L. (ed.), *Truth, Dare or Promise: Girls Growing Up in the 50s* (Virago, London, 1985).

Hey, V., *Patriarchy and Pub Culture* (Tavistock, London, 1986).

Howkins, A. and J. Lowerson, *Trends in Leisure, 1919–1939* (Sports Council/Social Science Research Council, London, 1979).

Humphries, S., *Hooligans or Rebels? An Oral History of Working-Class Childhood and Youth, 1889–1939* (Basil Blackwell, Oxford, 1981).

Humphries, S., *A Secret World of Sex: Forbidden Fruit: The British Experience, 1900–1950* (Sidgwick & Jackson, London, 1988).

Jones, S., *Workers at Play: A Social and Economic History of Leisure, 1918–1939* (Routledge & Kegan Paul, London, 1986).

Jones, S., *The British Labour Movement and Film, 1918–1939* (Routledge & Kegan Paul, London, 1987).

Kidd, A., *Manchester* (Keele University Press, Keele, 1993).

Lewis, J., *Women in England 1870–1950: Sexual Divisions and Social Change* (Harvester Wheatsheaf, London, 1984).

Lewis, J., *Women in Britain since 1945: Women, Family, Work and the State in the Postwar Years* (Blackwell, Oxford, 1992).

McCrone, K., *Sport and the Physical Emancipation of English Women, 1870–1914* (Croom Helm, London, 1988).

McKibbin, R., *Classes and Cultures: England 1918–1951* (Oxford University Press, Oxford, 1998).

Maitland, S., *Vesta Tilley* (Virago, London, 1986).

Malcolmson, R. W., *Popular Recreations in English Society, 1700–1850* (Cambridge University Press, Cambridge, 1973).

Mangan, J. A. and R. J. Park, *From 'Fair Sex' to Feminism: Sport and the Socialisation of Women in the Industrial and Post-Industrial Eras* (Frank Cass, London, 1987).

Neild, S., and R. Pearson, *Women Like Us* (Women's Press, London, 1992).

O'Connell, S., *The Car in British Society: Class, Gender and Motoring, 1896–1939* (Manchester University Press, Manchester, 1998).

Osgerby, B., *Youth in Britain since 1945* (Blackwell, Oxford, 1998).

Pegg, M., *Broadcasting and Society, 1918–1939* (Croom Helm, Beckenham, 1983).

Perks, R. and A. Thomson (eds), *The Oral History Reader* (Routledge, London, 1998).

Pimlott, J., *The Englishman's Holiday: A Social History* (Faber & Faber, London, 1947).

Portelli, A., *The Death of Luigi Trastulli and Other Stories: Form and Meaning in Oral History* (State University of New York Press, Albany, 1991).

Pugh, M., *Women and the Women's Movement in Britain, 1914–1959* (Macmillan, London, 1992).

Radway, J., *Reading the Romance: Women, Patriarchy and Popular Literature* (1984; Verso, London, 1987).

Richards, J., *The Age of the Dream Palace: Cinema and Society in Britain, 1930–1939* (Routledge & Kegan Paul, London, 1984).

Richards, J. and D. Sheridan, *Mass-Observation at the Movies* (Routledge & Kegan Paul, London, 1987).

Roberts, E., *A Woman's Place: An Oral History of Working-Class Women, 1890–1940* (Basil Blackwell, Oxford, 1984).

Roberts, E., *Women and Families: An Oral History, 1940–1970* (Blackwell, Oxford, 1995).

Rowbotham, S., *The Past is Before Us: Feminism in Action Since the 1960s* (1989, Penguin, London, 1990).

Rowbotham, S., *A Century of Women: The History of Women in Britain and the United States* (Viking, London, 1997).

Russell, D., *Popular Music in England, 1840–1914: A Social History* (1987; Manchester University Press, Manchester, 1997).

Rutt, R., *A History of Hand Knitting* (B. T. Batsford Ltd, London, 1987).

Stacey, J., *Star Gazing: Hollywood Cinema and Female Spectatorship* (Routledge, London, 1994).

Stanley, L., *Essays on Women's Work and Leisure and 'Hidden' Work* (Manchester University Sociology Department, Manchester, 1987).

Stanley, L. (ed.), *Feminist Praxis: Research, Theory and Epistemology in Feminist Sociology* (Routledge, London, 1990).

Stanley, L. and S. Wise, *Breaking Out Again: Feminist Ontology and Epistemology* (Routledge, London, 1993).

Summerfield, P., *Women Workers in the Second World War* (Croom Helm, London, 1984).

Summerfield, P., *Reconstructing Women's Wartime Lives: Discourse and Subjectivity in Oral Histories of the Second World War* (Manchester University Press, Manchester, 1998).

Tebbutt, M., *Women's Talk? A Social History of 'Gossip' in Working-Class Neighbourhoods, 1880–1960* (Scolar Press, Aldershot, 1995).

Tinkler, P., *Constructing Girlhood: Popular Magazines for Girls Growing up in England, 1920–1950* (Taylor & Francis, London, 1995).

Tomlinson, A. (ed.), *Leisure and Social Control* (Brighton Polytechnic, Brighton, 1980).

Tranter, N., *Sport, Economy and Society in Britain 1750–1914* (Cambridge University Press, Cambridge, 1998).

Vertinsky, P., *The Eternally Wounded Woman: Women, Doctors and Exercise in the Late Nineteenth Century* (Manchester University Press, Manchester, 1990).

Walton, J., *The Blackpool Landlady: A Social History* (Manchester University Press, Manchester, 1978).

Walton, J., *Lancashire: A Social History, 1558–1939* (Manchester University Press, Manchester, 1987).

Walton, J. and J. Walvin (eds), *Leisure in Britain, 1780–1939* (Manchester University Press, Manchester, 1983).

Walvin, J., *Beside the Seaside: A Social History of the Popular Seaside Holiday* (Allen Lane, London, 1978).

Walvin, J., *Leisure and Society, 1830–1950* (Longmans, London, 1978).

Wearing, B., *Leisure and Feminist Theory* (Sage, London, 1998).

Webster, W., *Imagining Home: Gender, 'Race' and National Identity, 1945–64* (UCL Press, London, 1998).

White, C., *Women's Magazines 1693–1968* (Michael Joseph, London, 1970).

White, J., *The Worst Street in North London: Campbell Bunk, Islington, Between the Wars* (Routledge & Kegan Paul, London, 1986).

Wilson, E., *Only Halfway to Paradise: Women in Postwar Britain, 1945–1968* (Tavistock, London, 1980).

Wimbush, E., *Women, Leisure and Well-Being: An Edinburgh Based Study of the Role and Meaning of Leisure in the Lives of Mothers with Pre-School Age Children* (Centre For Leisure Research, Dunfermline College of Physical Education, Edinburgh, 1986).

Wimbush, E. and M. Talbot (eds), *Relative Freedoms: Women and Leisure* (Open University Press, Milton Keynes, 1988).

Essays in edited collections

Alexander, S., 'Becoming a woman in London in the 1920s and 1930s', in G. Feldman and G. Stedman Jones (eds), *Metropolis, London: Histories and Representations Since 1800* (Routledge, London, 1989).

Anderson, K. and D. Jack, 'Learning to listen: interview techniques and analyses', in S. Gluck and D. Patai (eds), *Women's Words: The Feminist Practice of Oral History* (Routledge, London, 1991).

Borland, K., 'That's not what I said', in S. Gluck and D. Patai (eds), *Women's Words: The Feminist Practice of Oral History* (Routledge, London, 1991).

Bowden, C., 'The new consumerism', in P. Johnson (ed.), *Twentieth Century Britain: Economic, Social and Cultural Change* (Longman, London, 1994).

Bowker, D., 'Parks and baths: sport, recreation and municipal government in Ashton-under-Lyne between the wars', in R. Holt (ed.), *Sport and the Working Class in Modern Britain* (Manchester University Press, Manchester, 1990).

Bratton, J. S., 'Jenny Hill: sex and sexism in the Victorian music hall', in J. S. Bratton (ed.), *Music Hall: Performance and Style* (Open University Press, Milton Keynes, 1986).

Cunningham, H., 'Leisure and Culture', in F. M. L. Thompson (ed.), *The Cambridge Social History of Britain, 1750–1950. Vol. 2. People and Their Environment* (Cambridge University Press, Cambridge, 1990).

Davies, A., 'Leisure in the classic slum, 1900–1939', in A. Davies and S. Fielding (eds), *Workers' Worlds: Cultures and Communities in Manchester and Salford, 1880–1939* (Manchester University Press, Manchester, 1992).

Davies, A., 'Cinema and broadcasting', in P. Johnson (ed.), *Twentieth Century Britain: Economic, Social and Cultural Change* (Longman, London, 1994).

Deem, R., 'Feminism and leisure studies: opening up new directions', in E. Wimbush and M. Talbot (eds), *Relative Freedoms: Women and Leisure* (Open University Press, Milton Keynes, 1988).

Edwards, E., 'The culture of femininity in women's teacher training colleges 1914–1945', in S. Oldfield (ed.), *This Working-Day World: Women's Lives and Culture(s) in Britain, 1914–1945* (Taylor & Francis, London, 1994).

Finch, J. and P. Summerfield, 'Social reconstruction and the emergence of companionate marriage, 1945–1959', in D. Clark (ed.), *Marriage, Domestic Life and Social Change: Writings for Jacqueline Burgoyne* (Routledge, London, 1991).

Green, E. and S. Hebron, 'Leisure and male partners', in E. Wimbush and M. Talbot (eds), *Relative Freedoms: Women and Leisure* (Open University Press, Milton Keynes, 1988).

Griffin, C., 'Young women and leisure', in A. Tomlinson (ed.), *Leisure and Social Control* (Brighton Polytechnic, Brighton, 1980).

Griffiths, V., 'From "playing out" to "dossing out": young women and leisure', in E. Wimbush and M. Talbot (eds), *Relative Freedoms: Women and Leisure* (Open University Press, Milton Keynes, 1988).

Hargreaves, J., 'The promise and problems of women's leisure and sport', in C. Rojek (ed.) *Leisure for Leisure: Critical Essays* (Macmillan, London, 1989).

Hoher, D., 'The composition of music hall audiences, 1850–1900', in P. Bailey (ed.), *Music Hall: The Business of Pleasure* (Open University Press, Milton Keynes, 1986).

Howkins, A., and J. Lowerson, 'Leisure in the thirties', in A. Tomlinson (ed.), *Leisure and Social Control* (Brighton Polytechnic, Brighton, 1980).

Hughes, A. and K. Hunt, 'A culture transformed? Women's lives in Wythenshawe in the 1930s', in A. Davies and S. Fielding (eds), *Worker's Worlds: Cultures and Communities in Manchester and Salford, 1880–1939* (Manchester University Press, Manchester, 1992).

Hurstwitt, M., '"Caught in a whirlpool of aching sound": the production of dance music in Britain in the 1920s', in R. Middleton and D. Horn (eds), *Popular Music 3. Producers and Markets* (Cambridge University Press, Cambridge, 1983).

Jones, S., 'Working-class sport in Manchester between the wars', in R. Holt (ed.), *Sport and the Working Class in Modern Britain* (Manchester University Press, Manchester, 1990).

McIntosh, S., 'Leisure studies and women', in A. Tomlinson (ed.), *Leisure and Social Control* (Brighton Polytechnic, Brighton, 1980).

McKibbin, R., 'Work and hobbies in Britain, 1880–1950', in J. M. Winter (ed.), *The Working Class in Modern British History* (Cambridge University Press, Cambridge, 1983).

McRobbie, A., 'Working class girls and the culture of femininity', in University of Birmingham. Centre for Contemporary Cultural Studies. Women's Studies Group (ed.), *Women Take Issue: Aspects of Women's Subordination* (Hutchinson, London, 1978).

McRobbie, A. and J. Garber, 'Girls and subcultures: an exploration', in S. Hall and T. Jefferson (eds), *Resistance Through Rituals: Youth Subcultures in Post-war Britain* (Hutchinson, London, 1975).

Mason, J., 'No peace for the wicked: older married women and leisure', in E. Wimbush and M. Talbot (eds), *Relative Freedoms: Women and Leisure* (Open University Press, Milton Keynes, 1988).

Minster, K., 'A feminist frame for the oral history interview', in S. Gluck and D. Patai (eds), *Women's Words: The Feminist Practice of Oral History* (Routledge, London, 1991).

Morgan, M., 'The Women's Institute Movement – The acceptable face of feminism?', in S. Oldfield (ed.), *This Working-Day World: Women's Lives and Culture(s) in Britain, 1914–1945* (Taylor & Francis, London, 1994).

Oakley, A., 'Interviewing women: a contradiction in terms', in H. Roberts (ed.), *Doing Feminist Research* (Routledge & Kegan Paul, London, 1981).

Oram, A.,'Embittered, sexless or homosexual: attacks on spinster teachers, 1918–1939', in A. Angerman *et al.* (eds), *Current Issues in Women's History* (Routledge, London, 1989).

Osgerby, B., 'From the roaring twenties to the swinging sixties: continuity and change in British youth culture, 1929–59', in B. Brivati and H. Jones (eds), *What Difference did the War Make?* (Leicester University Press, Leicester, 1993).

Rollett, C., and J. Parker, 'Population and family', in A. H. Halsey (ed.), *Trends in British Society Since 1900* (Macmillan, London, 1972).

Stacey, J., 'Can there be a feminist ethnography?', in S. Gluck and D. Patai (eds), *Women's Words: The Feminist Practice of Oral History* (Routledge, London, 1991).

Stanley, L., 'The problem of women and leisure – an ideological construct and a radical feminist alternative', in Centre For Leisure Studies (ed.), *Leisure in the 1980s* (University of Salford, Salford, 1980).

Stanley, L., 'Historical sources for studying work and leisure in women's lives', in E. Wimbush and M. Talbot (eds), *Relative Freedoms: Women and Leisure* (Open University Press, Milton Keynes, 1988).

Tebbutt, M., 'Women's talk? Gossip and "women's words" in working-class communities, 1880–1939', in A. Davies and S. Fielding (eds), *Worker's Worlds: Cultures and Communities in Manchester and Salford, 1880–1939* (Manchester University Press, Manchester, 1992).

Warren, A., 'Mothers for the Empire? The Girl Guide Association in Britain, 1909–1939', in J. A. Mangan (ed.), *Making Imperial Mentalities: Socialisation and British Imperialism* (Manchester University Press, Manchester, 1990).

Warren, A., 'Sport, youth and gender in Britain, 1880–1940', in J. C. Binfield and J. Stevenson (eds), *Sport, Culture and Politics* (Sheffield Academic Press, Sheffield, 1993).

Wild, P. 'Recreation in Rochdale 1900–1940', in J. Clarke, C. Critcher and R. Johnson (eds), *Working-Class Culture: Studies in History and Theory* (Hutchinson, London, 1979).

Williams, J and J. Woodhouse, 'Can play, will play? Women and football in Britain', in J. Williams and S. Wagg (eds), *British Football and Social Change: Getting into Europe* (Leicester University Press, Leicester, 1991).

Woodward, D., and E. Green, '"Not tonight dear!" The social control of women's leisure', in E. Wimbush and M. Talbot (eds), *Relative Freedoms: Women and Leisure* (Open University Press, Milton Keynes, 1988).

Journal articles

Aston, E., 'Male impersonation in the music hall', *New Theatre Quarterly* (August 1988).

Bailey, P., 'Leisure, culture and the historian: reviewing the first generation of leisure historiography in Britain', *Leisure Studies*, 8:2 (1989).

Bialeschki, D. and K. Henderson, 'Leisure in the common world of women', *Leisure Studies*, 5:3 (1986).

Bolla, P., 'Media images of women and leisure: an analysis of magazine advertisements, 1964–87', *Leisure Studies*, 9:3 (1990).

Bruley, S., 'A very happy crowd: women in industry in south London in World War Two', *History Workshop Journal*, 44 (1997).

Chambers, D., 'The constraints of work and domestic schedules on women's leisure', *Leisure Studies*, 5:3 (1986).

Constantine, S., 'Amateur gardening and popular recreation in the 19th and 20th centuries', *Journal of Social History*, 14:3 (1981).

Daley, C., '"He would know, but I just have a feeling": gender and oral history', *Women's History Review*, 7:3 (1998).

Davidson, P., 'The holiday and work experiences of women with young children', *Leisure Studies*, 15:2 (1996).

Davin, A., 'Imperialism and motherhood', *History Workshop Journal*, 5 (1978).

Devault, M., 'Talking and listening from women's standpoint: feminist strategies for interviewing and analysis', *Social Problems*, 37:1 (1990).

Dixey, R., '"It's a great feeling when you win!" women and bingo', *Leisure Studies*, 6:2 (1987).

Geiger, S., 'What's so feminist about women's oral history?', *Journal of Women's History*, 2:1 (1990).

Gershuny, J. L. and K. Fisher, 'Leisure in the UK across the twentieth century', *Working Papers of the ESRC Research Centre on Micro Social Change* , Paper 99/3 (Colchester, University of Essex, 1999).

Giles, J., 'A home of one's own: women and domesticity in England, 1918–1950', *Women's Studies International Forum*, 16:3 (1993).

Goodman, P., '"Patriotic Femininity": women's morals and men's morale during the Second World War', *Gender and History*, 10:2 (1998).

Green, E., '"Women doing friendship": an analysis of women's leisure as a site of identity construction, empowerment and resistance', *Leisure Studies*, 17:3 (1998).

Harper, S. and V. Porter, 'Cinema audience tastes in 1950s Britain', *Journal of Popular British Cinema*, 2 (1999).

Hunt, G. and S. Saterlee, 'Darts, drink and the pub: the culture of female drinking', *The Sociological Review*, 35:3 (1987).

Lenskyj, H., 'Measured time: women, sport and leisure', *Leisure Studies*, 6:1 (1989).

Mangan, J. A., 'The social construction of Victorian femininity: emancipation, education and exercise', *The International Journal of the History of Sport*, 6:1 (1989).

Matthews, J., '"They had such a lot of fun": The Women's League of Health and Beauty between the wars', *History Workshop Journal*, 30 (1990).

Melling, A., '"Ray of the Rovers": The working-class heroine in popular football fiction', *The International Journal of the History of Sport*, 15:1 (1998).

Oliver, L., '"No hard-brimmed hats or hat-pins please": Bolton women cotton workers and the game of rounders, 1911–39', *Oral History*, 25:1 (1997).

Oram, A., 'Repressed and thwarted, or bearer of the new world? The spinster in inter-war feminist discourses', *Women's History Review*, 1:3 (1992).

Park, J., 'Sport, dress reform and the emancipation of women in Victorian England: a reappraisal', *The International Journal of The History of Sport*, 6:1 (1989).

Parratt, C., 'Athletic womanhood: explaining sources for female sports in Victorian and Edwardian England', *Journal of Sport History*, 16:2 (1989).

Parratt, C., '"Little means or time": working-class women and leisure in late Victorian and Edwardian England', *The International Journal of the History of Sport*, 15:2 (1998).

Proctor, T., '(Uni)forming youth: Girl Guides and Boy Scouts in Britain, 1908–39', *History Workshop Journal*, 45 (1998).

Rubinstein, D., 'Cycling in the 1890s', *Victorian Studies*, 21:1 (1977).

Sangster, J., 'Telling our stories: feminist debates and the use of oral history', *Women's History Review*, 3:1 (1994).

Scraton, S., 'The changing world of women and leisure: feminism, "postfeminism" and leisure', *Leisure Studies*, 13:4 (1994).

Sheridan, D., 'Using the Mass-Observation archive as a source for women's studies', *Women's History Review*, 13:1 (1994).

Stanley, L., 'Women have servants and men never eat: issues in reading gender, using the case study of Mass-Observation's 1937 day-diaries', *Women's History Review*, 4:1 (1995).

Stuart, M., '"You're a big girl now": subjectivities, feminism and oral history', *Oral History*, 22:2 (1994).

Summerfield, P., 'Mass-Observation: social research or social movement?', *Journal of Contemporary History*, 20:3 (1985).

Tinkler, P., 'An all-round education: the Board of Education's policy for the leisure time training of girls, 1939–50', *History of Education*, 23:4 (1994).

Tinkler, P., 'Sexuality and citizenship: the state and girls' leisure provision in England, 1939–45', *Women's History Review*, 4:2 (1995).

Wearing, B. and S. Wearing, 'All in a day's leisure: gender and the concept of leisure', *Leisure Studies*, 7:2 (1988).

Unpublished theses

Abendstern, M., 'Expression and control: A study of working-class leisure and gender, 1918–39. A case study of Rochdale using oral history methods', Ph.D. thesis, University of Essex, 1986.

Carrie, E., 'A study of women students' leisure', BA dissertation, University of Liverpool, 1954.

Harley, J. L., 'Report of an enquiry into the occupations, further education and leisure interests of a number of girl wage-earners from elementary and central schools in the Manchester district, with special reference to the influence of school training on their use of leisure', M.Ed. dissertation, University of Manchester, 1937.

Langhamer, C., 'Women and leisure in Manchester, 1920–*c*.1960', Ph.D. thesis, University of Central Lancashire, 1996.

Middleton, T., 'An enquiry into the use of leisure amongst the working classes of Liverpool.', MA dissertation, University of Liverpool, 1931.

Morgan, O., 'A study of the training for leisure occupations offered in a senior girls' school in an industrial area, together with an enquiry into the use made of this training by the girls, after their entry into employment', M.Ed. dissertation, University of Manchester, 1942.

Index

Note: 'n.' after a page reference indicates a note number on that page. Page numbers in italics indicate illustrations. Substantial references are indicated by bold. Works specifically cited in the text are shown under authors' names.